ROBERTO MAZZA is Assistant Professor of History at Western Illinois University. He holds a PhD from SOAS, University of London and is the co-editor of *Jerusalem in World War I: The Palestine Diary of a European Diplomat* (I.B.Tauris, 2011).

JERUSALEM

FROM THE OTTOMANS TO THE BRITISH

ROBERTO MAZZA

I.B. TAURIS
LONDON · NEW YORK

New paperback edition published in 2014 by I.B.Tauris & Co. Ltd
6 Salem Road, London W2 4BU
175 Fifth Avenue, New York NY 10010
www.ibtauris.com

First published in hardback in 2009 by I.B.Tauris & Co. Ltd

Copyright © Roberto Mazza 2009, 2014

The right of Roberto Mazza to be identified as the author of this work has been asserted by him in accordance with the Copyright, Designs and Patent Act 1988.

All rights reserved. Except for brief quotations in a review, this book, or any part thereof, may not be reproduced, stored in or introduced into a retrieval system, or transmitted, in any form or by any means, electronic, mechanical, photocopying, recording or otherwise, without the prior written permission of the publisher.

ISBN 978 1 78076 708 6

A full CIP record for this book is available from the British Library
A full CIP record for this book is available from the Library of Congress

Library of Congress catalog card: available

*For
Monica*

CONTENTS

List of Tables	ix
List of Maps	xi
List of Illustrations	xiii
Acknowledgements	xv
Glossary	xix
Introduction	1
1. Modernising Jerusalem: Administration and Population	11
From Ottoman to Egyptian rule and back	12
From the Tanzimat to the Young Turks through the Hamidian era: patterns of governance and administration	16
The Sancak and the Mutasarrıf	20
The Municipality of Jerusalem	22
The Councils ruling Jerusalem	26
The Notables of Jerusalem in the late Ottoman era	30
The People of Jerusalem (1905-1922): figures and definitions	34
2. Christianity at War	47
The Christian Churches of Jerusalem in history	48
Patriarchates between the Ottomans and the European Powers	51
The Churches and the Capitulations	54
'Peace' among Christians: the Status Quo, origins and developments	56
Christian Churches facing mobilisation and war	58
The Custody of the Holy Land	63
The Custody in the aftermath of the war: local and international dimensions	66
The strange allies: Arab Christians and Muslims together	68
3. Foreigners in Jerusalem	75
Visiting Jerusalem	77
Consulates	84

    Foreigners and the War   88
    Consul of War: Conde de Ballobar   97
    Consular missions in the aftermath of the War   107
4. The War and the British conquest of Jerusalem   111
    Preparing for war: mobilisation of human, material and ideological resources   113
    The real value of Jerusalem at the beginning of the war   121
    The British conquest of Jerusalem: 9 December 1917   124
    'Gerusalemme Liberata'   129
    'A dramatic incident of war': the surrender of Jerusalem   132
    Jerusalem conquered: local, British and international reactions   136
    The end of the last Crusade?   143
5. British Military Rule 1917-1920 and the case of the Nebi Musa Riots   147
    Military rule: 1917-1920   148
    The 'despot' ruler of Jerusalem: Ronald Storrs   158
    Planning Jerusalem   163
    April 1920: Nebi Musa Riots   165
Epilogue   179
Notes   183
Bibliography   233
    Private Papers   233
    Official Publications   233
    Newspapers   234
    Memoirs, Diaries and Tourist Guides   235
    Unpublished Material   236
    Internet sources   237
    Books   237
    Articles and Chapters   248
Index   257

LIST OF TABLES

Table 1: Population of city of Jerusalem from late Ottoman era to British census 1922.   37
Table 2: Schmelz's figures for the Jerusalem *kaza*.   38
Table 3: British census 1922.   38
Table 4: Breakdown of the figures of the British census within the walls.   38
Table 5: Breakdown of the figures of the British census outside the walls.   38
Table 6: Increase in the cost of living 1914.   119

LIST OF MAPS

Map 1: Ottoman administrative division of Palestine, Lebanon
and Syria 8
Map 2: Jerusalem 1912-1920 9

LIST OF ILLUSTRATIONS

Jerusalem. Street scene inside the Jaffa Gate (1909-1914)
Mayor of Jerusalem and Turkish Official, 1914-1917
Enver Paşa visiting the Dome of the Rock, 1916
Jews at the Wailing Wall
Mosque of Omar, northeast side
Ceremony of the Holy Fire at the Holy Sepulchre
St. George's Cathedral
Turkish column out to drill in Jerusalem, 1914
Ceremony of the Washing of the Feet. Holy Sepulchre, 1898-1914
Military review by Cemal Paşa and Kress von Kressenstein, 1917
Zaky Bey and his staff, 1914
Austrian Post Office in Jerusalem
Turkish troops Jaffa Gate
Turkish military. Man dancing with a sword, 1914-1918
Turkish prisoner of war, 9 December 1917
Turkish airplane in Jerusalem
American Consulate
British troops on parade, Russian Compound, December 1917
Military review by Allenby, 11 December 1917
Entry of Allenby in Jerusalem, Jaffa Gate, 11 December 1917
Franciscan monk reading the proclamation in Italian, 11 December 1917
Italian guard at the Church of the Holy Sepulchre, 1918
OETA Headquarters
Local Gendarmerie, Jerusalem 1918
Ronald Storrs at the Shrine of Nebi Musa, 1918

Last Turkish celebration of Nebi Musa, 1917
A Greek priest is searched, 8 April 1920
Nebi Musa festival, April 1920

ACKNOWLEDGEMENTS

Despite the fact that this is an academic book on Jerusalem, there is an intimate side embedded into it. In the summer of 2000 I was in Jerusalem with Monica, then my future wife; there was a general feeling of hope, soon to evaporate when the peace process collapsed and the al-Aqsa intifada began. I can still vividly remember watching the news and linking those pictures with my individual perceptions of Palestine, Israel and Jerusalem. I suppose it was the very beginning of a long path that eventually brought me to explore the history of the city, and to question a number of preconceptions in the media and academic literature.

This book officially started as a PhD dissertation at SOAS, and it would not have been possible to publish it without the help of many people. I am delighted to acknowledge the support and friendship of a large number of individuals. I should start thanking my PhD supervisor Dr Nelida Fuccaro, who read numerous versions of this work, in the form of a thesis and then as a book; she has provided me with precious and priceless suggestions, and is presumably now bored with the topic! Many thanks also go to the SOAS History Department, and in particular to Dr Benjamin Fortna for his support and for the opportunity I was given to teach what I like in a place that I love.

It is time to thank all who have made this book a reality. I have to express my gratitude to the CBRL (Council of British Research in the Levantine) and Senate House. They provided the necessary funds to travel around the world with the task of collecting as much material as possible. The CBRL, through the Kenyon Institute in Jerusalem, also offered me pleasant accommodation. I must express my thanks to the Vatican Archives and the Archives of the Italian,

Spanish and French Ministries of Foreign Affairs, which granted me access to their archival material. I need also to thank the Ottoman Archives in Istanbul, who helped me to find what I was looking for and who always provided me with excellent Turkish tea. I would also like to convey my gratitude to the Custody of the Holy Land in Jerusalem, as well as the personnel of the archives and libraries in Istanbul, Washington, Madrid, London, Jerusalem and Rome. I am particularly indebted to the Library of Congress, Washington DC, who made available for free the Matson photographic collection: a unique perspective on Jerusalem and Palestine from 1898 to 1946. Finally, I want to thank my editors at I.B.Tauris, Rasna Dhillon and Joanna Godfrey.

A book is not just the outcome of research, but I believe is more the concretisation of a dream. In my childhood I wanted to be and do many things, some of them quite unrealistic; I certainly could not aspire to being beamed aboard the Enterprise, but to have my name on a book has proved to be more feasible. Dreams, however, are not realised alone, and I want to thank Dr Vivian Ibrahim for providing precious advice, numerous corrections and priceless smiles that often brighten difficult moments. I am delighted to thank Dr Trudy Jacobsen and Dr Nir Arielli; they read early versions of this book, and their comments helped me to greatly improve it. Since I started my research I met so many people that it would be almost impossible to remember all of them, however, Dr Abigail Jacobson deserves special mention, as we share the same interest in Jerusalem and I benefited a lot from her work. I would also like to thank Dr Issam Nassar, Dr Eitan Bar-Yosef, Dr James Renton and Dr Yair Wallach: their works have been an inspiration for me, and chatting with them has given me even more than just an insight. I would also like to take the chance to thank my future colleagues in the History Department at Western Illinois University, Macomb IL; I am sure I will have the chance to share some future works with them. I would like to thank Lily Blouin, an exceptional grad student at Western who helped me with the corrections for the paperback edition of the book.

There is a vast community of 'Londoners' that I want to thank: first and foremost John Letizia, Guido Vezzoni and Cyp Stephenson. My gratitude also goes to the English basketball officiating community: officiating is not only a hobby; it gave me strength and some sort of discipline whilst carrying out my work. I would also like to thank the staff of the SOAS Student Union. To my friends back in Italy, who never asked me what my research was about, but who helped me to recharge my batteries every time I returned to my town, so that I could come back to London and restart my work with renewed strength. Some of these friends are no longer with us; however, I am sure Bruno is often laughing at what I am doing and is perhaps quite right.

Jerusalem was, and still is, a city of communities, with a great sense of family and home. There is a debt of gratitude which can hardly be paid back. I thank my parents Paolo and Carla Mazza who have always been supportive: they visited me during my research in Istanbul and Jerusalem, although they will never understand these few words as they do not speak English. Above all I am grateful to my wife: dear Monica, I cannot simply say thank you; in fact you are the one who has walked by my side everyday for the last few years, sharing failures and successes: I know a 'thank you' is not enough.

GLOSSARY

'aliyah: Jewish immigration to Palestine and then to Israel after 1948

A'yan: Notable Muslim and Christian families of Jerusalem and Palestine

Belediye: Municipality

Beylerbeylik: Territorial subdivision which corresponded to a greater province

Capitulations: Treaties or grants which established a system of privileges and reductions in custom duties, as well as extraterritorial jurisdiction, favourable to Europeans

CUP: Committee of Union and Progress

Custody of the Holy Land: Religious institution founded by the Franciscan order in the thirteenth century with the purpose to take care of Catholics in the Holy Land

Custos: Fr Superior of the Franciscans in the Holy Land; he is resident in Jerusalem and by internal constitution he must be an Italian citizen

Firman: Decree, order, issued by the Sultan in Istanbul and valid through the Ottoman Empire

Halukka: Collection and distribution of funds for the Jewish residents of Palestine and Jerusalem

Kaza: Administrative unit, a subdivision of the *sancak*

Meclis: Council

Meclis-i Idare: Administrative Council

Meclis-i Umumi: General Council, usually of the province

Millet: State recognised community, defined according to religion

Miri: State lands, owned by the Sultan and available on the market

Mutasarrıf: Governor of the *sancak* or *mutasarrıflık*; in Jerusalem he was appointed directly by Istanbul

Mutasarrıflık: Administrative unit corresponding to a province; synonymous with sancak

Mülk: Private property; privately owned land

Nüfus: Population register

Paşa: Highest official Ottoman military and civil title

Sancak: Administrative unit, Province

Status Quo: Set of rules and customs ruling the disputes over the control and management of the holy places in Jerusalem and the Holy Land

Status Quo Ante Bellum: Rules of military occupation

Tanzimat: Name given to a set of reforms carried out in the Ottoman Empire in the nineteenth century

Tapu: Land and property registry

Vali: Governor of the vilayet

Vilayet: Administrative unit, a larger province which included a number of *sancaks*

Waqf: Charitable endowment, lands not available on the market

INTRODUCTION

My arrival in Jerusalem occurred on 6 December 1322 [19 December 1906] and I am still within the seventh month of my appointment, which I know is a great act of grace bestowed upon me by His Majesty the Caliph. There is no denial, therefore, that the authority to study and examine such a major issue as the Jewish question in Jerusalem which a six-seven month experience can provide a weak man, especially such as your slave, is valueless to the point of being in effect non-existent. [This question] has perhaps no equivalent in the Empire and, without denial, is continuing to get more and more complicated and intricate, taking many different shapes and forms. It is always prone, because of the involvement of all powers in it, to become a major political problem and from all points of view, it is, in short, a most difficult and crucial one. (Ali Ekrem Bey, Governor of Jerusalem, 1906-1908)[1]

There are enough books on the history of Jerusalem to fill entire libraries, so it is fair to ask: do we need yet another history of Jerusalem? However, the large availability of works does not necessarily mean there is a thorough knowledge and understanding of the subject, even if these works are a reflection of its relevance and publicity.

There are several reasons why scholars, writers and readers have approached the history of Jerusalem. The different narratives available not only represent different styles, methodological approaches and focus; narratives are often, and foremost, the expression of different political and religious visions. These narratives have often been employed to make claims which served the purpose of those who wished to control the city and its meanings. In this context, Jerusalem has become an 'imagined community': in Andersonian terms, the city is imagined as there are many groups whose members do not necessarily know each other, but share strong feelings towards Jerusalem.[2] The city is also imagined as a community, irrespective of its manifest divisions, as it is conceived more as an ideal, where religious myths have been turned into collective memories, transmitted as history. Issam Nassar has noted how these narratives are in constant competition, as they connect the city with those groups who share the same history, thereby *de facto* isolating the history of different communities from the overall history of the city.[3] Is it then possible to write about Jerusalem without falling into these traps? Is it possible to avoid being subservient to a cause or a claim?

This book aims to discuss at least three issues rarely, if at all, touched on in the majority of works which relate to this popular city. Looking at the major literature on the history of Jerusalem, it is noteworthy that the particular period discussed in this work has often been neglected. There are several studies dealing with the late Ottoman history of Palestine, but the whole period of transition from Ottoman rule to British administration, and the period of the First World War, has been almost entirely overlooked. Rather than highlighting specific titles which have disregarded this period, it is more interesting to try and discover why this phase has been ignored. The question of periodisation is not only a practical or methodological issue: it is a choice of values and, to an extent, of claims to make. The division of history into periods is not something that is self-evident but rather – as E.H. Carr argues – a necessary hypothesis whose validity depends on interpretation.[4] This means that, beyond the simple task of dividing history on paper, what really matters is giving some meaning to the subdivision. While there is no issue with the idea of dividing history, the choice of the periodisation cannot be driven by political, ideological and religious claims. As it happens, concerning the available literature, there are not many claims to be made regarding Jerusalem during the First World War: there is indeed more to be said on the British mandate era, on early Jewish immigration, or on rising Palestinian nationalism. In view of this, ironically, the years of the war have been ignored for political and ideological reasons.

The choice of the periodisation links to the second issue debated in this work. In Jerusalem during the war, local issues like lack of food or the militarisation of the local environment overshadowed international questions such as the management of the holy places or Jewish immigration. This period, therefore, is less attractive to professional historians. This has to do with the dominant discourses in the historical works in relation to the city. There are more works dealing with Europeans and Zionists than with the local population regardless of their affiliation: it seems as if the natives or local residents were not to be considered as agents of change in this formative period. Jerusalemites have rarely been placed at the centre of attention, and tend to be shown only if interacting with Europeans or Zionists. However, there is also a problem in defining who a Jerusalemite actually is. Personally, I decided to use a broad definition and include not only natives but also permanent residents; it is the interactions of these people that made Jerusalem a lively place, rather than a large open-air museum, Pompei-style. Sometimes, certain narratives give the impression that the inhabitants of the city were supporting actors or extras performing walk-on parts and cameos. This has a major repercussion on the way in which Jerusalem becomes the focus of the production of historical narrative. Including Jerusalemites in the picture broadens the sources to investigate; it becomes necessary to move away from the traditional sources used in the discussion of the late nineteenth and early twentieth centuries.

The questions of sources and historiography are also debated. There are two major issues to discuss: the use of local sources, and the insufficient interaction between the historiographies available. The majority of the works available are based on European sources and accounts of Western travellers. In itself this is not a problem; it is the way these sources have been used that is the issue. For instance, consular sources have been employed mainly to explain political relations between international actors, to shed light on the battles between religious institutions, and regarding Zionism and Jewish immigration; sometimes, data and information on the local population have only been mentioned to support the benevolent effect of a European presence. The narrative of this book is based on a massive amount of data gathered through Western sources, but it focuses more on local issues, with a particular interest in what went on in the city during the war. The people of Jerusalem *were* the city, so it is necessary to take account of local voices expressed, mainly through diaries and memoirs. A good example is provided by the diary of the Spanish consul who resided in the city during the war; however scholars such as Abigail Jacobson, Issam Nassar and Salim Tamari have worked on diaries and memoirs of other local residents providing crucial information. Clearly, these sources are biased, and offer just one point of view: but it is the point of view of a local resident, and not of travellers imbued with religious fervour or a sense of *mission civilisatrice*. How can one write a history of Jerusalem without Jerusalemites, whether they are Orthodox monks, local businessmen or members of the Ottoman administration?

If sources are the main issue in writing the history of the city, in academic terms what should concern us is the production of narrative in different languages. Histories of Jerusalem have been written in several languages, notably English, Arabic, Hebrew, French and German, but some literature has also been produced in Italian and Spanish. Although most Israeli and Arab scholars have also published in English, what is really striking is the general lack of interaction between academics. In most of the literature in English, it is almost impossible to find references to French, Italian or Spanish narratives, whilst all of these narratives often feel obliged to quote from Anglo-Saxon works as English is the leading academic language. The works of Henry Laurens, Dominique Trimbur or Catherine Nicault are often unknown, while an article by Vincent Lemire and Yasemin Avcı seems to have been overlooked by Anglo-Saxon narratives. Indeed, different national narratives have different purposes: the French and the Italians have often focused on their activities in Jerusalem, while the British have focused on Jerusalem the biblical city or on the issue of Zionism. Arab and Israeli scholars have focused on political narratives, often relying on local sources to argue their cases, but *de facto* relying mainly on Anglo-Saxon literature for the historical context. Despite all possible attempts at interaction, what remains is an atomised academic field, unable to communicate. The landscape is neither clear nor idyllic. What I have attempted to do in this work is bring together as many narratives as possible; to process them, explore what they have to offer, and to merge these works with my own sources. To claim full knowledge of all available literature on Jerusalem would be a mistake. Also not all primary sources available have been directly scrutinised, such as the diaries of Wasif Jawhariyyeh or Ihsan Tourjman; however my hope is to have broken through certain academic dogmas, and open the field to new perspectives and more research.

This book is divided into five chapters, dealing with several aspects of Jerusalem: administration, Churches, foreigners, the war, and politics. Chapter 1 discusses the late Ottoman administration of Jerusalem. It presents an overview of the administrative machine, including the local inhabitants, with the long-term purpose of considering the changes and continuities between the Ottoman and the British administrations. As far as Jerusalemites are included in this narrative, it is crucial to define composition of the local population, both in terms of numbers and structure at the beginning of the twentieth century. Furthermore, in an effort to present a reliable and apolitical picture of the population, I have tried to gather and combine all sources available. In Chapter 2, the position of religious institutions in the city during the war is debated. My point is that these institutions, despite being alien entities in the city, with poor connections with the local population, had to change their attitudes during and due to the war, renegotiating their positions *vis-à-vis* local inhabitants. A case study is provided through the discussion of the Custody of the Holy Land during the war, which summarises all the paradoxes of the Christian religious institutions of Jerusalem. I also discuss the emergence of the Christian-Muslim associations in response to Zionist activities, less in political terms and more as local organisations reshaping the traditional alliances between the various communities in the city.

Chapter 3 introduces the question of foreigners in the city. It is clear that there is a need to differentiate between visitors and those who, for short or long periods, became residents. The agency of foreigners is scrutinised to show their impact on the city. I am particularly interested in those foreign residents who lived in the city throughout the war, like the American consul Glazebrook and the Spanish diplomat Conde de Ballobar. Each of them provides a different perspective on the city, but it is the young Spanish diplomat who offers a very interesting insight into wartime Jerusalem. Ballobar wrote a diary of his mission during the war, with plenty of comments about the military, administration, and the local people; in fact, he effectively became one of them. He reported on the social activities taking place in the city, primarily dinners or social gatherings between the local, Ottoman and foreign elites, shedding light on a little-studied phenomenon.

Chapter 4 discusses the overall impact of the war on the city of Jerusalem. The war is discussed from different perspectives. Jerusalem was never an open field for military operations; however, mobilisation, militarisation of the environment, and British plans and occupation had a massive impact on the local milieu. All aspects of daily life were renegotiated, and sectarian barriers were lowered. In the context of the war, it can also be seen how Jerusalem was deprived of its status as a real city of real people, and turned into a symbolic place, a prize for the ultimate winner. It is easy to observe the dichotomy of a city which was inhabited by local people and idealised by the new conquerors, who did not hesitate to define themselves as new crusaders.

Chapter 5 partly mirrors the first chapter, discussing the British military administration of the city. The war was over in Jerusalem in December 1917, with the British occupation of the city, but in fact, I argue that the war period continued until 1920, when a civil administration was established. The military establishment was simple, and worked efficiently though it had to face several problems. Once again, the administrative decisions taken in relation to the city are scrutinised, as is the impact they had on the local population. This means looking at the well known, but not often discussed, figure of the military governor of Jerusalem, Ronald Storrs, and his vision of Jerusalem, which was often translated into decrees with a long-lasting impact upon the city and its inhabitants. Eventually, the military administration was brought to an end by the explosion of violence between Arabs and Zionists in April 1920 – the Nebi Musa riots. A discussion of these events considers their dynamics, and the impact these riots had on the city and local communities, arguing that Ottoman Jerusalem was fading, giving way to a new city, with renegotiated local values and alliances, but not yet a divided city.

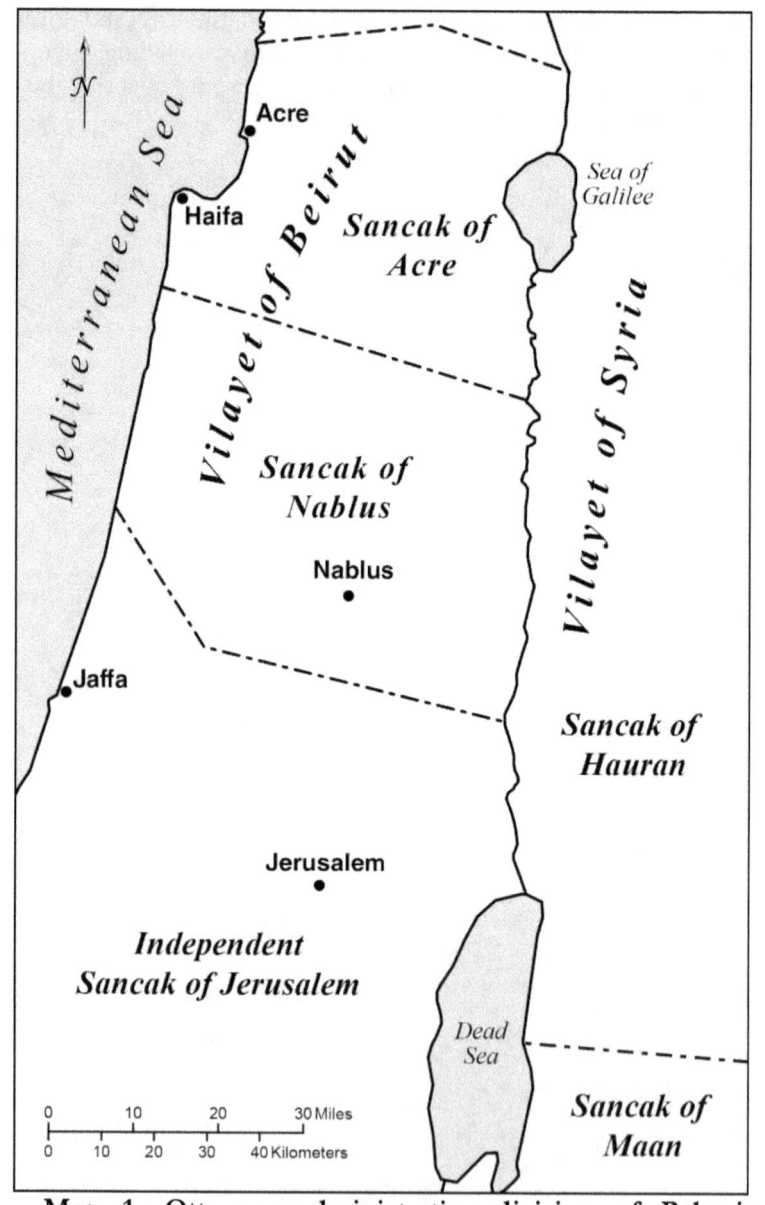

Map 1: Ottoman administrative division of Palestine, Lebanon and Syria ©Christopher J. Sutton

INTRODUCTION

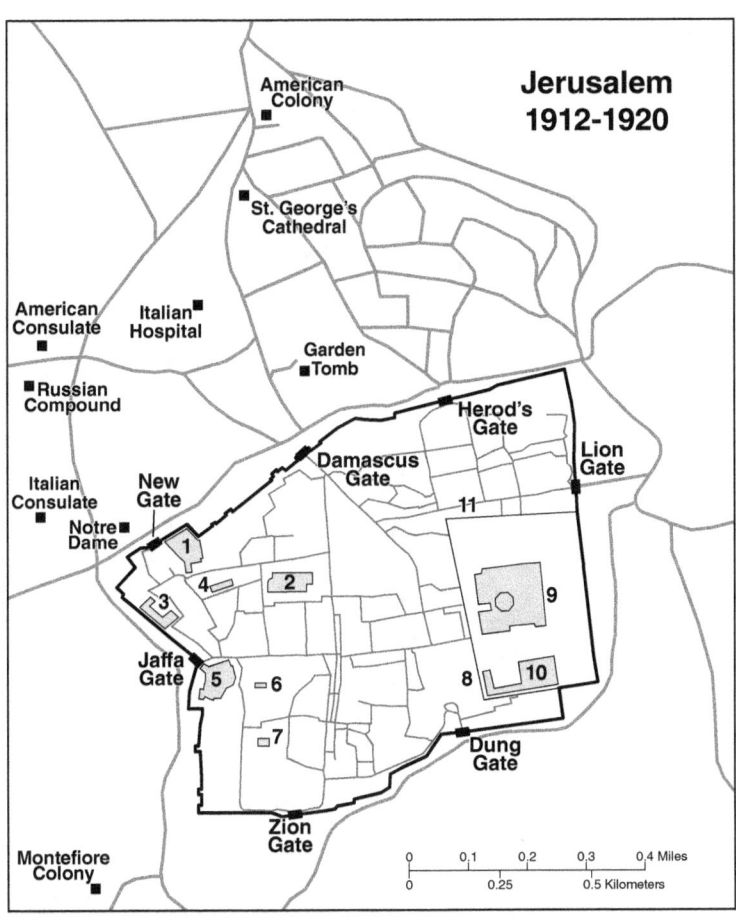

1 Custody of the Holy Land
2 Holy Sepulchre
3 Latin Patriarchate
4 Greek Orthodox Patriarchate
5 Citadel
6 Christ Church
7 St. James Cathedral
8 Wailing Wall
9 Dome of the Rock
10 Al-Aqsa
11 Via Dolorosa

Map 2: Jerusalem 1912-1920 ©Christopher J. Sutton

1

MODERNISING JERUSALEM: ADMINISTRATION AND POPULATION

Ölberg is the German for Mount of Olives. Jabal az Zeytun is the Arabic and Zeytindağı is just the name I gave to my book. There never was a Turkish Jerusalem. (Falih Rıfkı Atay 1894-1971)[1]

Historical writings on the modern period of Jerusalem are often based on historical accounts of religious myths and Western encounters with the city. These historical narratives have created tales in which the local population were almost invisible. While it is a fact that, at the beginning of the nineteenth century, Jerusalem was a small provincial centre, it is not necessarily true that Ottoman rule was backward and calamitous as has been previously portrayed. Looking at the sources available, most of the accounts depicting Jerusalem as a dreadful place misruled by the 'terrible' Turks are, in fact Western accounts. Are these accounts also the voice of the local residents? They might have had their grievances with the Ottoman administration and, indeed, Jerusalem was not as developed as European cities of the time, but at the beginning of the nineteenth century Jerusalem was in reality an Ottoman city, and not the product of biblical imagination or collective memories. What follows is not an example of a 'modernisation narrative', in which the focus is on the origins of this phenomenon, but rather a short study of the process of modernisation itself, and its impact on the local population.

One of the main problems in looking at the city of Jerusalem across the nineteenth and twentieth centuries is demography. Many historians have produced figures and statistics with the aim of strengthening specific claims, but what about studies that look at numbers just in terms of local inhabitants and dynamics, in order to explain processes such as the impact of modernisation on the population? Unfortunately not many of these works are available, as it seems that writing a history of Jerusalem means supporting the claims of one of the various communities' narratives. The challenge is to attempt to compile data unrelated to any particular narrative, to be used in the study of the everyday life of Jerusalem.

From Ottoman to Egyptian rule and back

The Ottoman history of Jerusalem begins with the occupation of the city by Sultan Selim I. Since 1260 the Mamluks had ruled Palestine from Egypt, but in 1517 Selim's army defeated them, ending their reign. However, it was not until the rule of his son, Kanuni Süleyman (the Law-giver, known as Süleyman the Magnificent, 1494-1566), that Jerusalem regained its importance after centuries in oblivion. He rebuilt the walls that still stand in the city today, improved the water system and established the foundations of the *millet* system, which regulated relations between the different religious communities.[2] The *beylerbeylik* (region) of Damascus, which included Palestine, was assimilated into the administrative structure of the Empire soon after the conquest of *Bilad al-Sham* (Greater Syria) although the Ottomans established a form of indirect rule, relying on local notables who remained important until the establishment of the State of Israel in 1948.[3] The *beylerbeylik* of Damascus was composed of 15 small administrative units known as *sancak*, while the *Sancak-i Kudüs-i Şerif* (Province of Jerusalem) was divided into a number of *nahiyes* (sub-districts), whose boundaries changed several times during Ottoman rule.[4] The two most important were Hebron and Jerusalem, each centred on the town it was named after.[5]

The Ottomans considered Jerusalem to be of great religious significance, as the city was regarded as the third holiest site in Islam after Mecca and Medina. However, it was not of paramount importance either strategically or economically to the new rulers, as Jerusalem was not at the centre of any important trading routes, and did not possess any military value.[6] The return of Palestine in general, and Jerusalem in particular, to the stage of international politics was triggered to an extent by the Napoleonic invasion of Egypt in 1798, which revived for Europeans, indirectly, the question of the Holy Land and of the holy places. The invasion of 1798 was carefully prepared by Bonaparte himself, gathering together troops, engineers, scientists, artists, economists, pharmacists, physicians, writers, interpreters and publishers. This was not meant to be a simple conquest of Egypt, but the transfer of contemporary French civilisation to the historic cradle of civilisation.[7] The legacy of the Napoleonic invasion, although studied intensively, has only recently been considered from the perspective of its long-term impact. The influence of the Napoleonic invasion on Palestine should not be overestimated, as the French adventure was short lived, ended in failure and had little influence on the modernisation of Palestine. Nevertheless, it has been argued that the local response to French invasion revealed the awakening of the local cultural life.[8]

The true legacy of Napoleon was picked up by Muhammad 'Ali, who became the viceroy of Egypt in 1805.[9] Muhammad 'Ali, who was of Albanian origin, came to Egypt with the Ottoman forces sent to fight against the French army in 1799, and seized power in Cairo in 1805 after the withdrawal of the French army in 1801, becoming virtually independent of Ottoman control.[10] In 1831 Muhammad 'Ali and his son Ibrahim Paşa invaded the region known as *Bilad al-Sham*, which included present-day Palestine and Syria. This proved to be a turning point in the history of modern Jerusalem. When the Egyptian army entered the city the population was fearful of what appeared to be a new invading European army: something last seen in the eleventh century, during the Crusades.[11] Muhammad 'Ali had, in the previous decades, carried out expensive reforms of the army, introducing a new style of discipline and military techniques, weaponry and uniforms; he also planned to produce armaments in Egypt, to avoid relying on European countries.[12]

In the nineteenth century, Jerusalem experienced two distinct periods of administrative, political, social, economic and military reform: the first was under the rule of Ibrahim Paşa, the then governor of Syria, while the second from 1839 until 1876, the so-called *Tanzimat* era. Following the administrative reforms imposed by the new rulers, the status of Jerusalem began to rise. Ibrahim Paşa abolished the Ottomans' administrative division of Syria and Palestine, which constituted two separate provinces. Instead, he appointed a Governor General over the entire region of Greater Syria who resided in Damascus. This process of administrative centralisation was balanced with the establishment of *maclis*, city councils, which included representatives of the elite families.[13] On a more local level, the Egyptians relied on a civil governor who was often chosen from among the local notables; the Egyptians adapted their idea of centralisation of the state according to local circumstances. However, the new rulers did not prove able to fully eradicate corruption, and had limited success in curbing the personal power of the local notables, although they did obtain positive results in some local contexts. Nevertheless, a number of changes specifically improved the status of the non-Muslim population, as Ibrahim Paşa hoped that favouring Christians would earn some European support for the Egyptian occupation of Palestine.[14] As a consequence of the elevated status of the Christian communities, as well as generally favourable conditions, the number of European visitors to the Holy Land and Jerusalem increased in the first decades of the nineteenth century.[15] However, this was not the only reason for a renewed European interest in the region: European intervention was directed primarily towards maintaining the integrity of the Ottoman Empire: its dismemberment would have likely caused a major conflict between European powers.[16] In order to extend trade with European countries the administration promoted strong religious tolerance, and new rights were granted to the *dhimmis*, non-Muslims under the protection of the state.[17] Under Egyptian rule, in the early nineteenth century the first European consuls were allowed to set up in Jerusalem as a symbol of a new approach towards Europeans and non-Muslims.[18] Particularly relevant for the city of Jerusalem was the removal of the centuries-old prohibition on building and repairing churches and synagogues and the abolition of other restrictions on non-Muslims.[19]

Besides administrative reforms, the Egyptians brought some economic developments, which were welcomed by local notables and entrepreneurs. Ibrahim Paşa promoted the introduction of new crops and new industries, with cotton and soap production proving to be the most successful.[20] Furthermore, the Egyptian authorities supported the idea of free trade, increasing access to foreign merchants.[21] Increased imports of European goods threatened local handicrafts, however, and the Egyptians encountered some opposition from local notables and inhabitants, who perceived these reforms as hostile and against their interests.[22] Furthermore Ibrahim Paşa introduced a progressive income tax to pay for increased military expenses, which hit the Palestinian elites hard.[23] Palestinians also revolted in 1834 against the military conscription imposed by the Egyptian rulers, and it took extreme measures on the part of Ibrahim Paşa to calm the insurrection.[24]

The new administration was also supported to deal with corruption and public security, as bribes, bandits and other similar problems were rife in the period preceding the occupation. In Jerusalem, the relative efficiency of the new system, and the introduction of income tax, led to the outbreak of a revolt in 1834, directed by Muslim notables of the city albeit with strong support from the peasantry.[25] The Husaynis, one of the most important families of Jerusalem, played a crucial role in the uprising. While planning the revolt against the Egyptians, the Husaynis duplicitously stated their support for the very regime they wished to overthrow; furthermore, they were trying to maintain a good relationship with the Ottomans, who eventually returned in 1840: a masterclass in Machiavellian machinations.[26] Something similar happened when the British took Jerusalem in 1917, and the burden of the surrender of the city was placed on the Mayor of Jerusalem, Husayni Salim Effendi al-Husayni.[27] After the revolt of 1834, two members of the family were included in the *maclis*, and Tahir al-Husayni was named *mufti* (leader of the local Muslim community) of Jerusalem.[28]

Egyptian rule in Jerusalem did not even last a decade (1831-1840), but its legacy reverberated throughout the administrative organisation of the city once it had been re-occupied by the Ottomans. Under Egyptian rule, the local governors fell under the purview of a council, the *meclis*, composed mainly of the Muslim elite, but also including some of the most influential Christian and Jewish members of the community. The Egyptians therefore introduced both elements of democratic representation: balances and checks.

Following the opening of the British consulate in 1838, other European powers followed, including France, Prussia, Austria and Spain, while the Russian government sent a diplomatic agent. These powers promoted business, protected travellers and supported the construction of hospitals and hospices for visitors and locals alike. The French opened three hospices between 1851 and 1889, as medical assistance granted the easiest and most direct access to local communities.[29] The activism of Europeans reinvigorated pilgrimages and tourism. Moreover, Jerusalem's increased importance on the international stage coincided with the Crimean War (1854-1856), which brought the issue of the control of the holy places to the forefront of intra-European politics. Jerusalem became the pretext for war between a Franco-Ottoman alliance against Russia. Despite the fact that the war was fought far from Jerusalem, the conflict impoverished Palestine: food, fuel and other resources were redirected to the frontlines. Jerusalem had to rely on aid from European countries, particularly Britain, France and Germany. Crime marked the emergence of new tensions between Muslims and Christians in the city, as the Greek Orthodox were accused of supporting fellow Orthodox Russia.[30] Nevertheless the Ottoman alliance with Britain and France, as well as the presence of a strong governor, prevented the situation from escalating to open violence against the Christians of the city.[31]

From the Tanzimat to the Young Turks through the Hamidian era: patterns of governance and administration

The reform movement known as *Tanzimat*, initiated in the Ottoman Empire in the first half of the nineteenth century, was linked to Muhammad 'Ali's rise to power in Egypt and his conquest of the

Bilad al-Sham. The *Tanzimat-ı Hayriye* (Auspicious Reordering) era began on 3 November 1839, when Sultan Abdülmecit promulgated the *Gülhane Hattı Şerifi* (Edict of the Rose Garden). Tax-farming was abolished, Ottoman subjects were granted security of life and property, and a new system of conscription was established. The edict also promoted the principle of equality before the law, which eventually meant the Ottoman subjects became equal.[32] Although this was a genuine attempt to promote reforms in the Empire, given the advanced process of decentralisation which had occurred in the eighteenth century, it was also part of a clear strategy adopted by the Ottomans to gain European support in their struggle against Muhammad 'Ali, who was threatening the core of the Ottoman Empire.

On 24 June 1839, Ottoman forces were defeated by the Egyptians at Nizip, in southeast Turkey. Only the intervention of the European powers stopped the advance of the Egyptian army towards the Ottoman capital. Meanwhile in the winter of 1840-41, British naval forces threatened the Egyptians, who eventually withdrew from the occupied territories of Syria and Palestine. In 1841 Muhammad 'Ali acknowledged the loss of the region, and accepted the hereditary governorship of Egypt from the Ottomans in exchange, even though he had been independent from Ottoman control. Egypt thus nominally remained a part of the Ottoman Empire until the beginning of the First World War, when the British declared the country a formal protectorate.

The *Tanzimat* reforms aimed to strengthen the Empire by implementing political and administrative centralisation. The deep essence of the *Tanzimat* was to change the very idea of the Ottoman state, which included the renovation and reinvigoration of old institutions that no longer worked and the establishment of new ones.[33] This was done through strategies including administrative reforms, development of infrastructures and economic improvements. The government was reorganised into ministries, and a Council of Ministers met in order to advise the Sultan; the government was presided over by the Grand Vizier. In the area of education, which was crucial for the modernisation of the Empire, schools were opened and new subjects taught by the mid-1850s.[34] Economic reforms proved to be hard to enforce, however. Despite the goodwill it created, the Capitulary system was a large impediment to Ottoman economic reorganisation.[35] In the mind of the Ottoman reformers, it was paramount to the idea that a more efficient and honest government would create a stronger Empire, composed of a population committed to the survival and development of the state itself. The *Tanzimat* also produced the supranational ideology of 'Ottomanism', which was designed to provide a non-religious identity to the subjects of the Empire.[36] The *Tanzimat* reforms were implemented throughout the Ottoman Empire until 1876, when Abdülhamid ascended the throne; however, despite his conservatism and the official halt to the reforms, it has been argued that the Hamidian period was the continuation of the *Tanzimat* era: he aimed to save the Empire with different means, focusing on Islam and its symbolic value to strengthen the Empire through a common religious identity.[37] Abdülhamid envisioned an efficient administration of the Empire through a strong process of reform of the bureaucratic system which, in fact, brought to fruition the previous reforms. Furthermore, the Hamidian regime was also based on personal loyalty towards the Sultan – which became almost indispensable for the ruling local elites and those wanting to join the civil service.[38] The main opposition to Abdülhamid and his regime was epitomised by the Young Turks and the Committee of Union and Progress (CUP), who staged a revolution in July 1908. The new regime envisioned a new idea of the state, with the leaders seeing themselves as the saviours of the Empire. While the revolution produced changes, it was more about restoring the Empire than changing it.[39]

The *Vilayet* law of 1864 reorganised the provinces of the Empire and remained the basis for local administration until the end of the Empire, following the First World War. The law aimed to define clear relations between the administrative units. Each *vilayet* was divided into *sancaks* or *livas* (interchangeable), then each *sancak* had several *kaza*, mainly villages.[40] The law also introduced a system of councils, which will be discussed later, to counterbalance the power of the governors. These officials were rotated so frequently that it was almost impossible to build any personal power or achieve great results in their work.[41] With the reform of the provincial administration, the ideas of the *Tanzimat* reached all regions of the Empire and became rooted in the local socio-political milieu.

With the Ottoman restoration after 1841, the *sancak* of Jerusalem regained some stability after the turbulent end of Egyptian rule. The *sancak* of Jerusalem was then composed of Jaffa, Gaza, Hebron and eventually Beersheba; following the establishment of a municipality in Istanbul in the late 1850s, Jerusalem soon followed suit.[42] Municipal government was a new institution across the Empire, as was the idea of an urban administration based on a territoriality separate from the provincial administration; it was not part of the Islamic tradition. Indeed, in Jerusalem the picture was quite different and the municipality, which was founded even before the issue of the law regulating the municipality, shows a genuine attempt to reform the Empire from the inside. Eventually, in Jerusalem the municipality became the most important local administrative body of the city, respected by both local citizens and foreigners, regardless of their identity.[43] Despite some limitations, the Jerusalem municipality contributed greatly to the development of the city and its living conditions in the late nineteenth century.[44]

It is not a simplification of the argument to say that, to an extent, administrative and local governance patterns did not alter radically throughout the three eras of the late Ottoman Empire. Centralisation and modernisation were instrumental to the survival of the Empire and were, though under different labels, promoted by *Tanzimat* reformers as well as by Abdülhamid and the CUP. The example of Jerusalem clarifies how cities were the most important recipients of all reforms carried out, and also the most important locus for tripartite competition between local elites, the Ottoman establishment, and foreigners.

The administrative units of Jerusalem have proved to be a crucial element in the process of modernisation of the city, but how can modernisation be defined and understood? Was it just imported from abroad or was it also the product of genuine internal reforms? In his seminal work on Jerusalem, Haim Gerber states that the *Tanzimat* reforms ignited a fast and lasting process of Westernisation of Jerusalem which was already underway, as a result of Egyptian rule in the 1830s, but also due to the strong impact of the West in the region since the early nineteenth century.⁴⁵ On the other hand, Nora Libertun de Duren, as well as the famous historian Martin Gilbert, have claimed that the real process of modernisation began with the arrival of the British.⁴⁶ According to these scholars, the period preceding the arrival of the British was not marked by the full imposition of the national state logic and state control, suggesting a different arrangement of people, institutions and territory. They have highlighted only the European influence, denying *de facto* an Ottoman process of state transformation.⁴⁷ A workable definition of modernisation can be summarised as a process of change which entailed the transformation of the traditional Ottoman administrative machine through the adoption of new legal and administrative tools. In this respect, modernisation is not viewed as a mere imitation of Western models but as the fruitful encounter between old and new forms of urban administration. Though Western administrative influence and cultural penetration in the Ottoman Empire was an undeniable development of the period, to equate modernisation with Westernisation is perhaps too far-fetched. At the same time, it would be an inaccuracy not to consider the *Tanzimat* as a modernising process partly inspired by Western ideals. Some processes and ideas were indeed brought to the region by Europeans but it was the local population which carried out and adapted these reforms, according to their needs and interests. Modernisation without a final recipient would be superfluous and meaningless, which is why this process could come to fruition only if linked with the final beneficiaries.

The Sancak and the Mutasarrıf

Following the end of Egyptian rule in 1841, the Jerusalem *sancak* started to enjoy a higher status amongst the other Palestinian *sancaks*, as a consequence of foreign interest in the city. In the summer of 1872, the *sancak* of Jerusalem was detached from the *vilayet* (Province) of Syria and placed under the direct control of Istanbul.⁴⁸ The *sancak*, or *mutasarrıflık* (both terms refer to the same institution) of Jerusalem was ruled by a *mutasarrıf* (governor). After the *sancak* was detached from the *vilayet* of Syria, the *mutasarrıf* of Jerusalem became unique amongst the other governors throughout the Ottoman Empire, as he was directly appointed and, therefore, responsible to the central administration in Istanbul, not to the *vali* of Syria.[49] Nevertheless, the Jerusalem *sancak*, though highly independent, was subordinate to the *vilayet* of Beirut in judicial matters, remaining so until 1910 when a Court of Appeal was established in Jerusalem. Furthermore, although troops were stationed in Jerusalem, the *sancak* was also dependent militarily on the authority of the Fifth *Ordu* (army), quartered in Damascus.[50]

The strength of the governors depended not only on their personal skills, but also on the authority given them by central government in Istanbul. *Mutasarrifs* who served in Jerusalem in the late nineteenth century were not particularly experienced, or homogeneous as a group, and none rose to a prominence in the central administration.[51] These governors were required, as part of their duties, to send the money collected from the taxpayers to Istanbul; furthermore, they did not have full control over other officials in the district.[52] They were more like administrators than powerful Paşas, framed in a complex picture which included several other actors such as notables, consuls and religious authorities, as well as the official policy of the Ottoman state, which was seeking to centralise its administrative units.

In the late nineteenth century, during the reign of Abdülhamid II, governors were appointed from among the palace secretaries of the Sultan, including Ekrem Bey, Governor of Jerusalem from 1906 and 1908. Later at the beginning of the twentieth century, governors were appointed by the Young Turks among Turkish officials.[53] It seems there were no marked changes in the character and performance of the nominated governors between the *Tanzimat*, Hamidian and Young Turks periods. It has been noted that during the last decades of Ottoman rule in Jerusalem, one or two governors were abject failures, such as Faik Bey, who in 1876 was accused of being extremely corrupt.[54] However, his successor, Rauf Paşa, who ruled Jerusalem from 1876 to 1888, was a clear exception and challenged the idea that governors were to hold the office only for a short time, proving able to control the notables and impose his authority over the powerful families.[55] Nevertheless, the process of modernisation that was taking place in the Empire improved the quality of the governors of Jerusalem (or at least the services provided), and from the *Tanzimat* era it is possible to observe an embryonic, modern pattern of public services, which followed the principle of standardisation. Governors had become more loyal to the duties of their position than to personal benefits.[56]

The municipality of Jerusalem

With the *mutassarıflık*, the largest and most important administrative unit of Ottoman Jerusalem, the municipality became the most influential and relevant institution of the city after the late 1860s. As explained earlier the idea of establishing local municipalities in the Ottoman Empire was revolutionary. In fact, according to Sunni Muslim tradition any legal entity other than the individual was unlawful.[57] The creation of this body illustrates how the *Tanzimat* reforms were successful in adopting European ideas and promoting internal reforms; eventually, the legal status of the municipality was granted using the law of the state, rather than religion. Indeed, the establishment of the municipality in Jerusalem is indicative of a trend towards modernisation in the social and administrative fields, in so far as it provided a degree of communal representation.[58] Furthermore, the establishment of municipalities across the Empire addressed the issue of the establishment and provision of public services, an indication of the centralisation and modernisation of the city's management.[59] The Jerusalem *belediye* (municipality) was one of the first to be established in the Ottoman Empire.[60] It has been suggested that the municipality was established in 1863, but only began to function fully later.[61] According to a letter sent by Ottoman governor Nazif Paşa to the Prussian consul in Jerusalem, it seems that the municipality of Jerusalem became fully operational only after 1867; however, French sources suggest an earlier date.[62] Although the municipality was established in the early 1860s, the law governing this institution was only passed in 1877, as part of legislation issued by Istanbul which regulated the reforms of the local councils across the Empire.[63] The provincial administration was restructured several times before the issue of the *Vilayet Belediye Kanunu* (Provincial Municipal Ordinance) of October 1877, defining the authority, competence, budget and legal limits of the municipality.⁶⁴ The European powers did not initially welcome the municipality, as article 19 of the 1877 law forbade those who belonged to the municipal council from being employed by or becoming a protégé of a foreign country.⁶⁵ This was meant to prevent Europeans from directly influencing the municipality. The Ottomans had already fought the power of the foreign consuls, so they did not want an internal battle with Ottoman citizens.

The *belediye* was responsible for the cleanliness of the town, maintenance of the roads and distribution of water, supervising public health, cafés and restaurants, commercial activities, urban planning, and other public services.⁶⁶ The municipality also controlled a local police force, which supervised urban communities, and sanitation of the city. From the 1880s sanitation began to improve thanks to the paving of main roads.⁶⁷ Although Jerusalem had several hospitals, in 1891 the municipality established a Municipal Hospital accessible to all the inhabitants irrespective of religion or nationality. The visit of the German Emperor in 1898 resulted in some improvement in the sanitary conditions of the city, as extensive cleaning operations were carried out inside and outside the walls. Due to the expansion of the city outside the walls, in 1905 the municipality made plans for the sanitation and lighting of the new areas, the cost of which would be split amongst the owners of the properties located outside the walls.⁶⁸ In 1911, when a cholera epidemic struck the city, the municipality intensified its efforts to clean streets and other public facilities.⁶⁹ In 1915 after war had already broken out, a local body was appointed for the distribution of provisions to the Muslim community, and informed by the municipality to save a portion of the provisions for the Municipal Hospital, managed directly by the *belediye*.⁷⁰ The municipality was also active in guaranteeing water supplies; foreign companies were called upon to help in improving the water supply for the city.⁷¹ The question of water, both its distribution and availability, became a central issue for the municipality at the beginning of the twentieth century. Water in Jerusalem was scarce and its availability affected rural as well as urban populations: scarcity of water meant less agricultural produce and therefore less tax to be collected.⁷² The newly established (1909) *Chambre de Commerce, d'Industrie et d'Agriculture de Palestine* considered access to water a primary concern for the socio-economic development of Jerusalem.[73] Nevertheless, a solution was far from being adopted: the Ministry of the Public Works delayed the works several times.[74] Only in January 1914 was the French Périer Company awarded three concessions to develop and manage electric tramway, electric light and water supply services for the municipality of Jerusalem, to the great satisfaction of the local residents.[75] Unfortunately, the war halted these works almost immediately.

In 1886 the municipality was responsible for the establishment of the first professional police force in Palestine. This police force was generally held in good regard by local and foreign residents, though the governors of Jerusalem thought otherwise. Ekrem Bey complained to his superiors in Istanbul that the police were weak and deficient.[76] Because municipal policemen were recruited from the urban population, residents believed the police force to be honest; it was often compared favourably to the detachments of the Ottoman army camped outside the city.[77] As time passed engineers, physicians and veterinarians became advisers of the *belediye*; there was also a specific municipal office in charge of registering street names and house numbers, as well as births and deaths. For instance a municipal engineer was appointed in order to control the construction of buildings, which were previously approved by means of permits issued by the municipality.[78]

In order to provide these services the municipality began to tax residents, and eventually the budget of the municipality needed to be approved by the administrative council, which also meant it could be rejected if the administrative council was required to guarantee debts contracted by the municipality.[79] The main revenues were from taxes imposed on the sale of livestock, slaughter of animals, charters and other means of transport and the lighting and cleaning of streets, but also from the issue of permits and from tolls.[80] Sometimes the municipality encountered fiscal resistance from part of the local population, namely the consuls. As noted earlier, in 1905 the municipality intended to carry out work to improve sanitation and street lighting outside the walls, charging the owners of the buildings located in those areas. Traditionally, the owners of buildings within the walls of the city were not charged for these services; the consuls thus tried to oppose the new proposal made by the municipality. Eventually the municipality was able to establish its authority, but before doing so it had to change the nature of taxation as well as adjust its monetary requirements.[81] In fact, the municipality had ample autonomy in fixing its budget, but its every decision was then challenged by other political and administrative institutions.

At the head of the municipality there was the mayor, who was under the supervision of the *mutasarrıf*. The office of mayor, although without a salary, was considered very influential; as such, the most important families of Jerusalem regarded it as a source of power and competed for appointment to this office. Until 1908, the municipal council was composed only of Arab Muslim and Arab Christian members;[82] however later in this year Jews also took part in the elections and eventually the first Jewish councillor was elected.[83] Following the Provincial Municipality Law of 1877, members of the municipality were nominated through an electoral process.[84] According to this law, the number of elected members ranged from six to 12, based on the city's population size. Only Ottoman subjects could participate in the elections. According to Yellin, a Zionist of the 'first hour' and a teacher at the Alliance Israélite Universelle, male citizens and residents over 25 years of age, paying a property tax of over 50 Turkish piastres, were eligible to vote.[85] The municipal council in Jerusalem, meanwhile was composed of ten members; candidates could be any Ottoman subject aged over 30, paying at least 150 Turkish piastres annually.[86] Members were elected for four years in a rotation, with five being replaced every two years. Eventually, the municipality became dependent on the municipal council, as well as on the governor of Jerusalem and the central government in Istanbul, as well as the attitudes of the foreign consuls and religious authorities.

The municipality was very dynamic, focusing not only on the modernisation of the city, but also on the wellbeing of its inhabitants. Despite its limits and problems, the municipality was indeed an arena for public discussion, aiming to involve the inhabitants in provision of the services required: it was a space for negotiation, rather than the polarisation of interests.

The Councils ruling Jerusalem

From the 1870s there were three councils based in Jerusalem. The *Meclis-i Belediye* (Municipal Council), discussed previously; the *Meclis-i Umumi*, the General Council of the *vilayet*; and the *Meclis-i Idare*, the Administrative Council of the *sancak*. The *Vilayet* Law of 1864 created clarity in the hierarchy of the provincial offices, resulting in the establishment of the *Meclis-i Umumi* and the *Meclis-i Idare*.[87] Nevertheless, the functions and the structure of these bodies were clearly defined with the issuing of the 1871 *Vilayet* Law, which introduced a number of regulations for city administration. The General Council of the *vilayet* of Jerusalem, the *Meclis-i Umumi*, however, became fully operational only after the issue of the *Vilayet* Law of 1913, which was passed by the Young Turks.[88]

The *Meclis-i Umumi* was meant to meet once a year for a period of no more than 40 days. Originally, the members of the General Council should have been elected on the basis of proportional representation, one representative for every 12,500 males, but the system was dropped after its inception in 1913 and the council was eventually composed of representatives from the various *kazas* (sub-districts). The original law had stated that membership in the council was to be shared on a religious basis between Muslims and non-Muslims, according to the population in the *kazas*, since Muslims were not the majority in every village.[89]

Besides the *Meclis-i Umumi*, the law of 1913 established a provincial committee (*Encümen-i Vilayet*) which would continue working whilst the General Council was not in session; its function was to check the annual budget and expenditure.[90] Rather than passing laws this assembly was meant to give approval to the governor's actions, and it has been claimed that it was nothing more than a rubber stamp.[91] However, the report of the American consul in Jerusalem to the Department of State for the year 1914 suggests that this body was fully functioning. Unfortunately, from the sources available it is not possible to gauge the real influence of the governor upon the council; nevertheless the council was vital and clearly proactive:

I have the honor to report that in accordance with the new provisions of the Vilayet Law, the general Council for the Province of Palestine has just completed its 40 days session; besides approving the Concessions for tramways, electric light and water works, several important allowances from the general budget were made as follows: An appropriation of $1,826.00 to establish a breeding farm for horses and donkeys. For the establishment of an agricultural school, $13,200.00 and the transfer of the model farm from Arteef to Sajed and from Jaffa to Hebron. For the purchase of agricultural instruments $2,640.00. Small sums were appropriated for the repairing of the roads between Hebron and Beth Jibrin, Jaffa and Gaza, Jaffa and Sabil Abu Nabbott and Hebron and the Valley of El Kort. The work of the Council produced general satisfaction as it gave the central authorities an idea of the general needs of the Province and appropriations were made to that effect.[92]

The General Council for the *vilayet* was involved in financial and budget supervision, but did not make final decisions on it, which was still the prerogative of the governor. Nevertheless, it had considerable power because, through the approval or rejection of the budget, the council could greatly affect the implementation of the administrative decisions of other governmental bodies.

The *Meclis-i Idare*, the Administrative Council of the Jerusalem district, was set up as a result of the issue of the *Vilayet* Law of 1864. The *Meclis-i Idare* included both *ex-officio* (members by virtue of holding official positions) and elected members. Among the *ex-officio* members were the *mutassarif*, a *kadi* (the judge), a *mufti* (the religious leader) and a representative of the Christian Churches and the Jewish communities. There were four elected members; generally one or two were Christians and the others Muslims. Overall there were seven Muslim members and five non-Muslims.[93] Access to the franchise was based on the ability to pay at least 150 Turkish piastres in taxation; this possibly means that only 5% to 10% of the population was involved in this process, so ultimately the members of the *Meclis-i Idare* were leaders of the local communities.[94] However, the notables represented only the wealthy constituencies, as the process allowed for only a small number of Jerusalemites to have their say, rather than the whole of the population, considering that only 1,000 of 40,000 inhabitants took part at the end of the nineteenth century.[95] In this context the *Meclis-i Idare* became a sort of 'balancing institution' between the *mutasarrıf* and the local elite, an arena where the two could meet and compete over deliberations on public works, police, land registry, agriculture, finance and tax collection. The council had the authority to appoint officials in charge of the city, but only to a limited extent: the *Meclis-i Idare* could appoint municipal policemen and gendarmes, but not other public officials.[96]

The members of the *Meclis-i Idare* spent most of their time in discussions relating to financial matters, as did their colleagues in the *Meclis-i Umumi*; however, they had control over the financial resources collected through taxation, as well as, to an extent, the power to impose taxes. Although the municipal budgets were quite limited, the *Meclis-i Idare* could deliberate on and approve those budgets, showing either its support for the municipality or its disapproval, which reflected internal battles between the notables. The council also had considerable power in matters of land holding, and the final word in issuing cadastral certificates (*tapu*) defining the value and the ownership of land and house properties, giving it responsibility for the control of the population, mainly the immigrants.[97] Jewish immigration was, of course, particularly under scrutiny as, at the turn of the century, the majority of Jewish immigrants were from Russia, the biggest enemy of the Ottoman Empire.[98] On the eve of the First World War, the *mutasarrıf* of Jerusalem, Macid Bey, wrote to the Ministry of the Interior that the Jewish immigrants were under surveillance, as were the Jews who were Ottoman subjects, in order to verify their loyalty to the Ottoman state. However, the governor also highlighted that he would not tolerate 'whoever was to make any exaggeration about the Jews as malicious people in order to raise a Jewish question'.[99]

The Establishment of the Italian hospital in Jerusalem provides an opportunity to look at the powers and mechanisms of the *Meclis-i Idare*. In 1911, the Italian Government together with the *Associazione Nazionale per Soccorrere i Missionari Italiani* (National Association for the Assistance to Italian Missionaries) planned to build a hospital in Jerusalem. The first step taken by the Italian authorities was to change the status of the land, which was the property of the consulate, from *mulk* to *mukataa*: from private land exempt from state control (the land was a property of the consulate) to a tax farm which could be developed.[100] Although the works began, the completion of the hospital was delayed as a result of the Italian-Libyan war (1911-1912) and the ensuing financial strains on the Italians.

In 1914, the National Association for Assistance to Italian Missionaries intervened, offering financial help for the hospital.[101] The following year, the members of the *Meclis-i Idare* visited the hospital whilst it was still under construction, fixing, at 3,050 francs, the tax on the value of the building (estimated at 305,080 francs). The Italian consul Conte Senni wrote immediately to the *mutasarrıf* complaining that the hospital was not yet ready; therefore it was unlawful to tax it.[102] After some time, the *Meclis-i Idare* again demanded the Italians pay, but in the meantime Italy had joined the war against the Turks; even though circumstances had changed, the Turkish authorities still sought the money. In July 1915 Senni reported that the Turkish authorities were claiming payment of 16,364 piastres as taxation on the land and the hospital.[103] Not surprisingly, the Italian Foreign Office ordered the consul not to pay the tax on the hospital building, as it was closed and sealed; in an unexpected turn, however, the Italian Government authorised the consul to pay tax on the land.[104] The hospital remained closed until the end of the war.

Although most of the material available for the *Meclis-i Idare* concerns minutes of a trivial nature, it does not necessarily mean that the council dealt only with matters such as the amendment of entries in the Population Register or the issuing of 'good behaviour' certificates.[105] Its members were often employed as intermediaries, or served on *ad hoc* committees, as in the case of the Italian hospital, where the tax committee visited the Italian building in person to determine the amount of taxation to impose.[106] The council was not an executive one, but mostly functioned passively, meaning that it usually reacted to problems submitted by other actors, such as the municipality, the *mutasarrıf*, consular agents or even private citizens.[107] Unlike the municipality, these councils were more detached from the local population, though the issue of Jewish immigration could still easily inflame debates between their members. Despite this apparent distance from the population the decisions taken, whether positive or negative, impacted on the local environment and population.

The overview of the administrative structure of Jerusalem in the late Ottoman Empire has clearly shown that reformers aimed primarily to centralise and reorganise the Empire. Eventually, it was up to the local governors to implement these reforms, becoming, in a passive way, agents of modernisation, though some proved to be quite proactive. Besides governors, local notables also became agents for change in Jerusalem, as they played the role of intermediaries between the Ottoman establishment, foreigners and the local population. Last, but not least, European consuls and individuals were also powerful agents of modernisation. It was the rise of European interest in the region that brought about dramatic changes, as a European presence meant not only direct influence over the Ottoman administration, but also economic integration into the world market. It would, however, be unfair not to stress the significance of the Ottoman reforms and local efforts, and simply to attribute the modernisation process to external actors. The creation of new urban institutions as a result of centralisation brought the elites and the educated population of Jerusalem much closer to the political centre of the Ottoman state. Also, individuals, through the creation of associations and an increasingly strong press, played a role in the promotion of a genuine locally based process of modernisation. The emergence of a local intelligentsia made Jerusalem the centre of cultural and intellectual ferment and competition.[108]

The Notables of Jerusalem in the late Ottoman era

If, on the one hand, Jerusalem was ruled by Ottoman officials as well as by religious authorities and foreign consuls, their power was also balanced by the presence of local groups possessing, to different degrees, social and political influence.[109] These groups, who formed the backbone of the local elites, were a class of notables who functioned as intermediaries between the population, the Ottoman administration, and other powerful agencies. These notables, whose political profile was rather complex, derived their power from economic sources and from their religious legitimacy. The concept of 'politics of notables' in the Arab Middle East was coined by Albert Hourani, in order to explain the political configuration of Arab cities under Ottoman control. According to Hourani, the 'politics of notables' needed specific conditions, first when a social milieu was ordered around patronage; secondly when urban society was dominated by members of influential families who were able to control the rural hinterland; and thirdly when these local notables could act freely in the political sense.[110] The notables were thus an informal elite, composed of the richest, most powerful and prestigious families of the Arab cities.[111] Local notables mediated between the society that they represented and the state authority that often appointed them. As intermediaries, they had both to possess the political qualities to represent their constituencies and to be able to bargain with their counterparts.

The socio-political elite of Jerusalem was composed of two groups: the Muslim religious leadership (*ulama*), who provided a voice for popular grievances and demands mainly through the Friday prayer, but also from Christian leaders; and the secular notables (*a'yan, amirs*), families or individuals whose power was rooted in the genealogic memory of the ancestors (the *asabiyyah* of the family), who controlled the wealth, and commodities such as land and commercial activities. A third group of notables would base their power on the control of local military garrisons (*aghwat*); however, as the military command for the region was based in Damascus, there were no military notables in Jerusalem and the local notables could not build their power on military strength.[112] Jerusalem was not of any particular military or strategic value and, therefore, Ottoman troops were camped in other towns and cities, leaving Jerusalem practically undefended.

The notables of Jerusalem were predominantly Muslim and Christian, but there were also some Jewish families included in this group, like the famous Valeros.[113] These elites were not officially organised, and worked on an informal basis. They were open groups, and mobility within and between them was not only allowed but promoted (the only boundaries not crossed were of a religious nature, and intermarriage between people of different religious backgrounds was not common); movement thus occurred in groups belonging to the same religion. These families, regardless of their creed, not only knew each other very well, but were connected by means of frequent meetings, business, and exchange of services and favours.

In the case of Jerusalem, the question of the local notables fits into the framework presented by Hourani, albeit with some specific exceptions. The notables of Jerusalem in the late Ottoman era were mainly from three families, who occupied most of the available agencies: the Husaynis, the Khalidis and the Nashashibis.[114] As Jerusalem was very far from important commercial routes, these notables did not base their power on wealth from trade, but on land ownership in the rural hinterland of the city. It was the control of the key administrative, political and religious posts that conferred their authority over the population and consolidated their position as intermediaries with the Ottoman administration from the end of Egyptian occupation in 1841.[115]

Ottoman officials held the main administrative positions, such as that of governor of the province and of *kaimmakams* (district governor or senior officials). However, Jerusalemite Arabs, mainly Muslims, were allowed to be part of the lower ranks of the administration, like a *müdür* (director of school).[116] The Turkish governors always tried to balance the power of the different families by playing them off against one another, guarding against any single family becoming too powerful. They would also assign notables to key positions within the province and rotate them periodically, to prevent a single family monopolising certain positions.[117]

The Arab notables were largely found in the spheres of law and education. They presided over the religious courts (*qadi*) as well as the religious and state schools. During the *Tanzimat* era, when education was secularised and brought under the control of the central government, the Arab notables found a way to adapt to the new system.[118] The Khalidis supported the reforms of Ali and Fuad Paşas whilst the Husaynis, claiming a direct link with the Prophet, opposed both the Egyptian and *Tanzimat* reforms due to their secular character.[119] With the end of the *Tanzimat* era in 1876,

Sultan Abdülhamid II turned against the supporters of the previous regime, with the Khalidis suffering the most as they lost their primacy among the notables of Jerusalem whilst the Husaynis monopolised the function of *mufti* and became the administrators of the mosque of Nebi Musa.[120] The Hamidian regime significantly reshaped the image and career patterns of the notables in the Arab lands.[121]

The notables of Jerusalem proved to be the cornerstone of Jerusalem's fragmented social framework. Both under Ottoman and British rule, the notables of the city struggled to retain their pre-eminence, as the demographic realities of the city were changing as a result of Jewish immigration. To this effect, the speech of Ruhi al-Khalidi (Bey), elected to the Ottoman Parliament in 1908 following the CUP revolution, is quite instructive. Ruhi Bey warned that Palestine was in danger because of Zionism and the number of settlers coming to Palestine.[122] Though the majority of the inhabitants of Jerusalem, towards the end of the nineteenth century, were not Arab Muslims, the notables managed to keep control of the Administrative Council with six Muslim members and only two Christians and two Jews.[123]

With the advent of the Young Turks in 1908, the status of Jerusalem's notables underwent, once again, some radical changes, with the Khalidis now back on the main stage of Jerusalem's political scene. The first phase of Young Turks' rule was welcomed by the local population at the end of the Hamidian police regime.[124] However, following the 1909 failed attempt at a counter-revolution inspired by Abdülhamid in Istanbul, the Young Turks started to promote a different idea of Ottomanism, which focused essentially on the promotion of the Turkish identity and thereby undermined the power of the Jerusalem notables. Following the prohibition on political associations, issued in the same year, as a result of rising opposition to the Young Turks, some local notables became Arab activists in secret societies, promoting early Arab nationalist ideals in Jerusalem.[125] These societies promoted Arab autonomy and/or independence and were composed of notables as well as teachers, students and Arab army officers.[126] Interestingly, however, some of these associations predate the Young Turks revolution: in 1905 an Arab association called *Ligue de la Patrie Arabe* wrote an open letter to Arabs under Turkish rule, accusing Abdülhamid of being a usurper and a tyrant.[127] Nonetheless, it seems that this was an isolated case, as it was the later betrayal of the Ottomanist idea by the Young Turks, and then by the CUP, that led many Arabs to become activists.[128] A report by the British Arab Bureau in Cairo, gathering enquiries made through natives of Jerusalem living in Cairo after the autumn of 1914, describes the notable families as not being pro-Turk, but being compelled to support the Turks.[129] Some less prominent members of the Husayni family were arrested in the last days of Ottoman rule, accused of being pro-British: they hoped that a British victory would end Turkish rule.[130] The problem with these reports is that they do not investigate the reasons why notables turned against the Ottomans, showing just a superficial and propagandistic side of a more complex situation involving this class at the end of Ottoman rule.

The People of Jerusalem (1905-1922): figures and definitions

In the cities of Palestine there was a strong tradition of urban local patriotism, and the idea of being a Jerusalemite was thus deeply rooted among the local population.[131] However, considering the particular character and nature of Jerusalem, the question of who the Jerusalemites were is complex. The local population under the Ottoman government, following the general rule of the *millet* system, was divided along religious lines. Using cultural patterns, the population of Jerusalem can be considered to have been portioned along two axes: the first representing a religious cleavage, the second representing ethnic and linguistic cleavages. The first subdivision corresponded with the official one enforced by Ottoman religious law, as exemplified by the *millet* system; the second represents the divisions which reflect ethnicity, nationality and language, while self-representation also played a major role in the definition of the various communities residing in Jerusalem. An additional element was the presence of foreigner communities, further complicating Jerusalem's demographic landscape.

The following tables present a collection of data on the demography of Jerusalem from the beginning of the twentieth century until 1922, including the data provided by the first British official census. The main purpose of this reconstruction is to analyse the structure and composition of Jerusalem in the transitional period from the Ottomans to the British. Unfortunately, population statistics are often used as evidence to support claims over the city, rather than for the study of the everyday life of the local population.

The main issue about the demographic history of Jerusalem is, that up until 1922, the date of the first British official census, there are no official statistics available. Most of the available information comes from Western travellers, consuls or residents. On the Ottoman side, a register was held for the urban population called *nüfus*. The General Administration of Population Registration (*Sicill-I Nüfus Idare-I Umumiyesi*) was established during the Hamidian period in the late nineteenth century as part of the system of control created for the empire; however, only Ottoman subjects were recorded.[132] In 1905 there was an attempt to update the *nüfus*, adopting the European census style. Every individual Ottoman subject was recorded according to sex, year of birth and marital status: Jews and Christians, coming from foreign countries but considered as permanent residents, were not recorded.[133]

The influential work of Schmelz is one of the most important sources for the demographic history of Jerusalem, as he has worked thoroughly on the Ottoman sources available from the *nüfus* and the 1905 census and offers statistics regarding the population of the region (*kaza*) of Jerusalem. As is apparent to the readers, the main problem with Schmelz's work, as far as Jerusalem is concerned, is that the statistics available do not detail figures for the urban population, but only for the Jerusalem region.[134]

Relying on a vast set of various sources, Table 1 reports the figures of all the sources it has been possible to gather from 1905 to 1919. Table 2 presents Schmelz's figures for the Jerusalem region, to be used for a comparison with the figures available for Jerusalem as urban centre. Table 3 shows the figures of the British census of 1922. Tables 4 and 5 present the breakdown of the figures of the census of 1922 in relation to the city within and outside the walls. The main division of the population is based on religious lines, but where other criteria have been taken into consideration, notes are provided.[135]

Table 1: Population of city of Jerusalem from late Ottoman era to British census 1922.

Source	Year	Muslims	Christians	Jews	Others	Total
Robinson P.[136]	1905			45,000		66,000
Gueyraud[137]	1909			50,000		
Schölch A.[138]	1910	12,000	13,000	45,000		70,000
British consul[139]	1911				350[140]	80,000
Luncz[141]	1913	10,050	16,750	48,400		75,200
Biger G.[142]	1914					80,000
Bish. Blyth[143]	1914			60,000		75,000
Matson O.G.[144]	1914	10,000	15,000	50,000		80,000
Arab Bureau[145]	1914	20,000	25,000	45,000		90,000
War Office[146]	1914	9,000	14,000	57,000		80,000
Bentwich N.[147]	1914			60,000		100,000
American consulate[148]	1914					90,000
American consulate[149]	1915					85,000
Ruppin A.[150]	1915			45,000		80,000
Storrs R.[151]	1917	11,000		30,000		
Zionist Org.[152]	1917	10,600	11,663	31,147		54,410
Segev[153]	1917			27,000		55,000
Biger G.[154]	1917					55,000
Andrews F.F.[155]	1918			40,000	*[156]	60,000
Bentwich N.[157]	1919			30,000		60,000

Table 2: Schmelz's figures for the Jerusalem *kaza*.

Source	Year	Muslims	Christians	Jews	Others	Total
Schmelz U.O.[158]	1914	79,000	42,000	45,000		165,000

Table 3: British census 1922.[159]

Muslims	Christians	Jews	Total
13,413 (24,45%)	14,699 (23,50%)	33,971 (54,30)	62,578

Table 4: Breakdown of the figures of the British census within the walls.

	Muslims	Christians	Jews	Others	Total
Male	5,159	3,809	2,673	1[160]	11,642
Female	4,186	3,453	2,966		10,605
Total	9,345	7,262	5,639	1	22,247

Table 5: Breakdown of the figures of the British census outside the walls.

	Muslims	Christians	Jews	Others	Total
Male	2,645	3,792	14,040	489	20,969
Female	1,423	3,645	14,292	5	19,362
Total	4,068	7,437	28,332	494[161]	40,331

These tables show figures over a relatively long period, but the data from 1914 and 1917 show the changes in the pattern of the population during the transition from Ottoman to British rule. It is reasonable to argue that the urban population of Jerusalem in 1914 was approximately 80,000 people. The exceptions are represented by the estimates provided by Norman Bentwich, a senior British official in the British administration of Palestine and a Zionist activist, who places the population of Jerusalem at approximately 100,000 individuals. Unless one is considering the inhabitants of the city's immediate hinterland as part of Jerusalem, the figure provided by Bentwich is unreliable; furthermore it is not clear where Bentwich gathered this data from.[162] The American consulate and the Arab Bureau present an estimated population of 90,000 people living in Jerusalem. It seems, however, that the Arab Bureau relied on the information provided by the American consul in the monthly Consular Sanitary Report which reported on contagious diseases and deaths. As Americans included some villages close to Jerusalem in the report, it is not an exaggeration in the estimation, but rather a result of counting in a larger area.[163] The figure of 80,000 people living in Jerusalem by 1914 becomes reliable once some clear miscalculations have been discarded. Furthermore, it is necessary to consider the slow but constant increase of the population in Jerusalem due primarily to Jewish immigration. Fr Robinson, a clergyman of the Custody of the Holy Land, estimated that there were 66,000 people living in Jerusalem in 1905.[164] By 1910, according to Schölch, there had been an increase of 5,000 individuals.[165] According to Luncz and Bishop Blyth, 75,000 inhabitants lived in Jerusalem by 1913, which means another increase of 5,000 in less than three years. In view of this, an estimate of 80,000 inhabitants in 1914 appears, after all, to be the closest to the actual number of people living in the city.[166]

Between 1905 and 1914 the Jewish population of Jerusalem was between 45,000 and 50,000, representing the majority.[167] In 1914, however, the figures for Jewish inhabitants in the city are quite conflicting: they range from 45,000 to 60,000 individuals. According to the sources available, a figure of around 50,000 Jews would perhaps be a fair assessment because in 1914 the Ottoman government enforced laws against Jewish immigration, so the number of Jews moving to Jerusalem decreased (even though restrictions did not always work). Figures of 60,000 Jews living in Jerusalem, therefore, appear to be unrealistic. Furthermore according to the Ottoman data elaborated on by Schmelz, the 45,000 Jews living in the *kaza* of Jerusalem were concentrated in the city of Jerusalem in 1914, giving more credibility to smaller figures.[168] Christians and Muslims were more or less equally divided, although figures available for the same year are, once again, conflicting. However, relying on previous and subsequent figures, it appears that, with a total population of 80,000 people (of whom 50,000 were Jews) there were approximately 15,000 Muslims and 15,000 Christians. Considering that the majority of the Christian population of Jerusalem was Arab, it is not unreasonable to suspect that mistakes could have been made through confusing Christian Arabs with Muslims.

The statistics available for 1917 and 1918 suggest that a sudden decrease occurred in the population. The figures of 55,000-60,000 inhabitants in Jerusalem after the British conquest appear to be reliable and consistent with the inevitable reduction of the population caused by the war: deportation of Jews and other subjects, alongside the military mobilisation of Ottoman subjects, may have led to a plausible decrease of 20,000-25,000.[169] Upon their arrival the British, therefore, found a city that had lost almost a third of its inhabitants. Particularly impressive is the diminution in the number of Jews (which had halted by 1918) although they still formed the largest community in Jerusalem. According to the figures provided by the British census of 1922, the population of Jerusalem increased very slowly due to a difficult recovery in the aftermath of the war. The figure of 62,000 inhabitants registered in 1922 is not far from the 55-60,000 registered in 1917, but considerably fewer than the 80,000 inhabitants of 1914. Indeed, this reduction has been the object of much speculation, as many historians claimed this was the result of extensive deportation or massacres committed by the Ottomans during the war.

The figures for the inhabitants of Jerusalem suggest that it is necessary to find some general guidelines and cleavages that can lead us to the definition of the social, ethnic and religious identities of the Jerusalemites. Regarding the Muslim community, despite the presence of a very small minority of North Africans and Indians, the great majority of the Sunni Muslims in Jerusalem were of Arab origin, although there was also a small community of Turkish officials who shared this religious affiliation with the local population. No Shi'a Muslims have ever been reported as resident in the city.[170] While the Muslims of Jerusalem may have appeared to be a solid monolith, they were divided in terms of loyalties towards their notables and religious leaders. Ronald Storrs, the first British governor of Jerusalem, noted in his diary that the Muslim community in Jerusalem was unlike the Jewish and the Christian communities; Muslims were not subdivided into rites and denominations, but into two partisanships loyal to the Husayni and the Nashashibi families.[171]

The Jewish community was the largest in the city. Nevertheless the Jews were not a homogeneous community, as they were divided by their ethnic origins and their degree of piety and involvement in religious activities. In terms of origins, the Jewish community was divided between Ashkenazim and the Sephardim, and other smaller groups such as the Yemenites and Bukharians.

The Ashkenazi Jews of Jerusalem were of east-central European origin. The name Ashkenaz was applied in the Middle Ages to the Jews living in Northern France and Western Germany. Eventually, by the eleventh century, these Jews had moved to Poland, Lithuania and Russia. The Ashkenazim spoke Yiddish, a combination of German and Hebrew. Generally speaking, the term Ashkenazim was used for Jews of European, mainly German, origins.[172] The history of the Sephardim Jews is quite different. Some Jews, after the Diaspora of 70 AD, settled on the coast of North Africa, Spain and Portugal. After the Christian *reconquista* of 1492, some moved to Venice or London, where it was easier for them to settle; others remained under Muslim, and then Ottoman, rule in North Africa, and other Middle Eastern areas such as Palestine or Persia. Sephardim spoke a combination of Spanish and Hebrew known as Ladino. Most of the Jews living in the Middle East also spoke Arabic.[173]

According to Ronald Storrs, governor of Jerusalem from 1918 to 1926, in 1917 Jerusalem there were 16,000 Ashkenazim and 14,000 Sephardim, while the Israeli scholar Ben-Arieh states that there were 13,446 Sephardim and 13,125 Ashkenazi Jews in Jerusalem in 1916.[174] The Sephardim community was the largest in Jerusalem at the beginning of the twentieth century, but, following the Jewish immigration from central Europe, the Ashkenazim Jews became the majority.[175] The first wave of Jewish immigration (*'aliyah*) started in 1882, driven mainly by Zionist ideals and pogroms, which brought around 25,000 Ashkenazi Jews to Palestine. The second *'aliyah* took place between 1904 and 1914; some 40,000 Jews moved to Palestine, mainly from Russia, following the outbreak of pogroms and anti-Semitism.[176]

The Yemenite and Bukharian were two small Jewish communities, the former from Yemen and the latter from Bukhara in Central Asia.[177] The Yemenites arrived in Jerusalem in the 1880s whilst the Bukharians made their appearance in the city in the late 1860s, establishing a small quarter.[178] The Sephardic Jews of Jerusalem were mainly organised into independent communities, based on their place of origin. Besides the Bukharian and Yemenite communities among the Sephardim, there were the Jews from Kurdistan, Damascus, Georgia, Persia and Morocco. Among the Sephardim Jews of Jerusalem, it seems that subdivisions were conceived along geographical origin, but the general Sephardim identity united them when necessary, as in the case of the distribution of the *halukka* (organised collection of funds in Europe and America for the indigent Jews of Palestine). The money sent from the Jewish communities outside Palestine to the Sephardi leadership was divided into three parts, according to different needs, such as municipal expenses or support to religious scholars.[179]

With few exceptions, all the Jews of Jerusalem belonged to one of these communities or *kollelim* (Jewish community defined according to the particular religious rite followed). However, Ashkenazi were also organised according to country of origin, like the Sephardim, and sources of financial support.[180] It was among the Ashkenazim that a full range of orthodox, ultra-orthodox, Hasidism and Agudists, who refused to use Hebrew for any purpose except prayer, and, eventually, secular Jews, were to be found.[181] The Jewish community of Jerusalem was therefore atomised into countless groups and sects. Membership of these groups ranged from several thousand to several families, such as the Karaites Jews, an ancient sect composed of around 50 people at the beginning of the twentieth century.[182]

In Jerusalem, Christianity was also affected by the same atomisation that shaped the Jewish communities. Some of the Christian denominations were defined according to geographical provenance, others according to religious tradition. The three main Christian communities of Jerusalem were the Armenians, the Greek

Orthodox Church and the Latins (Roman Catholics).[183] The Christian Churches during the war will be discussed separately; nevertheless, in the context of the current analysis of the population of Jerusalem, it is important to note who these Christians were. The Armenian community was composed mainly of clergy, up until the years of the war; in fact, lay Armenians were not allowed to settle permanently in the Armenian convent area.[184] Armenians were among the first pilgrims to visit Jerusalem after the fourth century.[185] The Armenian quarter, located in the old city, was thus used as shelter for pilgrims and visitors. Furthermore, after the British conquest of Jerusalem, there was a consistent influx of the survivors of the killings of 1915 in Eastern Anatolia: 20,000 Armenians reached Palestine as refugees.[186]

If the Armenian Church represented a solid and homogeneous institution, the cases of the Greek Orthodox Church and the Latins were quite different. The Greek Orthodox Church represented the majority of Christians in Jerusalem. In 1914, out of 15,000 Christians, there were approximately 7,000 Greek Orthodox.[187] The large majority of the Greek Orthodox laity and the lower clergy were of Arab origin, whilst the hierarchy was ethnically Greek. The Arabs were not involved in the administration of the Church at a higher level; therefore, a conflict between the two groups developed in the middle of the nineteenth century, and continued to exacerbate relations between the two.[188] Another interesting feature of the Greek Orthodox Church in Jerusalem was that, in the nineteenth century, Russia had assumed the role of protector of the Orthodox population of the Ottoman Empire.[189] This was a political manoeuvre enabling Russia to exert more influence over Istanbul. With the end of both the Russian and Ottoman Empires, the Greek Orthodox community of Jerusalem went through a period of great uncertainty, exacerbated by serious financial difficulties.

The Catholic community was not the largest in Jerusalem, but was regarded as the most powerful. Before the war there were approximately 4,000 Roman Catholics and 500 Uniate Catholics.[190] There were Arabs among the Catholics, although not in the same number as those belonging to the Greek Orthodox Church; other members of the church included clergy and laity from many different countries. The majority of the Catholics in Jerusalem were of the Latin rite; however a significant number of Catholics belonged to Uniate Churches of Oriental rite, such as the Armenian Catholics, the Greek Catholics, and the Maronites. A second split in the Catholic Church is represented by place of origin.

The European countries, through the protection of their subjects in Palestine, attempted to influence both Ottoman and Church politics in the region. France was, by tradition, the protector of Catholic interests in the Holy Land. However, other governments did not hesitate to intervene in local issues on an *ad hoc* basis to protect their own interests. The majority of the Catholics were Italian, French, Spanish, and Austrian, but there were clergy and laity from virtually all over the world. Indeed, the very meaning of Catholic as 'universal' perfectly fits Jerusalem.

Other Christian communities were living in Jerusalem, some of them very small, like the Ethiopians and the Copts; however, relative newcomers such as the Protestants and Anglicans were both numerically and socially relevant. The German Protestants and the English Anglicans began to establish their presence in Jerusalem in 1841, with the establishment of a Bishopric, but after its dissolution in 1887, both Anglicans and Protestants established their own institutions. In 1914 there were about 1,500 Anglican/Protestants in the city.[191] They were concerned mainly with missionary and social activities, directed towards the population of Jerusalem. Although there were some conversions amongst the Arab population, the Anglican-Protestant communities comprised mainly German, English and American citizens, who had moved to Jerusalem animated by religious fervour.

A second group of residents were members of the Ottoman administration. Although there are no official statistics regarding the members of the Ottoman establishment living in the city, it can be assumed that before the war there were 1,000-1,500 individuals.[192] Apart from the different religious authorities residing in the city, there was a tiny, but powerful, community representing foreign countries. This included not only consuls, or consular agents (who will be discussed in detail in the following chapters) but also members of the Ottoman Public Debt Administration, the institution which had, since 1881, managed the Ottoman finances. There were also members of the Zionist Organisation, who were investigating the possibility of Jewish immigration to Palestine. The majority of these individuals, though not settled on permanent basis, invested money and resources whilst in Jerusalem, as in the case of the early British consul J. Finn, while others established businesses. Businessmen of French, British, German, Italian and American citizenship were also part of the Jerusalem environment; if Jaffa was the main commercial centre, it was in Jerusalem where the political game was played: therefore, traders needed to have offices and representatives in order to lobby the Turkish, and then the British, government.[193]

Analysis of the population of Jerusalem from 1905 to the 1920s clearly highlights a complex and rapidly changing picture, with an apparent pattern pointing towards the growth of the Jewish population, a reflection of decisions taken outside Palestine. The early-modern history of Jerusalem was marked first by its re-establishment on the world map as a primary religious and political centre, as a result of the Napoleonic invasion of Egypt, the rule of Muhammad 'Ali and then by the emergence of the Jewish question on the international stage, which had profound effects on Palestine. The changing structure of the population of Jerusalem brought new opportunities of economic development and of modernisation; however, the newly emerging social composition of the city was responsible for newer and stronger divergences among the different communities living in Jerusalem. The Ottoman administration through the municipality attempted to consider Jerusalem as a community composed of different sections; however this idea of civil unity was washed away by the war and replaced by the Jerusalem of biblical images and collective memories.

2

CHRISTIANITY AT WAR

> Pray for the peace of Jerusalem:
> They shall prosper that love thee.
> Peace be within thy walls,
> And prosperity within thy palaces.
> (Psalms 122:6-7)

In 1914, the Christian Churches of Jerusalem were an integral part of the social, political and religious landscape of the city, despite the fact that, since the very beginning of the Christian era, Christianity had been divided. Christian religious institutions have been often, if not always, studied in the contexts of religious, archaeological, legal and political fields; but seldom in relation to the local milieu. Most of the literature on Jerusalem seems to have forgotten that these institutions were part of the local social fabric: the clergy might have been alien, but they still lived in the city and most of the followers were local residents. Although most of these institutions were *de facto* national agencies 'unofficially' representing European governments, the Churches were also involved in local issues. In the period preceding the war, the borders between local and international issues which were debated and affected the Christian institutions of Jerusalem were clearly marked; however, with the war as a catalyst, relationships between different actors were renegotiated and reshaped following the new situation in the post-war period. Looking at Christian Jerusalem, the study of a representative institution will provide details of the complexity of the internal and external relationships and the associations with the local population. Secondly, the focus will shift to how local Christianity reacted to some of the outcomes of the war, and how the Arab-Christian identity of local residents was set aside in favour of a shared identity with the Arab Muslim section of the population. This particular discussion aims to challenge the common misperception that it was primarily Muslims who opposed Zionism and Jewish immigration.

The Christian Churches of Jerusalem in history

To understand how the war helped the renegotiation of the relationships between the Christian institutions and the local population of Jerusalem and how these institutions were reshaped, it is necessary to go back into the distant past. In the fourth century, with the edict of 313 the Roman Emperor gave legal recognition to the faith, moved the imperial capital from Rome to Byzantium and called the first Ecumenical Council of Nicea to elaborate on the contents of the faith.[1] Once Christianity had been declared legal, contest for control of the holy places began, and Jerusalem, being the place where Jesus lived and died, was granted special status by the first Christian communities. Even before Constantine took an interest in the city, Christian pilgrims were already visiting Jerusalem: indeed, Constantine was instrumental in raising the status of the city itself.[2] After the Council of Chalcedon in 451, five major Episcopal Sees had been recognised as having priority status – among them Jerusalem, which was granted patriarchal status. Political and doctrinal struggles between Rome and Constantinople (the new name for Byzantium) became rife in the following centuries, ending with the schism of 1054. Jerusalem, which had fallen under Muslim rule in the seventh century, carried on with the eastern tradition. Despite being ruled by Muslims, the Patriarchate endeavoured to secure the highest degree of autonomy possible from the Muslim governments, in order to control the holy places and avoid interference in the internal affairs of the community.[3]

Following the schism of 1054, the Catholic Church in Jerusalem separated from the Greek Orthodox Church. The Latin Kingdom of Jerusalem was established by the Crusaders in 1099, and the Catholic Church began to implement policies which would 'latinise' the local Church, damaging the Eastern (Greek-speaking)

Churches. Most of their clergy were banned from the Holy Sepulchre and other places, and the Greek patriarchs of Jerusalem were exiled to Cyprus in 1291 after Acre was lost to the Muslim armies.[4] It seems that the local population, both Greek and Latin, accepted the authority of the new Patriarch.[5]

In 1187, when the Muslim military commander Salah al-Din reconquered the city, Christians and Jews were granted the status of *dhimmi*: protected people as *ahl al-kitab* (people of the book). Islam established the legal superiority of Muslims over *dhimmi* but granted privileges of protection over non-Muslim subjects.[6] As long as Christians accepted Muslim rule, they were allowed to practise their religion and control matters regulating personal status, but were limited in their expressions of religiosity in the public arena. Salah al-Din prescribed that the Greek Patriarch would represent all Christians in Jerusalem, and restrictions were imposed on the display of Christian symbols such as the Cross, while very strict laws regulated the construction and restoration of churches.[7] Christians were also excluded from military service, prohibited from carrying weapons, and were required to pay a special tax. These limitations established their legal and social inferiority in Jerusalem, as well as across the *Dar al-Islam*.[8] The Latin Patriarchate moved to St John of Acre until 1291, when the Crusaders were expelled from the city by the new Muslim power: the Mamluks.[9] In this period, the Greek Orthodox Patriarchate of Jerusalem became very closely linked to Constantinople and the Byzantine political and religious tradition. When Constantinople was captured by the Ottoman Turks in 1453, the link between the two cities was severed and the Patriarchate of Jerusalem became destitute. The situation changed in 1517 when the Ottoman Sultan, Selim I, took Syria and Palestine from the Mamluks. The Patriarchate of Jerusalem underwent major changes which reshaped its authority, image and role in the city.

Under Ottoman rule, Christians remained second-class subjects, but their condition improved considerably compared to previous periods. The Ottomans consolidated the status of *dhimmi* through the establishment of the *millet* system, a semi-independent religious organisation for *ahl al-kitab* communities, which granted legal recognition to these particular religious communities throughout the Empire.¹⁰ Initially only four *millets* were recognised: the Muslim, Greek Orthodox, Armenian and Jewish, although the Catholics were nominally part of the Greek Orthodox *millet*. Rapidly, the Christian *millets* increased in number due to pressure from the religious authorities and various European countries.¹¹ Each community was responsible for the allocation and collection of taxes, the educational system and religious matters. The *millet* organisation applied only to Ottoman subjects, however, in fact foreigners had been under the jurisdiction of the Capitulations (see below) since the sixteenth century.¹² The *millet* system itself lasted until the end of Ottoman rule, although it did witness considerable transformation in the nineteenth and twentieth centuries as a result of the *Tanzimat* reforms, the influence of the Young Turks rule, and the Balkan Wars in 1912-1913.¹³

After the Latin Patriarchate had moved, first to Cyprus and then to Rome in 1374, it was only with the Franciscans that the Catholics regained a foothold in Jerusalem. Although the history of the Custody of the Holy Land will be discussed in more detail later, it is important to underline that it was the establishment of the *Provincia di Terra Santa* (Province of the Holy Land) in the first General Chapter in 1217 and the visit to the Holy Land, though not to Jerusalem, by Saint Francis of Assisi in 1219 that slowly reopened the doors of the city to the Latins. Eventually, the Franciscan apostolate replaced Christian military expeditions.¹⁴ With the two papal bulls 'Gratias Agimus' and 'Nuper Charissimae' in 1342, Pope Clement VI granted the Franciscans the guardianship of the holy places. The Franciscan institution became known as the 'Custody of the Holy Land' led by a Custodian called *Custos*.¹⁵

By 1912, the 15,000 Christians who lived in Jerusalem belonged to the following denominations: Greek Orthodox, Roman Catholic, Armenian Catholic, Greek Catholic, Armenian Orthodox, Coptic, Ethiopian, Syrian, Anglican and Protestant.¹⁶ However, the size of the city's Christian communities did not determine their political and religious influence; rather, it was the degree of control exercised by their clergy and the European powers over the holy places which determined their importance. The Copts, for instance, were a very small group, but had held the right to display hanging lamps in the Holy Sepulchre from the sixteenth century or even earlier. They also possessed a small thirteenth-century chapel behind the aedicule where they were allowed to organise a procession on Good Friday. All this gave them a status never achieved by the larger Anglican community, which still does not enjoy such rights.[17] It was a matter of prestige rather than power, yet occasionally prestige was transformed into real power.

The Greek Orthodox and Roman Catholics represented the largest and most powerful Christian communities in the late nineteenth and early twentieth centuries. The Armenian Church grew in importance during the First World War as a result of the fierce conflict between Ottomans and Armenians, culminating in massacres and forced deportation of Armenians throughout the Empire.

Patriarchates between the Ottomans and the European Powers

At the beginning of Ottoman rule, the authorities in Jerusalem supported the Orthodox Church against the Latins, who were identified with the European powers. In the seventeenth century, the Ottoman Sultans also restored some possessions and rights to the Greek Orthodox Patriarchate, which had been given to the Catholics by local authorities.[18] Sultan Ahmet I, for example, issued a *firman* in 1605, giving the Greek Orthodox Church control over the northern part of the Calvary in the Holy Sepulchre, while another *firman* of 1637 issued by Sultan Murad IV gave the Orthodox the possession of the Stone of Unction and the whole of the Calvary.[19] At the same time, however, the residence of the Patriarch was moved from Jerusalem to Istanbul, consolidating the tight links between the Patriarchate and the Ottoman state.[20] The appointment of the Patriarch of Jerusalem was decided by the Ecumenical Patriarch of Constantinople; the latter was dependent on the Ottoman authorities.

The Ottoman administration was inclined to play the Orthodox and Catholic Churches off against one another, according to the interests of the Ottomans but also according to the pressure exercised from the European powers.[21] Following the Ottoman occupation of Jerusalem, the Catholics looked for support from

Venice, Genoa, Austria and, eventually, France, which emerged as the protector of Catholic interests in the sixteenth century, following the stipulation of Capitulations.[22] For much of its long history, the Greek Orthodox Church was not under the influence of the European powers, but, from the early eighteenth century, Russia strove to become the protector of the Orthodox subjects of the Ottoman Sultanate.[23] After the Treaty of Küçük Kaynarca of July 1774, marking the end of the Russo-Turkish war (1768-1774), Russia accomplished its goal: in 1845 a Russian protégé, Cyril, was elected Patriarch of Jerusalem, marking the entry of Russia into the religious politics of Jerusalem. This coincided with the return of Jerusalem to the European stage: in 1847, Pope Pius IX re-established the Latin Patriarchate in the city, while the first Protestant missions started to operate in Palestine with the establishment of the joint Anglican-Protestant Bishopric in 1841.[24] Following these events, the Greek Orthodox Patriarch of Jerusalem, resident in Istanbul, was forced to move back to Jerusalem on account of Russian pressure.[25] At the end of the nineteenth century, conflict between the Arab laity and the Greek hierarchy became apparent, exploding violently with the deposition of Patriarch Cyril in 1872 through intrigues of the Russians, which angered the local Orthodox Arab laity.[26]

The history of the Catholics in Jerusalem was linked to the politics of the European powers much more consistently than that of the Orthodox Church. The Capitulations – commercial treaties between the European powers and the Ottomans – granted privileges to foreign traders and diplomats, but did not cover religious affairs; yet the European governments took advantage of these treaties in order to intervene in religious issues.[27] The Capitulations gave the French government a 'moral duty' to intervene and protect the Latins, particularly the Franciscans.[28] Furthermore, following the Ottoman conquest of Palestine in the sixteenth century, the question of the control and possession of holy places became an international question. The Franciscans, the only Catholic representatives in the city, were not only a monastic order, but also political actors. As Franciscan friars came from various European countries, they could appeal to their own governments, projecting the Custody of the Holy Land, and the order itself, onto the international stage.²⁹

Catholics in Jerusalem competed with the other denominations for control of the holy places. However, unlike the Orthodox Church, they did not experience any substantial internecine struggles in the nineteenth century. While the Greek Orthodox Patriarchate of Jerusalem was controlled by Greek clergy, Ottoman authorities and Russian diplomats, the Catholic Church was paradoxically freer from any direct interference. In fact, despite attempts by European governments to control the Custody, the Franciscans managed to maintain a good balance. Still, Catholics were generally not regarded as a local community but rather a foreign enclave, despite their attempt to employ the Arabic language in their relations with the local population.³⁰

From the mid-nineteenth century until the outbreak of the First World War, several Catholic institutions established various seminaries, convents, hospices, schools, orphanages and, also, small factories throughout Palestine, in an attempt to establish stronger control over the Holy Land.³¹ A good example is the establishment of the massive building known as Notre Dame de France in the late 1880s just outside the walls. This building was designed to lodge pilgrims, but also to show French power in the city and to compete with other institutions, but was located between the Russian Compound and the Old City, a statement against Orthodox expansion.³² These institutions were particularly active in promoting pilgrimages, as they were a great source of income.³³ Thanks to collections of money, Catholic institutions, towards the end of the Ottoman era, were able to run charitable activities for the poor. Like all other Churches, Catholic institutions survived thanks to contributions from European countries and the United States. For example, the Custody of the Holy Land collected funds to support its activities through commissariats (local branches) across the world.³⁴ This situation was to change with the outbreak of the First World War.

Following the Ottoman conquest of Armenia in the sixteenth century, relations between the two groups were strained. The Ottoman government forced the upper echelons of the clergy residing in Armenia under the control of the newly established

Armenian Patriarchate of Constantinople (Istanbul); even the Armenian Patriarchate of Jerusalem, established in the fifth century, eventually accepted the authority of Istanbul.[35] The Armenian laity of Jerusalem never exceeded 1,000 people under Ottoman rule. Following the clashes between the Ottoman army and the Armenians in east Anatolia at the end of the nineteenth century, their number rose as Armenian refugees arrived in Palestine, many taking permanent residence in the Armenian quarter of Jerusalem.[36] Despite what was happening in Anatolia, in the city, the relationship between Armenians and the Ottoman establishment was relatively peaceful; both represented a small minority of the population, and to the Ottomans as well as the Arabs the Armenians did not represent a major threat. Even in 1915, when the Turkish army came into direct conflict with the Armenians living in north and northeast Anatolia, it seems that the communities of Jerusalem were not subject to persecution or physical threats.[37]

The Churches and the Capitulations

The position of Christianity in Jerusalem was defined by the Capitulations – treaties between the Ottoman Empire and the European countries – and the Status Quo: a set of rules which regulated the ownership, control and management of the Christian holy places in Jerusalem.

As mentioned earlier, the Capitulations were bilateral treaties between sovereign states, but also unilateral concessions granted to groups of merchants.[38] Known in Turkish as *ahdname* or *imtiyazat*, the Capitulations had precursors in the early Muslim tradition in the Fatimid and Mamluk governments.[39] The first Capitulations were mainly commercial agreements which allowed Italian, and then French, citizens the right of residence and trade in the Ottoman Empire, allowing them to enjoy rights of extra-territorial jurisdiction in the Empire.[40]

After the French signed capitulary treaties, other European countries followed suit. In the sixteenth century, the Ottomans granted England and Holland capitulary rights; in the eighteenth century, Capitulations were also granted to Austria, Sweden and the

Kingdom of the Two Sicilies.[41] The Capitulary regime initially favoured the Ottomans, but became increasingly disadvantageous as it was exploited by the European powers. The Capitulations originally granted the Ottomans an opportunity to share the benefits of world trade, in the fifteenth and sixteenth centuries, with Florence, Genoa, Venice, the Netherlands, France and Britain.[42] They also allowed European countries to maintain consular posts in Ottoman territories, although there was no reciprocation granted to the Ottomans, who only started to establish representatives in Europe at the end of the eighteenth century.[43] The rise of a stronger Europe from the fifteenth century coincided with the beginning of the decline of the Ottoman Empire, and the Capitulations mirrored this situation in the nineteenth century when the capitulary regime became the most important European instrument for economic and political penetration into the Empire.

In Jerusalem, the regime affected the foreign communities living in the city, primarily in the religious sphere. With renewed European interest in the Holy Land, the British Government opened the first consulate in Jerusalem in 1838, during the rule of Muhammad 'Ali. It was followed by the arrival of a considerable number of European and American citizens. They were not simply Christian pilgrims, however, as they planned to settle in the city and to work as physicians, teachers and businessmen.[44] Under the protection of the Capitulations and foreign consulates, educational and health institutions were built by European entrepreneurs and governments. The Capitulations granted Europeans substantial cuts in tax and custom duties, as well as rights of extra-territoriality.

Capitulations were seen by locals as a restrictive measure and an interference by foreigners in several areas; they were, however, instrumental in the establishment of infrastructures and services also enjoyed by the local population. By late 1914, services in Jerusalem such as post offices and higher education institutions were in the hands of the Europeans, who promoted their own interests. In the summer of 1914 the Ottoman government exploited the outbreak of the war in Europe to abolish the capitulatory system throughout the Empire. That September the Ottoman Ministry of Foreign Affairs sent the foreign embassies of

Istanbul a note stating that the Capitulations would be abolished on October 1. The Governor of Jerusalem, Macid Şevket, wrote to the foreign consuls informing them of the closure of the foreign post offices, which was tantamount to the abolition of the most visible capitulary privileges.[45]

The Imperial order abolishing the Capitulations was read to the people of Jerusalem in an official ceremony held in the garden of the municipality. After the governor had read the document, Said al-Husayni, a local member of the Ottoman parliament, delivered a speech on the value of this measure, but also invited the crowd to show respect for the foreigners.[46] As elsewhere in the Empire the abrogation of the Capitulations was hailed as the beginning of a new era; religious orders, foreign clergy and laity had to deal with this new situation without relying on any foreign help.[47] Among the Christians, panic spread rapidly as demonstrations against the Europeans were staged throughout the city, while during the mobilisation for war, Ottomans occupied schools and hospitals previously under the protection of the European governments.[48]

'Peace' among Christians: the Status Quo, origins and developments

The so-called 'Status Quo' of the Christian holy places was the result of treaties and customary practices which regulated the right of control and access to the Christian places of worship in Jerusalem, as well as in the Holy Land in general, between the various Christian Churches. These rights reflected both the divisions between the Churches and the external support granted to them by the European powers.[49] The Status Quo was established progressively by the issue of several documents during Mamluk rule and of *firmans* by the Ottoman dynasty, the last of which was promulgated in 1852 and confirmed the state of affairs existing in 1757. The codification of these agreements into a body of official regulations was only proposed during the drafting of the charter for the British Mandate in Palestine in early 1920, including Article 14, which envisaged the appointment of a special commission to define the rights and claims on the holy places.[50]

In 1852 Sultan Abdülmecid despatched a *firman* to the Governor of Jerusalem, Vizir Hafız Ahmet Paşa, establishing the rights of several Churches in relation to the holy places, and it confirmed, to a large extent, the course of policy advocated in 1757 by Osman III.[51] The question of the holy places led to a major European conflict in Crimea, with Russia on one side and Britain and the Ottoman Empire opposing.[52] As a result, the Status Quo received formal recognition at the Conference of Paris in 1856, and was later confirmed at the Congress of Berlin in 1878.[53]

When General Allenby entered Jerusalem in December 1917, he confirmed the existing provisions so as not to change the balance between the Christian communities in favour of any particular confession. The proclamation read:

> Since your city is regarded with affection by the adherents of three of the great religions of mankind and its soil has been consecrated by the prayers and pilgrimages of multitudes of devout people of these three religions for many centuries, therefore, do I make it known to you that every sacred building, monument, holy spot, shrine, traditional site, endowment, pious bequest, or customary place of prayer of whatsoever form of the three religions will be maintained and protected according to the existing customs and beliefs of those to whose faith they are sacred.[54]

The British authorities were fully aware of the complexity and instability of the balance between the Christian Churches of Jerusalem and the international dimension attached to the issue. An interdepartmental commission, known as the De Bunsen Committee, established in 1915 to discuss British policies in the Middle East, recommended that the holy places should be placed under international control.[55] Mark Sykes, a member of the De Bunsen Committee, was aware that the Italian and French governments would compete for the control of Catholic institutions. In November 1917 he proposed that Jerusalem be kept under martial law, in order to avoid direct confrontation between French and Italian diplomacy, but also to give these two countries direct control over their unmixed institutions, which were Christian institutions with a clear majority of members from a specific country.⁵⁶ British officials were aware that the Status Quo could become a trap, a net without escape as the granting of rights to a confession was likely to trigger the objection of another Church and, thus, European states. Furthermore, in the light of the Balfour Declaration, which reinforced British commitment to the Jewish cause, the British Government needed as much support as possible from the Christian Churches in order to counteract Arab resistance.

Overall, the Status Quo was instrumental in regulating the relations between the various Christian denominations in the holy places, which were often a reflection of the political relations between the European powers. The Status Quo had no direct impact on the local population; however its indirect impact was felt as it was instrumental in marginalising the local Christian communities, which were not part of the decision making in relation to the holy places.

Christian Churches facing mobilisation and war

The process of mobilisation for war began early in the summer of 1914, when the Turkish authorities imposed martial law. After the abolition of the Capitulations, on several occasions the Austrian and German representatives intervened on behalf of the Christians despite the fact that, as noted by the German consul Brode, the local Catholics, as well as other Christian denominations, were possibly pro-French.⁵⁷

The first Christian group to be affected by the war were the Anglicans as they were citizens of an enemy power living on Ottoman soil. The Church Missionary Society and the London Jews Society were advised by the Foreign Office to remove their missions in September 1914.⁵⁸ French and British Catholic clergymen were also ordered to leave; however, the *Custos* of the Custody of the Holy Land travelled to Istanbul and managed to obtain the temporary suspension of the expulsion of French and British friars.⁵⁹ As a result, the Anglican clergy were the only Christian residents to abandon the city in the first stages of the war. While Ottoman officials seized Anglican buildings and possessions, members of the Church moved to Egypt. The newly appointed

Rev. Canon Rennie MacInnes, who succeeded George Francis Popham Blyth as Anglican Bishop in Jerusalem in 1914, also settled in Cairo.[60] Upon his appointment, Bishop MacInnes began to establish a relief fund for the Holy Land.[61] Despite being banned from Ottoman territory, the Anglicans maintained contacts in Jerusalem with Arabs converted to Anglicanism and the so-called Hebrew Christians, a group of Christians supporting Jewish immigration to the Holy Land, who supplied vital information to British intelligence.[62] Although members of the Anglican Communion were not significant in number, they provided many services to local communities, particularly schools and hospitals. St George's College, where local children played cricket and football, was turned into a military camp, leaving Jerusalemite children without a popular playground.[63] Indeed, the departure represented a major blow for the local population.

Late in 1914 the Turkish authorities ordered that all religious orders were to abandon their convents and gather in residences in Jerusalem, to make it easier to control them.[64] The Franciscan pilgrim house and convent Casa Nova & St Saviour Convent hosted members of different religious congregations still present in the city. For a while it looked as if the situation was stabilising. However, according to the last Ottoman governor of Jerusalem: 'At the beginning of the war churches were respected and even sealed up, but later, as Turkish officers took possession of them, robberies of church ornaments, robes etc. began'.[65]

The Greek Orthodox Church was particularly affected by the war. The Greek Orthodox Patriarchate, at the outbreak of the hostilities, found itself in dire financial straits. Pilgrimages, which were its main source of income, halted, and the Patriarchate was increasingly forced to borrow money.[66] During the war it borrowed more than 100,000 French francs from individuals and institutions including Almiso Zarfudhaki in Alexandria (a Greek Orthodox businessman), Credit Lyonnais bank, and the Greek and Russian governments. Russian diplomats were expelled from the city as Russia joined the war against Turkey; they did not return to Jerusalem following the Bolshevik revolution.[67] In the meantime, the Christian Orthodox population, who were mostly Ottoman subjects, had to pay a heavy exemption tax in order to avoid military service.[68] The political crisis between the Arabs and the Greek hierarchy, which dated back to at least the nineteenth century, intensified during the conflict, as attempts by the Arab laity and lower clergy to take control of the Patriarchate were countered by the Greek hierarchy.[69] Due to financial constraints, Patriarch Damianos secretly began to sell land to the Zionists, widening the rift with the Arab laity. Financial problems left the Church effectively inoperative during the three years of war. Evidence suggests that the Arab laity worked towards the protection of local interests, while the Greek upper hierarchy tried to save ecclesiastical properties from requisition by the Ottoman authorities.[70] Although Greece remained neutral, Turkish officials began to look suspiciously at the Greeks living in Jerusalem.[71]

Religious events were celebrated as usual, despite the distress. In April 1915, the Spanish consul Ballobar witnessed the religious procession of the Holy Fire led by Patriarch Damianos, noting that the procession was not as animated as in the past, because of the absence of pilgrims from outside the Empire.[72] By 1917 the celebrations for the Greek New Year were mainly restricted to Ottoman officials and the high clergy. Celebrations among the laity, meanwhile, were very sober given the high prices of essential foods and other goods caused by the general paucity of provisions.[73] Financial help from Orthodox private donors and associations based in the United States came after repeated appeals from the Patriarchate through the American consul Dr Otis Glazebrook.[74] The worst came in July 1917 when Greece finally joined the war against Turkey, and Russia had already been shaken by the February revolution which led to the collapse of the monarchy: the Patriarchate of Jerusalem was left completely alone. As an institution which was under direct control of the Ottoman authorities, the retreating Ottoman troops ordered the Patriarch to leave, and left the institution itself under the control of the Greek clergy.[75] The Latin Patriarch, Mons Camassei, shared the fate of his Greek Orthodox counterpart, and was deported in November 1917. The Latin Patriarch appealed to the German General Von Falkenhayn but the Ottomans were determined to carry out the deportation order. Cemal Paşa himself, military governor of Syria and commander of the Fourth Army, visited Mons Camassei and forced him to leave for Nazareth.[76]

However, some Christian groups coped quite well during the war, and were even able to offer services to their co-religionists and to the local population. Despite not being part of any ecclesiastical establishment, the members of the American Colony, who were mainly Protestants, offered their services to the population regardless of religious affiliation.[77] In 1915 the US Secretary of State instructed Glazebrook to investigate whether the American Colony was in need of funds as they operated several soup kitchens and fed more than 2,000 people every day.[78] The American Colony raised funds from the United States which they used to aid refugees and wounded. Early in 1917, when it became clear that the United States was to join the war against Germany, German officials began a campaign against the Americans residing in Jerusalem.

When the United States declared war on Germany in April of that year, the soup kitchens run by the American Colony were closed on the orders of the German military command, leaving many poor people to die from starvation and disease.[79] Bertha Vester Spafford and her husband, the leaders of the Colony, met Cemal Paşa asking him to allow them to assist the wounded. Until then, the American Colony was the only institution which had the funds to continue charitable work. Cemal accepted the offer and put at their disposal the Grand New Hotel, inside Jaffa Gate, for use as a hospital. Apart from attending to the sick and wounded, members of the American Colony ensured that burial traditions were respected: Jews would not be buried by Muslims, or Catholics by Greek Orthodox.[80] As soon as the city had been occupied by the British army, the Colony sought the support of the British, through General Shea, and 20 truckloads of food and medical supplies were sent soon after to Jerusalem from Egypt. The American Colony also became involved in the 'Syria and Palestine Relief Committee', an Anglican institution founded by Anglican Bishop Rennie MacInnes and based in Cairo, designed to help the reconstruction of Jerusalem after the war. Despite the stringent religious and social character of the American Colony, evidence suggests that the work of the Colony was always genuinely impartial, working towards the wellbeing of the people, regardless of religion, nationality and politics; a very peculiar characteristic in Jerusalem.

Among the small Christian communities of Jerusalem was the Ethiopian Church, an ancient institution dating back to the early Christian era, which had claimed a small chapel in the church of the Holy Sepulchre from at least 1172.[81] During the war, the Church was handed over to Turkish officers, and one building was converted into a hospital.[82] According to a British report written soon after the occupation of the city, the Abyssinian communities, of both Catholic and Orthodox rites, were in good condition, relatively untouched by deportation and disease.[83]

During the war thousands of Armenians were deported to Palestine from Anatolia because of the bloody conflict unfolding there between Armenians and the Ottoman army. Some of them reached Palestine in extremely poor health.[84] Allegedly, as a result of the friendship between Cemal Paşa and the former Armenian Patriarch, Maghakia Ormanian, the Armenian residents of Jerusalem were not forced to leave the city for remote locations.[85] In 1916, when epidemics of typhus and cholera hit the city, it appears that the Armenians living close to the Church of the Holy Archangels were particularly badly affected. In the aftermath of the war about 10,000 Armenian refugees arrived in Palestine, many of whom were gradually moved to a camp in Port Said; about 4,000 were accommodated in Jerusalem.[86]

Considering the upheavals that Jerusalem faced, how was Christianity affected during the war, and how did it react to war conditions? All Churches experienced lack of provisions, while deportations and requisitions linked them more directly with the local population; although some of them were able to keep a public profile, others could only just cater for the basic needs of their followers. A good example of how the war affected Christian institutions is provided by the Custody of the Holy Land. Traditionally the *Custos* was required to keep a diary, which has proved to be significant in the historical reconstruction of war conditions in Jerusalem. The Custody of the Holy Land will be discussed as a case study below, thereby providing more details on the Christian institutions during the war.

The Custody of the Holy Land

Among the Christian institutions of Jerusalem, one of the most rooted in the social fabric of the city at the beginning of the twentieth century was the Catholic *Custodia Terrae Sanctae* (Custody of the Holy Land), belonging to the Franciscan order founded as a Franciscan Province during the thirteenth century by St Francis of Assisi.[87] Since its establishment the highest authority of the Custody, the *Custos*, has always had to be an Italian subject. Membership of the council which regulated the life of the Custody was also based on nationality. In the period under discussion, the Custody was administered by a Discretory composed of the *Custos*, one French vicar, one Spanish procurator and six members: one Italian, one French, one Spanish, one German, and, after 1921, one British and one Arabic-speaking member.[88] The *Custos* had religious jurisdiction over the Catholics of Palestine, parts of Egypt, Jordan, Lebanon, Cyprus, and Rhodes, which meant a degree of competition occurred with the Latin Patriarch. The *Custos*, alongside the Greek Orthodox Patriarch and the Armenian Patriarch, became responsible for the enforcement of the Status Quo regarding the holy places.

The Custody managed a complex relationship with the European governments. The balance in the ruling council of the Custody was quite fragile, as these governments attempted, through its members, to influence the institution. However, it was the very trans-national nature of the Custody that ensured its survival throughout the centuries. As an institution ruled by Ottoman law, the Custody was not allowed to own properties such as convents, schools and other buildings. Only individual friars were allowed to own properties in their name, and the choice of who should be entitled to ownership was taken by the Custody according to nationality. The international character of the Custody meant that every decision was subject to international scrutiny. During the war, however, the Custody was left somewhat to its own devices, although the Spanish and Austrian consuls did intervene to support the Custody when harassed by the Turkish authorities. During the war, Spain donated at least 60,000 French francs to the Custody, whilst the central powers, mainly Austria, supported the organisation financially.[89]

When the conflict broke out, the Ottoman Army began to seize the buildings and properties of the Custody that were registered in the name of friars of Allied citizenship.[90] The Vatican, concerned with the future of the Holy Land, urged Cardinal Dolci in Istanbul to explain to the Ottoman authorities that an infringement of property rights was to be considered an act of defiance against the Vatican state, which claimed ownership of these properties regardless of Ottoman terms.

Through the diary of the *Custos*, it is possible to study the Custody throughout the war in a way that is not possible with other institutions. The diary of Fr Eutimio Castellani between 1914 and 1918 is written in the form of a chronicle, and includes notes updated on a daily basis.[91] Following the Ottoman government's entry into the war, the Custody found itself isolated internationally; the main framework of political and religious action became Palestine, and particularly Jerusalem. The financial situation of the Custody began to worsen, as its main sources of income such as pilgrimages and agricultural production were no longer available. Early in September 1914, the Custody reduced the activities of its workshops producing wheat, fabrics and other commodities, reducing the wages of its employees by 15%.[92] In November the same year the Turkish authorities ordered religious congregations scattered around Jerusalem to gather in the city centre. The Franciscans hosted the clergymen in the convent of St Saviour and the clergywomen in the Casa Nova. A few days later the police registered all names of the clergy living in the two houses.[93] Visits to the convents by local police became common events throughout the war, often for the purpose of seizing provisions and supplies: with winter approaching, for instance, the military requisitioned coal from the Custody, and their mill worked for five days in order to supply the Ottoman troops in Jerusalem with flour and bread.[94]

When Italy joined the war alongside the Allies the situation worsened, as the Ottomans saw the Vatican as an ally of the Italian government.[95] Although the Ottomans had seized schools, convents and hospitals as part of the process of mobilisation, Cardinal Dolci obtained permission to reopen the convents in

Jerusalem belonging to the Custody. However, the order which came from Istanbul was not followed by prompt action on the part of the local authorities in Jerusalem, and most of the convents remained closed.[96] The few British and French missionaries among the Franciscans were ordered to leave in 1914 since they were subjects of hostile nations, though their departure was delayed thanks to external intervention.[97] While the Ottoman order only concerned men, it also stated that 'all nuns, the women who are not nuns and the male children below 18 years of age, who may desire, must also be sent away out of the country'.[98] Later on, Turkish troops seized nearly all property in the form of buildings and supplies, *de facto* mobilising for the war effort all human, ideological and material resources 'offered' by the Custody.

The summer of 1915 proved to be difficult for the Custody as Italy joined the war against Turkey in late August, and the Ottoman authorities ordered that all clerics of Italian nationality, mostly Franciscans, should leave Jerusalem. However, thanks to the American and Spanish consuls, and the decisive intervention by the Austrians, they were allowed to remain.[99] Hence in 1915 the Franciscans living in the city comprised 72 Italians, 17 Ottoman subjects, 4 Portuguese, 31 Spanish, 13 Germans, three Americans, and 5 Dutch.[100]

In 1916, the Custody suffered a tremendous blow. In April the pharmacy at St Saviour was looted and then closed down; in June Turkish troops occupied St Saviour and Casa Nova, which were subsequently converted into hospitals, leaving only ten rooms in the two convents for the use of friars and nuns.[101] Despite these precarious conditions, the Custody continued to run a soup kitchen for Jerusalemites. As the activities of the Custody were reduced drastically, the entries in the diary for 1917 also fell, mainly dealing with news coming from outside Jerusalem. Realising that the British army was not far from the city after the evacuation of Jaffa in March 1917, the locals hoped that the British would soon free Jerusalem.

The Custody in the aftermath of the war: local and international dimensions

As soon as the city was captured by the British forces in December 1917, the Custody had to deal with Jerusalem's internal situation and re-establish its connections outside the region. One of the most urgent questions was the religious protectorate over the Catholics in the Holy Land, which had been granted to France for a century. A few weeks after the British conquest the Franciscan order named Fr Ferdinando Diotallevi as the new *Custos*. The Vatican Secretary of State Cardinal Gasparri kept the activities of the Custody under strict control, as the Vatican hoped to deter the influence of Italy, Spain, France and Great Britain, all of which were attempting to use this institution to gain more influence in Palestine.[102]

A British report on the Custody estimated damage of £10,000 due to Ottoman activity. The convents Casa Nova and St Saviour did not suffer any major damage during the occupation but all furniture, table linen and silver as well as the cellars were decimated.[103] According to this report, the workshops run by the friars, and exploited by the Turkish troops, were not entirely destroyed as most of them had been closed during the war. Once Fr Diotallevi reached Jerusalem in 1918, he wrote a report for the General of the order Fr Cimino, the former *Custos* before the war. He again stressed that all their properties had suffered looting, but also emphasised that the Franciscans were still able to serve one daily meal to the needy. Diotallevi also reported that the Franciscans took care of both Abyssinian and Armenian Catholics.[104]

Politically, the *Custos* reported that the Status Quo had been maintained; furthermore, he stated that the voice of the Custody was not as strong as it had previously been. As a matter of fact, the Latin Patriarch was still in the hands of the retreating Turkish troops; the Vatican was carefully monitoring events in Palestine, with particular attention to the international dimension, but also observing the conditions of the local population.

As soon as the war was over the Custody came to the forefront of the international politics surrounding the future of the holy places, the question of Zionism, and the conflict with the Latin Patriarchate, as well as other issues. In Rome Cardinal Gasparri genuinely believed that the administration of the holy places would be given to the Vatican. In fact, he believed that an internationalisation of the city would be almost impossible to achieve. Furthermore, he believed that the French protectorate over the Catholics would expire, now that Palestine was in the hands of the British. Apparently with this in mind, the General of the Franciscan order, Fr Cimino, sent a telegram to the *Custos*, Fr Diotallevi, stating that: 'Turkish domination in Palestine having ceased, the ancient French protectorate has ceased also'.[105] Furthermore, the Holy See had already, in early 1917, clarified to the French authorities the intention to stop French protection if the Ottomans were to leave Palestine permanently.[106] Officially, the French protectorate over the Catholics was part of the privileges granted by the Capitulations, which had officially been abolished by Art. 28 of the Treaty of Lausanne in 1923, but also by Art. 8 of the Mandate for Palestine.[107] The British military and the Foreign Office, concerned with public security, invited the Custody and the Vatican to raise the question. The liturgical religious honours (a set of religious privileges granted by the Church to individuals belonging to a particular nation) towards the French were kept alive until 1924 despite great opposition from both the Custody and the majority of the non-French Catholics following the instruction by Gasparri.[108] In 1926, France and the Vatican reached an agreement to the effect that liturgical honours throughout the Ottoman territories could be reinstated, with the permission of local governments.[109] This effectively marked the end of the centuries-old French protection over Catholics in Jerusalem and the region at large.

The activities of the Custody have rarely been studied in a local context, as the international dimension of this institution has taken centre stage. The diary kept by the *Custos* Ferdinando Diotallevi from his appointment in 1918 until 1924 is clear evidence of the predominance of international and diplomatic issues.[110] Looking at Diotallevi's diary, it is striking that there is no mention of the local community. The editor of the diary, Daniela Fabrizio, has rightly pointed out that relations with both Catholic and non-Catholic

Christian institutions were the two main concerns of the *Custos*. One last point to underline is the apparent lack of interest on the part of the *Custos* Diotallevi concerning the Zionist issue, unless it directly involved the holy places.[111] It was the Vatican and the Latin Patriarchate that became more involved in the controversies surrounding this question.

The strange allies: Arab Christians and Muslims together

Study of the Custody of the Holy Land shows the internal dynamics of this religious institution, and how the war was instrumental in the renegotiation of relations with the local community. However, the war had a major impact on the local Christian communities through the renegotiation of local alliances and the de-marginalisation of the Christians, who subsequently became an active part of the emerging Arab nationalist movement. The war had a profound ideological impact on Jerusalem's Christian communities; in fact, it was during the war that local Christian Arabs anxiously received rumours concerning Jewish immigration, which later turned into more consistent news. When the Balfour Declaration became public knowledge in late 1917, even though it was only published in Palestine in 1920, the attitude of local Arab Christians towards the Jews changed, as they felt threatened by Jewish immigration. Local Christian notables in Jerusalem joined their Muslim counterparts in political, cultural and literary associations which opposed Jewish immigration.

The notables of Jerusalem were both Muslim and Christian, and some Jewish families were also relatively important; they were the cornerstone of Jerusalem's fragmented social framework, and its rapidly changing demographic structure. They represented a mixed population which included around 15,000 Christians and 15,000 Muslims in Jerusalem at the outbreak of the war, as opposed to 50,000 Jews.[112]

Muslim and Christian Arabs acknowledged the common threat represented by Zionism. Despite political differences and the divisions among different Christian denominations protected by European countries, the anti-Zionist struggle became a critical concern.[113] The creation of Muslim-Christian associations was part of the development of the Palestinian national movement, which started to take shape during the last phase of Ottoman domination.[114] It is important to stress that, although Zionism shaped to an extent the national Palestinian movement, this movement did not emerge solely as a response to the two different phenomena of Zionism and Jewish immigration. Khalidi argues that Palestinian identity was also the outcome of the increasing identification with the new boundaries set in the post-First World War period.[115] Nevertheless, evidence suggests that, within months of the British capture of Jerusalem, local Muslim and Christian notables began to organise their response to Zionist activities.[116] One of the main problems of these associations was the political vision of their Muslim members concerning the future of Palestine. Despite the importance of Christianity in the social and religious life of the area, Muslims tended to stress the Islamic character of Palestine. Some local Muslim leaders encouraged Palestinian Christians to convert to Islam, as they regarded the Christian faith as closely intertwined with European interests in the region and therefore corrupted.[117] Further, the activities of these associations were affected by the rivalries between the great (Muslim and Christian) Arab families of the city, such as the Husaynis, the Nashashibis and the Khalidis.[118]

This phenomenon was not confined to Jerusalem. Many committees including Arab émigrés, again both Muslim and Christian, were formed around the world with the aim of supporting the emergent Palestinian cause. One of the main purposes of these groups was to lobby British authorities in the territory and outside Palestine, as well as other Western powers, and other nations not involved in the conflict. For example in Mexico, the 'Hijos de Palestine', which mainly included Christians of Palestinian origin, wrote to the Latin Patriarchate of Jerusalem in 1919 questioning the rights of Russian Jews to the possession of Palestine.[119] Similarly, a group of about 4,000 Christian Palestinians living in Bolivia wrote to the Vatican stressing that Palestine should not be ruled by the Jewish population.[120] Ultimately, these associations were not particularly successful in attracting international support; however, they indicate the strength of feeling aroused globally by the emerging Palestinian question among émigré communities.

The Muslim-Christian associations which operated in Jerusalem did not succeed in attracting similar global attention. However, their constant lobbying and actions raised the issue of Palestine and Zionism, and opened a serious debate among the countries with a stake in Palestine. The first official Muslim-Christian Association was formed in 1918 by the Arabs of Jaffa and Ramallah, with the purpose of fighting Zionism and Jewish immigration, but also to counter the British argument that Arabs in Palestine were divided along religious lines.[121] Early in November 1918, an Arab delegation walked to the Headquarters of the British military governor, Ronald Storrs, and delivered a speech and a note protesting about British plans regarding the division of Palestine.[122] Some time later, similar associations were formed in Jerusalem.[123] At least six organisations operated in the city. In 1918, the two most important associations were the Arab Club (*al-Nadi al-'Arabi*) and the Literary Club (*al-Muntada al-'Arabi*), but by 1920 other organisations had also gained prominence, such as the Association of Brotherhood and Chastity (*al-Akh wa al-'Afaf*), the Arabic Association of Ladies, the Educational Club and the Arabic Association of Jerusalem. These associations were chaired by notables who were at the forefront of the emerging national movement. Members of the Nashashibi family, for instance, chaired the Literary Club, while the al-Husaynis chaired the Arab Club.[124] Interestingly, there was a degree of division amongst the local Catholic Church in relation to the future of Palestine. From the beginning of the 1920s the Greek-Catholic Patriarch, Demetrios Qadi, began to pressure the Vatican to abolish the Latin Patriarchate, in favour of the more locally based Greek-Catholic, which was of the Oriental rite and, indeed, Arabic in culture, language and tradition.[125] Nevertheless, following a meeting between the Latin and Greek hierarchies, a common political position in relation to Palestine was found, and the Greek-Catholic appeal faded away.[126] Yet the local Palestinian Catholic community did not give up to the petition for the election of an Arab Latin Patriarch.[127]

A Supreme Committee of the Arab Societies in Palestine was established in November 1919 in Haifa, as an umbrella organisation to coordinate their activities. Writing to the government of the United States, they first made a statement of support towards the Allies, then, following Woodrow Wilson's idea of self-determination, asked for the independence of Palestine, its territorial integrity, and the prohibition of Jewish immigration.[128] Despite the diplomatic tone of the letter, it is clear that these associations were eager to move from diplomacy to action if necessary, as suggested by the concluding statement: 'we hereby declare that we are irresponsible for any trouble or disorder that may occur in this country as a consequence of the obvious general excitement and dissatisfaction'.[129] This does not necessarily mean that these associations had little control over the population; on the contrary, it suggests that these associations would be able to control a significant number of people and, if necessary, they would not prevent demonstrations against British and Zionists. A letter sent from the Literary Club, based in Jerusalem, to the American representative in the city in August 1919 shows the militancy of these associations, as stated by the opening line: 'We live as Arabs. We die as Arabs.'[130]

The same associations attempted to put pressure on other governments. In 1919, before the Versailles Peace Conference, the Supreme Committee wrote to the Pope asking him to intercede on behalf of the Palestinian people to save their country from Zionists.[131] A statement by the Committee after the Versailles Peace Conference, also sent to the Vatican, can be read as an attempt to provide a political rationale for the disturbances already taking place, like the Nebi Musa Riots of April 1920:

> The decision of the Conference of San Remo regarding the Arab countries generally and Palestine specially is to us a sentence of gradual death. We ask you to decide for us a quick death which would spare us all pain [...] The transformation of Palestine into a National Home for the Jews is a source of great troubles and serious disturbances in the land where the prophets lived and where Jesus Christ was born and crucified. Disturbances have already started in several towns, notably in

Jerusalem on 4th April 1920. The responsibility of this is yours and not that of Arabs who are defending their rights and doing everything in order to revive their nationality. History shall blame you for your deed. [...].[132]

The document mentions Jewish immigration, the Balfour Declaration which allowed the establishment of a Jewish national home in Palestine, and the Conference of San Remo in which the British, French and Italians discussed the future of the Middle East. However, this document also brings into the political scene an important religious element. As this letter was addressed to the countries involved in the Peace Conference, which was convened to discuss the future plans over the Ottoman Middle East, the petitioners underlined the status of Palestine as the land where Jesus lived and died, thus using Christianity to gain support for the emerging Palestinian cause.

Throughout 1919 the Literary Club, among other associations, continued to urge the Vatican to intervene against Jewish immigration, but by early 1920 the tone of their statements, which in the early stage was conciliatory, had changed as a result of the outcomes of the Peace Conference.[133] During a meeting held at Nablus, the Supreme Committee of Arab Societies decided to boycott Jewish economic activities and publicise their decision both in the Arabic press and the British official news, in order to oppose Zionist immigration.[134] With the fourth anniversary of the Balfour Declaration approaching, the Zionist leadership announced a great celebration in Jerusalem as they had done in previous years. The Palestinian Association of Egypt, which included Christians and Muslims and was one of the numerous groups to emerge during the war, sent a circular recommending that the occasion be treated as a day of mourning and that all Arab shops should close. This particular occasion turned out to be relatively peaceful; 'only' one Arab was killed in the Jewish quarter of the city.[135]

The impact of these Muslim-Christian associations on urban politics was substantial, as they became 'transreligious' gatherings which supported and fomented the evolution of national sentiment in the formative years of the Arab Palestinian movement. The role of Christian activists, however, appears to have been fairly marginal. The war changed inter-communal relations between Muslims and Christians, which had been characterised by suspicion and, at times, open conflict, into a more balanced relationship. Internal dynamics were also affected; Catholics of Latin and Eastern rites, acknowledging the common Zionist threat, joined forces to ask that Palestine be united with Syria.[136] Christians were originally over-represented during the establishment of the nationalistic Muslim-Christian Associations; however, by the late 1920s, and more so in the 1930s, Muslim notables gained control of the nationalist movement.[137] These associations were important insofar as they sanctioned the first alliance between Christians and Muslims against the threat of Zionism. These groups increasingly targeted and opposed Zionism as a political movement, creating a great deal of tension with Jewish residents. Nevertheless, the Muslim-Christian associations made distinctions between local Jewish residents and Zionist immigrants, as suggested by a note from General Money, chief administrator of OETA (Occupied Enemy Territory Administration).[138] However, tension escalated, culminating in episodes of violence, demonstrations and riots, such as the Nebi Musa incident of 1920, which saw major clashes between Arabs (Muslim and Christian) and Jews. This could be considered a watershed in the history of Jerusalem, as it marked the beginning of a latent clash which developed into a full-scale conflict in the following decades.

3

FOREIGNERS IN JERUSALEM

> From Bethlehem to Jerusalem is a journey of about three miles. The whole way is full of vineyards and orchards. The vineyards are like those in Romagna, the vines being low but thick. [...] The inhabitants, I am told, number about four thousand families. [...] Jerusalem, notwithstanding its destruction, still contains four very beautiful, long bazaars, such as I have never before seen, at the foot of Zion. [...] Most of those who come to Jerusalem from foreign countries fall ill, owing to climatic changes and sudden variations of the wind, now cold, now warm. All possible winds blow in Jerusalem to prostrate itself before the Lord.
> (Obadiah Yareh di Bertinoro, *circa* 1450)[1]

As seen earlier, Jerusalem was inhabited by a varied community at the beginning of the twentieth century, which included a large number of foreigners (that is, non-Ottoman citizens). If the picture of the population of the city was far from unitary, the foreign community was even less homogeneous. Foreigners living in Jerusalem did not belong to local groups, they did not speak in local idioms and they did not share the customs of the natives.[2] However, they believed they were familiar with the environment, claiming to possess knowledge of the local setting and its history, and hoped to redefine the image of Palestine in order to include themselves within the landscape.[3] Foreigners were both visitors and permanent residents who, by the outbreak of the war, made Jerusalem a cosmopolitan city; however, the local population was often excluded from this portrait. The war brought even more foreigners to the city, first in the form of the military of the Austro-

German armies, and then the British; foreigners were no longer just visitors, but (nearly) permanent administrators.

The relationships between these foreigners and the local communities were extremely complex. I will discuss some of the foreign visitors and residents with the aim of understanding their interactions with the local population specifically during the war period. To do this it is necessary to try and shift the focus away from international issues, like the question of the holy places, the protectorate over particular religious groups and the Capitulations, which often do not fully take into account the needs of local inhabitants. I will attempt to do this, while also exploring new historical sources.

Visitors in their various guises – whether tourists, pilgrims, businessmen or clergy – are indeed important; however, more focus is placed on consuls and their work aimed at the local population during the war. Before the war, consuls, it will be shown, proved to be the main channel through which the foreigners of the city attempted to redefine its image and its environment. The consuls helped make the land more accessible and attractive for visitors; facilitating travel and businesses in the Holy Land, they often served the purposes of their own governments, but also became part of the development of eschatological plans of religious groups. It seems that, although the Ottomans controlled the administrative apparatus of the city, it was the foreign population that managed its ideological machinery, as suggested by the introduction in Jerusalem of the European concept of 'modernity'. The war acted as a catalyst for rapid and radical change. Foreign presence in the city proved to be a permanent feature, and is possible to argue that foreigners represented a strong form of continuity in the transitional period from Ottoman to British rulers.

During the war, consuls, as well as other foreign actors, changed their attitude towards Jerusalem and its inhabitants. International issues became less prominent, leaving more room for local ones. Isolation, lack of resources and uncertainty about the future brought the consuls closer to the local inhabitants, sharing with them the unexpected consequences of the war. The war did not reduce the foreign presence but merely changed the composition of the city, with fewer civilians and more military, as well as changing the national representation, with Germans and Austrians becoming the majority of foreigners by the end of 1914.

Overall, many historians discussing foreigners in the Holy Land, regardless of the period under scrutiny, equated their presence with the development of the process of modernisation. This is not only reductive, but also incorrect. Jerusalem, until the mid-nineteenth century, was a destination for pilgrims travelling from both Christian and Muslim lands, seeking to experience the city's historic spirituality; modernisation was not an issue for these people. However, with the establishment of convents, hospitals, schools and new businesses linked to foreign enterprises, Jerusalem was then projected outside its own stage, in some way *de facto* becoming a European city. In 1839, the British Government felt that the time was right to open a consulate in the city. The doors of Jerusalem were thus opened to the presence of new types of foreigners: diplomats, scholars and tourists. These newcomers had different backgrounds, purposes and ideologies from the previous stereotype of the foreign resident; however, all of them aimed to modernise Palestine and Jerusalem according to their own values.[4] These foreigners acted more as agents of modernisation and westernisation, and thus helped the partial fusion of Palestine with Europe.[5]

Visiting Jerusalem

Once Jerusalem became more accessible in the nineteenth century – a result of new routes and modes of transport with faster steamships and new railways in the Ottoman Empire – at least three kinds of visitors and non-permanent residents are discernible: tourists, pilgrims and scholars. During the war the flow of visitors obviously ceased, but looking at the influx of visitors at the beginning of the twentieth century in the light of the policies adopted by the British military administration from 1917 to 1920 in relation to visitors enables us to gain a better understanding of the impact of these people on the city and its population.

Pilgrims are in a different category from tourists. It is not just the purpose of the visit, but the services required which differentiate them. For the most part, pilgrims were also tourists; but tourists were not necessarily also pilgrims.[6] Pilgrimage is strictly linked to the idea of a sacred space, with the journey towards this space playing an essential role in the process.[7] Pilgrims to Jerusalem would sometimes have to face long journeys, lasting weeks or even months, during which, through prayer and fasting, they prepared themselves for the meeting with the sacred.

There were myriad reasons for performing a pilgrimage to Jerusalem: some looked for a safe seat in the afterlife; others were asking for grace and blessing; while many were sick, travelling to Jerusalem in hope of a cure and a miracle. Some were just looking to spend the final days of their lives near the sacred space; it was considered a special honour to die and be buried in Jerusalem, the very site of the manifestation of God. Pilgrimage was also about returning home with souvenirs and stories to share, and not based on class division, because the pilgrimage was undertaken by poor and rich alike.[8] The Austrian and German emperors visited Jerusalem at the end of the nineteenth century as part of a political visit to the Ottoman Empire, also taking the opportunity to go on pilgrimage. Considering the sacred meaning of Jerusalem for Christians, Muslims and Jews, it is unsurprising that the city was a very popular destination. Christian pilgrims from Europe and the United States represented the majority of the visitors at the turn of the twentieth century; however, both Jews and Muslims held their own pilgrimages too. Jews from Central and Eastern Europe, as well as from America, visited the city during the Passover and other important religious occasions, while the most important Muslim religious pilgrimage was the Nebi Musa festival, held at the same time as the Jewish Passover and Christian Easter.[9]

Throughout the late Ottoman period pilgrims were primarily Russians, despite some large pilgrimages organised in France and Italy. The Russian Orthodox Church believed that Russia, as a state, was to play an eschatological role in imposing Christian orthodoxy on the world, and that Jerusalem would be the place for the second coming of Christ. For the Russian Empire, however, Palestine was of strategic importance, possibly playing a crucial role in the weakening of its Ottoman opponents.[10] The British consul reported in 1910 that, of 33,000 pilgrims visiting the city, 12,000 were Russian subjects. The second most populous nationality was

Greek, with 3,500 pilgrims, showing the huge numerical gap between the Russian pilgrims and those of other nationalities; in contrast it is worth noting that only 500 French pilgrims visited the city in 1910.[11] The impact of these pilgrims on the city became increasingly apparent. Pilgrims affected the urban environment, economics, politics, cultural and social relationships. Pilgrims were, according to the Capitulations, under the protection of the consulates of their own countries. Pilgrims, most of them poor, brought with them offerings gathered before their departure for the pilgrimage. This money was destined for the main Christian religious institutions in the city, and the Greek Orthodox Patriarchate supported itself mainly through the money donated by pilgrims.[12]

The European powers sponsored pilgrimages to the Holy Land. French, Russians, Italians, Austrians, and other European nations, began to build infrastructure for pilgrims as a response to the needs of these people.[13] This was, however, also used quite openly to create a base in Palestine and Jerusalem, influence Ottoman policies, and compete against each other. For instance in 1902 a large Italian pilgrimage sparked the anger of the French, and above all the local French-speaking clergy, who felt threatened in their authority over the protection of the Catholics.[14] The large presence of pilgrims in Jerusalem became a strategic phenomenon, exploited through the establishment of foreign consulates in the city from the mid-eighteenth century. Consulates were not the only foreign institutions that were opened. They were accompanied by the establishment of hospices and guesthouses for pilgrims. One positive outcome of these policies was that the local population enjoyed access to some of the services provided.[15] In 1884 the French began to build the Hospice of Notre Dame, an impressive building just outside the walls near Jaffa Road. Notre Dame was, by the end of the Ottoman administration, the largest building in the city, with more than 400 rooms available for pilgrims. However, the French did not stop their activity there; the French St Louis Hospital also offered its services both to pilgrims and to the local population.[16] The Franciscans built their Casa Nova hospice in order to host more pilgrims, while Italians, through the Italian National Missionary Aid Society, began to build a hospital designed by the famous architect Antonio Barluzzi in the Renaissance style; meanwhile a square tower built next to the hospital recalled the tower of Palazzo Vecchio in Florence.[17]

Given the large number of Russian pilgrims, from 1864 an entire area outside the walls close to the Jaffa Road, known as the Russian Compound, was converted into a massive pilgrimage service area.[18] The Compound was composed of the Russian consulate, a Cathedral, a hospital, three hospices for pilgrims, and other buildings.[19] Russian pilgrims were allowed to stay in the Russian Compound for two weeks free of charge, then usually charged a nominal sum.[20] Other foreign governments and private citizens contributed to the development of facilities for pilgrims. In some cases, the reception of pilgrims became a business: some Jewish and Christian entrepreneurs from Jerusalem began to export religious artefacts for both Christians and Jews and, in the mid-1890s, this business reached the value of £20,000.[21]

If pilgrimage was a popular activity, tourism at the end of nineteenth century became the new fashion for rich Europeans and Americans willing to spend large sums of money to sate their spirit of adventure. The famous British travel agent Thomas Cook organised visits to the Holy Land towards the end of the nineteenth century, and the first *Baedeker Guide of Palestine and Jerusalem* was published in London in 1876.[22] Tourism in Jerusalem was an elite phenomenon, as opposed to the pilgrimage which was open to everybody. Among the tourists visiting Jerusalem was the author Mark Twain, who visited Palestine and the city in 1867 as member of a group of American travellers crossing the Middle East, and cynically depicted Palestine as 'monotonous' and 'uninviting'.[23] Twain was disappointed as Jerusalem could not offer many of the facilities available in his own country, not to mention the adventure he was looking for. In his 1912 work on Jerusalem, Charles Moore Watson (1844-1916), a Colonel with the Royal Engineers who had vast experience exploring Egypt and Palestine, claims that tourists were normally disappointed when visiting Jerusalem as they had little knowledge of the history of the city and found it a dirty and rather disagreeable place.[24] Tourists, as well as pilgrims, needed basic services, so hotels began to be built by European entrepreneurs, and private houses were converted into guesthouses.

The tour operators hired interpreters and guides from among the local population. In 1898, when the German Emperor Kaiser Wilhelm II visited Jerusalem, it was a boom year for tourism with hotels fully booked for weeks and visitors needing to hire tents.[25] In anticipation of the visit, the city was thoroughly cleaned and a number of public works were carried out; however these works were primarily short-term and their benefits soon disappeared: problems such as poor sanitation and lack of access to water remained almost unsolved.

In the years preceding the outbreak of war, tourism began to have a more substantial effect on this city, but it still could not be described as a large industry. According to a report by the British consul, Harold Eustace Satow, in 1911, 5,595 tourists visited Jerusalem between June 1908 and May 1909, increasing to 7,196 the following year; however, numbers dropped in 1911 to 5,759 as a result of the Balkan Wars and the Turco-Italian war in Libya. The consul also reported that, in 1911, tourists visiting Jerusalem included 1,626 Americans, 957 British and 895 Germans.[26] In the same report, Satow stated that among the people who travelled on the Jaffa-Jerusalem railway in 1911, there had been 6,700 tourists and 33,500 pilgrims travelling as second-class passengers between the two cities.[27] The Jaffa-Jerusalem railway was the fastest way to reach Jerusalem once travellers or goods had disembarked at Jaffa port. Although the number of tourists was a mere fraction of the pilgrims, these tourists represented a good source of income; according to the Jewish paper *Ha-Or*, the shopkeepers of Jerusalem were looking forward to serving British tourists, who were quite free-spending.[28]

Tourist services at the turn of the century did not have a great impact on the amelioration and urbanisation of the city, a task that was left mainly to the municipality and some private enterprises, though it is undeniable that the city enjoyed some improvements from this industry.[29] Although, as explained earlier, locals were employed in tourist services such as hotels or as guides, at the beginning of the twentieth century tourism was not a major economic activity compared with the olive-soap industry or the production of handicrafts.[30] The growth of the tourist industry, however, led to an increasing need for tourist services, and numerous tourist agencies were opened along the Jaffa Road.[31] The most popular accommodations on the Jaffa Road, or just inside the Jaffa Gate, were the Grand New Hotel, sponsored by Cook's Agency, the Jerusalem Hotel and the Hotel Palestine. Souvenir shops like the Oriental Bazaar, the White Store and the Kurt & Eftemios shop were situated near Jaffa Gate.[32] Despite all these activities, two British reports of 1900 underlined how the local population suffered from lack of similar services, while tourists were relatively well catered for.[33] For tourist agencies locals were not a source of revenue and for those charged with the task of providing services to the population, it may be said that prestige was more attractive than duty.

As the Ottoman administration did not have enough funds to deal with visitors, the development of the infrastructure to facilitate tourism was left to foreign institutions such as consulates or foreign private companies, which ultimately worked towards the development of their own interests. Europeans established sea routes to Palestine with fast steamships, invested money in infrastructure, built hotels and organised tours; the local administration was, however, in charge of courses for interpreters and guides from the 1890s.[34] In 1889 in Paris the *Société du Chemin de Fer Ottoman de Jaffa à Jérusalem* was established. It was a French enterprise that was granted the concession to build the railway from Jaffa to Jerusalem.[35] The railway never turned into a commercial success as it was very expensive to run. During the war tourism, as well as pilgrimage, halted completely. The American consul stated that, in 1914, 500 German tourists arrived in Jerusalem in July and left in August, and no new arrivals to the city were recorded.[36]

A third category of non-permanent residents of Jerusalem includes explorers and researchers. Research on Palestine and Jerusalem was, unsurprisingly, biblically oriented. The main purpose of the explorers, geographers and archaeologists was to study the Bible, using empirical data gathered through surveys of the Holy Land. Although there was some genuine scientific interest, this activity was mainly geared towards the discovery of evidence to support the authenticity of the Bible. The first British, German and American explorers of Palestine in the mid-nineteenth century were moved by the desire to better understand and analyse the Bible through the study of the Holy Land from geographical and archaeological perspectives.[37] Biblical archaeology used the techniques of mainstream archaeology, but it was intentionally confined to the areas relevant to the Bible stories.[38] Although the main focus of these scholars was the archaeology of the Old Testament, biblical sites relevant to the New Testament were also considered. In the 1840s a Protestant researcher, Edward Robinson, aroused some controversy over the authenticity of the site of the Holy Sepulchre; leading to some Protestants and Anglicans searching for an alternative place where Jesus might have been buried outside the walls of the city.[39]

European nations competed with each other in the exploration and study of Palestine in the nineteenth century. In 1865, the British Government founded the Palestine Exploration Fund, while in 1877 the Germans founded their own German Society for the Exploration of Palestine.[40] It was only in 1900 that the Americans established the American School of Oriental Research. Dominicans of French nationality founded the *École Pratique d'Études Bibliques*, thereafter known as the *École Biblique*. Other new societies were formed, such as the Russian-Orthodox Society of Palestine in 1882, and existing institutions, such as the Custody of the Holy Land, began to devote part of their activity to the exploration and study of the Holy Land.[41]

The role of these institutions was mainly to support archaeological discovery, and they had little interaction with the local population.[42] The surveys carried out in the city shed light on its evolution through different historical periods in order to substantiate biblical stories. The Palestine Exploration Fund, founded to uncover biblical sites, first investigated the possibility of mapping Palestine in 1871. By 1876 it had surveyed the Eastern part of the country, while the map of Western Palestine was published in 1877.[43] As early as the 1870s, the British War Office provided funds for this project, since the mapping of the Jordan Valley was considered to be of strategic value.[44] This mapping activity also became crucial to the process of acquiring land and claiming rights on land, houses and properties by Jews migrating to Palestine and Jerusalem, and, from the mid-nineteenth century, Jewish organisations and Jewish private citizens began to purchase land in Palestine and the city despite the obstacles placed by Ottoman legal practices.[45]

The impact of this search for biblical roots was felt across Europe and America. Reports of discoveries were published and publicised in the press. The image of Jerusalem was oriental and romantic, as the interest was in an idealised city of biblical times. The scholars visiting Jerusalem were imbued with the romance of archaeology and the adventure of discovering the past.[46] Nonetheless, the role played by these associations was crucial in mapping, surveying and retracing the history of the city, and in promoting new studies of it. In the short term this work of research had a little direct impact on the local population; however, in the long run the findings and results produced by these scholars, groups and associations were also appropriated by local communities who started to make a variety of claims to reshape the concept of local identity.

Consulates

Amongst all foreign enterprises in the Middle East, the most powerful and, indeed, the most durable and efficient was diplomacy. As a result of the new interest in Jerusalem, the European powers began to establish their own consulates in Jerusalem, starting with the British. The establishment of consulates was a response to an increase in activity in the economic, social and religious spheres of the foreign subjects in Jerusalem and the surrounding areas. The British consulate was first established in 1839; in the following two decades, another four followed: the German in 1842, then those of France, Piedmont and Sardinia in 1843, the Austrian in 1849 and the Russian in 1858. The Americans opened their consulate in 1844 but it only became fully functioning in 1856.[47] Other, smaller consulates opened in the early twentieth century. A Swedish consulate was opened in 1904 and, in 1909, after its separation from Sweden a Norwegian consulate was established; in the same year, a Belgian consulate was established and given to Dr Mancini, an Italian subject who was also the physician of the Custody of the Holy Land and the son-in-law of the French consul Autrey. A Brazilian consular agency was also opened in Jaffa in 1907, and managed by a French subject with the purpose of caring for Brazilian pilgrims.[48] Consuls derived their authority from the Capitulations that granted extraterritorial status to them: freedom of movement, trade and settlement to the consuls and their protégés. Consuls usually dealt with all aspects of the personal status of the individuals under their protection. Furthermore, consulates were the seats of consular courts, which dealt with all civil and criminal cases regarding foreign subjects. Consuls also presided over mixed courts which adjudicated cases involving Ottoman and foreign subjects.[49] By the outbreak of the First World War, there were in Jerusalem six General Consulates – a clear indication of the prestige attached to the city – whose consuls were directly responsible to the Ministry of Foreign Affairs of their own countries rather than to the ambassadors in Istanbul.[50]

Paramount among the European powers which developed interests in Jerusalem from the mid-nineteenth century were Britain, Germany, France and Russia. Britain was looking after its strategic, economic and political interests in the Eastern Mediterranean.[51] Germany was trying to establish itself on the Ottoman scene as an emerging nation. From the 1840s, the Prussian state and, subsequently, Germany supported the Ottoman Empire and favoured the settlement of its citizens, both Jews and Christians, in the region.[52] France, through its role as a traditional protector of Catholics in the Holy Land, was looking to maintain influence in the region and among the local population. Meanwhile, the Russian government continued its protection of the Orthodox Church, trying to weaken the Ottoman Empire further after the Crimean War.[53] At the turn of the twentieth century, the United States was not interested in politics or strategic positions, and the American consulate mainly promoted American economic interests and assisted American travellers, pilgrims and scholars.[54] After the unification of Italy in the 1860s, the Italians expanded their interests in Palestine and Jerusalem in particular, where they competed with the French government for the right to protection of the Catholics.[55] Spain also opened a consulate in 1854, with the intention of catering for the different Catholic institutions of the city, and to compete with France and Italy for the protection of the Catholics.

As representatives of their governments, consuls had to deal with both the Ottoman authorities and the local population. Their most important relationship was with the *mutasarrıf* of Jerusalem. The case discussed in Chapter 1 in relation to the proposed taxation for services on foreign residents outside the walls, highlights how the governor was the only Ottoman authority who could deal directly with the consuls as the representative of the central Ottoman government.[56] Given the frequent rotation of Ottoman officials, the consuls were always careful and thorough in their assessment of the officials appointed to the governorship of the *sancak*. The main activity of a governor, in dealing with the consuls, was attempting to circumvent the Capitulations through the enforcement of measures restricting the free movement of foreigners or imposing special taxes on foreign businesses.[57] Usually, the consuls had the upper hand in updating their capitulary rights. Only on a few occasions did the governors win their legal cases against the foreign consuls.[58] In 1905, the Governor of Jerusalem, Reşid Bey, amid great dissent from the consuls, managed to impose on those foreign residents outside the walls a tax on street lighting and sanitation, proposed by the municipality.[59]

One particular issue which caused friction between the parties was Jewish immigration to Palestine. Most of the foreign consulates favoured Jewish immigration under the umbrella of the Capitulations, as these Jewish immigrants were citizens of different European countries. The first to favour Jewish immigration were the British.[60] Following a Christian religious revival during the 1820s, a number of British citizens arrived in Palestine in order to proselytise to the Jewish population through the 'London Society Promoting Christianity', an association whose primary aim was to convert Jews to Christianity.[61] Under the heavy influence of the people involved in this particular movement, such as Lord Ashley (Earl of Shaftesbury), the British Government started to actively support Jewish immigration to Palestine.[62] The Ottomans attempted to counteract Jewish immigration with strict laws prohibiting movement, and limits to land and house purchases by Jews. In October 1913 the local Ottoman authorities in Palestine were ordered by Istanbul to stop the system of issuing 'red papers', which granted Jews entering Palestine permission to visit for a limited period, as long as they surrendered their passports.⁶³ Despite instructions from the authorities, Ottoman governors often had to succumb to consular pressure.⁶⁴ Consuls were, in general, highly critical of the Ottoman administration, and dismissive of the local government, as reflected by this statement from the Italian consul in 1896: 'It is general opinion that the Ottomans will not obtain any efficient result from the reforms [...] the new administrative system will upset the population. Likely, the reforms will be delayed.'⁶⁵ Although consuls were critical, in the end they had to accept the final decisions of the Ottoman rulers. While this stemmed from some genuine respect for Ottoman authority, it is also quite apparent that it was easier for consuls to blame local authorities when things were turning negative.

It was partly because of the constant pressure from consuls and foreign citizens that the municipality of Jerusalem worked towards the improvement of services like lighting, cleanliness and public security. Consuls genuinely supported local development, but also never forgot to protect their interests. The British consul supported municipal efforts to improve the lighting of the city; however, he also advocated the implementation of the capitulary regime with regard to the enforcement of tax cuts on real estate in favour of Ottoman and foreign subjects alike.⁶⁶

Consuls also directed relations between the local authorities and the European firms that managed the city's public services.⁶⁷ There was great competition among the consulates to win concessions from the Ottoman administration. Early in 1914, for instance, a large project was finally granted to the French Parisian bank Périer to construct a tramway line, fit pipes to bring potable water to the city, and expand and electrify street lighting, after fierce competition between a number of European companies. However, the project was halted by the outbreak of the war.⁶⁸ In this agreement the municipality of Jerusalem would have acquired control of both services and infrastructure, after a period of ten or fifteen years.⁶⁹ The municipality was thus trapped in a vicious cycle of dependency created by the capitulary system which, through political means, had greatly favoured the penetration of foreign capital. In 1906, the Governor of Jerusalem, Ali Ekrem Bey, wrote to Istanbul arguing that in a country where more than half of the population was foreign, it was impossible in questions relating to the municipality to treat foreigners as though they did not exist.[70]

It is difficult to assess the relationship between consuls and the local population. Consuls often dealt with local entrepreneurs and members of the notable families but, occasionally, they also dealt with ordinary citizens. As argued later in this chapter, the Spanish consul had limited contact with the local population, whilst his American colleague was less involved in official business but more connected to some of the local communities and their needs. Unfortunately, sources available cannot be considered particularly reliable in shedding light on this area; in fact, in official correspondence this relationship was rarely discussed, unless related to consular activities. Indeed, some consuls might have chosen to be completely isolated from the local scene. They could not, however, choose to remain apart from Jerusalem and its environmental problems, such as lack of water or periodic epidemics. Consuls were residents, whether they liked it or not.

Foreigners and the War

As soon as the war broke out in Europe, the city of Jerusalem was placed under military administration. It was not clear whether the Ottoman Empire would join the war, and if so on which side; therefore, once mobilisation started, the consuls undertook intensive activity aimed at protecting their own countries' interests and protégés. Confusion, everywhere, was the main feature in the short time before Turkey began to fight alongside Germany and Austria. As soon as martial law was proclaimed in the city, at the beginning of November 1914, the foreign consuls informed their own protégés not to interfere in local military operations. All economic activity was halted, affecting both local and foreign inhabitants. For the few weeks between the proclamation of martial law and the actual declaration of war, Jerusalem was caught in a position of impasse. By October, Jerusalem was cut off from the rest of the world: the foreign postal services were closed, and there was no mail delivery. The actual order to close the foreign post offices was sent by the Governor of Jerusalem to the consuls on 22 September.[71] Services like electricity and water were reduced, and only two hotels and two hospices were able to employ small generators to provide for themselves. Telephone lines, previously owned by foreign companies, fell under local Ottoman management, although the new management was not able to provide a proper service as the necessary equipment was in storage in Antwerp.[72] Under Ottoman management during the war, telephone lines never worked properly.[73] Schools managed by foreigners were closed, and only Ottoman schools remained open.

The worst for the foreigners, however, was still to come: in September 1914 the Ottoman government sent all foreign embassies in Istanbul a note stating that with effect from 1 October 1914, the Capitulations were to be considered unilaterally abrogated. When the circular reached Jerusalem, the news was welcomed by the Muslim population, whilst among foreigners and Ottoman Christians and Jews panic spread, as they feared actions against them.[74] The people most affected were the Jews, who had traditionally lived thanks to the support of the *halukka*.[75] Charity from abroad was not halted, but its distribution was affected by war conditions.

Although war had not yet been declared, foreign subjects, mainly of the Allied powers, were advised by their own consulates to leave the city.[76] At the same time, all consuls complained to Ottoman authorities about the abolition of the Capitulations. Even Germany and Austria, who were allied with the Ottoman Empire, had to accept the abolition of privileges granted by the Capitulations. The German and Austrian consuls, as a sign of protest, handed back to the Ottoman governor the official decree which abolished them. The American consul, Otis Glazebrook, undertook a campaign against the abolition of the Capitulations, supported by the American ambassador in Istanbul, Henry Morgenthau. The ambassador proved to be a strong opponent of the Ottoman decision, arguing that the Capitulations could not be abrogated without the consents of the countries that signed those treaties.[77] Even after the war, when the British took over, the Americans still campaigned against their abolition.[78] Since the Americans were not involved at the outbreak of the European conflict, they felt it was unfair to suffer the consequences of the abolition of the capitulary regime which had granted them a considerable commercial presence in the area. The abolition was felt to be a breach of the plurisecular tradition of foreign privileges in the Ottoman Empire. However, apart from a formal reaction from all consulates, and with the only strong opposition aired by the Americans, the consuls merely acknowledged the Ottomans' last full act of sovereignty.[79] At this stage, the consuls endeavoured to protect some of their employees who had Ottoman citizenship and were called to serve in the Ottoman army, declaring them as their protégés. They also protected their own and their protégés' properties by prevailing upon the local administration and notables.[80]

On 3 November 1914, the British consulate in Jerusalem received a telegram informing them that the Ottoman Empire had declared war against the Allies.[81] The British, French and Russian diplomats and residents began their operations of evacuation. On 30 October, the British consul received a coded telegram instructing him to burn all ciphers and confidential archives; following these instructions, William Hough set a huge fire in his garden and, in mid-November, left the city.[82] The French consul, George Gueyraud, and the director of Credit Lyonnais, Miguel Antonio Guerassimo, also left the city alongside Hough.[83] The American consul, Glazebrook, took charge of British and French interests in Palestine.[84] However, most of the properties belonging to British and French citizens were seized by Ottoman officials after being evacuated. Some residents, mainly Jewish protégés of the consulates, were deported to Damascus, their properties either seized or demolished.[85] Furthermore, an official order of Cemal Paşa claimed that all enemy subjects would be kept as hostages to guard against the bombardment of open ports.[86] The same day that the British and French diplomats departed, the Latin Patriarch Camassei, the Spanish consul Conde de Ballobar, and the Italian consul Senni, held a meeting in the residence of the American consul. They signed a document asking the Entente powers not to bombard the Ottoman open ports in exchange for the freedom of prisoners held by the Ottomans.[87] Eventually, Ottoman authorities deported the prisoners to Syria.

In addition to the representatives of neutral countries such as Italy, the United States and Spain, representatives of Germany and Austria, the allies of the Ottoman Empire, remained in the city.[88]

These consuls had a hard task; they had to deal with Ottoman officials and military authorities, the consuls of neutral countries and, to an extent, the local population. Despite being allies, the German and Austrian consuls, Johann Brode and Friedrich Kraus, were cut out of any decision-making process, with Turkish officials adopting a more aggressive attitude towards foreign nationals, including Germans and Austrians, reflecting the independent and unpredictable character of Cemal Paşa.[89]

One of the main activities of the consuls in Jerusalem during the war was to provide aid and relief to the local population. Despite the censorship, the difficulties in communication, and the orders coming from their own countries, the consuls continued to play an important political role, and they retained a structured competition among themselves. Under war conditions, the distribution of aid and the protection of the civilian population became the main political issues among the consuls. Relief usually arrived from neutral countries via the port of Jaffa, through sea transports declared safe by the warring factions and then managed and distributed by the foreign consuls in Jerusalem. Notably, the largest part of the aid delivered went to the Jewish communities. The local Muslim community also received provisions, which were managed by a local Commission composed primarily of local notables.[90] Although there is no direct evidence to reveal exactly which of the notables were involved in this commission, it is not unreasonable to suspect that the main families involved in this process were the usual people: the al-Husaynis, Khalidis and Nashashibis.

The United States was the primary relief provider, and paid special attention to the Jewish population, regardless of whether they supported Zionism. Furthermore, the ambassador in Istanbul was the leading Jewish American Henry Morgenthau, who strongly advocated for this help to be distributed.[91] A cargo organised by two Jewish-Americans, Levine and Epstein, landed in Jaffa in May 1915. The proportion of distribution was 55% for Jews, 26% for Muslims and 19% for Christians.[92] It was the Jerusalemite Jews who suffered the most from the war conditions, as a result of the restrictive measures imposed specifically by the Ottoman government on the Jewish population. The Christians, either Ottoman subjects or citizens of other countries, were under the legal protection of the neutral countries, as well as Germany and Austria.⁹³ Nevertheless, they were not often successful in their dealings with the Ottoman authorities: in October 1915 the Austrian consul Kraus and the Spanish consul Ballobar petitioned the Ottomans to stop the occupation of a Franciscan convent in the city. They failed and the building was eventually seized.⁹⁴ The Austrian consulate also worked for the relief of the Jewish population of the city, providing them with financial aid and food. Furthermore, although Kraus and Brode could not prevent the expulsion of the Jewish population from Jaffa under orders from Cemal Paşa in 1917, they managed to avoid a major catastrophe which could have ended in a massacre.⁹⁵

There were several reasons behind the assistance provided to the Jewish population. All the countries represented in Jerusalem had large numbers of citizens who were Jewish, and there was widespread anti-Semitism in these countries. The powerful myth of Jewish supremacy – the idea that the Jews could influence world politics – was well known, as was the idea that the Jews, as a race, and with a strong sense of unity, could influence those governments that were still neutral in the conflict.⁹⁶ Ultimately, the protection of the Jews was a political, rather than humanitarian, manoeuvre. Zionism was gaining ground in Germany as well as in Britain, and there was fierce competition between countries to grant protection to the Jews. From the perspective of this competition, it seems that the Balfour Declaration, issued in 1917, allowed the British Government to monopolise the Zionist cause.

The Ottomans, perfectly aware of the rising Zionist activity before the war, first tried to stop Jewish immigration, and then attempted to expel Jews from Jerusalem and Palestine. In December 1914, neutral countries were ordered to notify any Jews under their protection that they were to leave the country within three days.⁹⁷ All consuls protested against this measure, however, and it was withdrawn.⁹⁸ Throughout the war there were many episodes like this. Towards the end of the conflict and, above all, after the discovery of the Nili spy network, Ottomans became harsher and the job of the consuls increasingly difficult, as they could no longer influence the Ottoman authorities.⁹⁹ At the end of March 1917, Cemal Paşa ordered the evacuation of Jaffa; Ballobar and his German and Austrian colleagues complained, but they could not change this decision. The refugees were allowed to go to Jerusalem and Galilee, though no food or shelter were provided.[100]

To help the relief activity, two important organisations were established: the Muslim Commission and the Central Committee for the Relief of Jews. The first was a local body, managed by notables with the purpose of distributing aid and relief to the local Muslim population. Although it was under the control of the Ottomans, it was able to act quite freely.[101] The Ottoman governor, who was distrustful of the Arab notables, asked the American consul to verify whether the Commission was working according to the rules, and to make sure that some of the rice and sugar available would go to the Municipal Hospital, which accepted Jews and Christians as well.[102] The Central Committee was an international organisation, composed mainly of Jewish Americans, established by Zionists to help all Jews in Palestine, regardless of their support of Zionism.[103] Nevertheless, local authorities wanted to maintain some control over these activities; therefore Glazebrook was asked by the local authorities to send them a list showing the payees and the amount of money sent.[104]

The activity of this particular body was quite complex, and loaded with political connotations. The American ambassador in Istanbul, Henry Morgenthau, was the first to appeal to American Jews after the outbreak of the war, in order to help all Jews living in Palestine, while the British agreed to grant free passage to vessels carrying food, medicine and other commodities provided by the American Jewish Committee. This agreement, signed in 1915, was made on the condition that the distribution was done under the supervision of the American consul, and without any interference on the part of the Ottoman authorities.[105] An enormous amount of money was sent, and the efforts to aid the Jews of Palestine proved successful. Reports on the activities of the Central Committee suggest that it succeeded in restoring the lives of Jews in Jerusalem to a state of normality, at least in 1915.[106]

It was also common, as far as the war conditions allowed, for private citizens in the United States, as well as Germany, to send money directly to particular individuals living in Jerusalem. Normally the money was paid to the American ambassador in

Istanbul, and then transferred to the consul in Jerusalem. Then, under the instructions of the private citizens who had sent the money, it was paid to the beneficiary.[107] In February 1916, for instance, the sum of $110 was made available to be paid to Gerschan Heyman and Neo Sheorim, two Jewish inhabitants of Jerusalem. The money was sent first from Gerschan's son, Louis Heyman, who was living in the United States, to the Central Committee for the Relief of Jews Suffering throughout the War, then from the Committee to the American consulate in Jerusalem.[108] The Central Committee for the Relief of Jews Suffering Throughout the War was formed in the United States in 1914, and was part of the Joint Distribution Committee, alongside the American Jewish Relief Committee and the People's Committee.[109] The Joint Distribution Committee had been formed in November 1914, chaired by Felix Warburg (a member of the Warburg banking family, of German origin), with the purpose of coordinating the activities of the three relief committees.[110]

A key figure in the distribution of aid was the American consul Otis Allan Glazebrook. He was born in Virginia in 1845 and educated at the Virginia Military Institute and the Virginia Theological Seminary. Glazebrook was deeply religious: he served for seven years in missionary fields in Virginia after the civil war and was eventually ordained in 1869. Glazebrook was a young civil war veteran who, after the conflict, founded the Alpha Tau Omega Fraternity, an organisation designed to reunite the Southern and Northern parts of the country using Christian principles.[111]

From 1914, as a personal friend of President Woodrow Wilson, Glazebrook served in the American Foreign service. It seems that the president appointed him to Jerusalem due to their shared faith. Glazebrook arrived in Jerusalem in April 1914 and left the city when the United States joined the war in April 1917; he returned in December 1918, remaining there for almost exactly two years, after which he was assigned to Nice, and later Monaco. Glazebrook died on 26 April 1931, on his way back to the United States.[112]

As consul, Glazebrook played a crucial role in the city after the outbreak of the war. The main activities of Glazebrook in Jerusalem related to the distribution of relief aid from the United States, destined for the Jewish communities, and tending to the needs of the American Colony.¹¹³ His job was difficult given Ottoman mistrust of American help towards the Jews. Paradoxically, at the beginning of 1917, when it was clear that, sooner or later, the United States would join the war, some of Glazebrook's activities were halted by the Germans, who interrupted relief distribution, whilst the Ottomans allowed American relief to continue in Jerusalem, as the local population, including the same Ottomans officials, benefited from this relief.¹¹⁴

Glazebrook was quite different from his Spanish counterpart still in the city, Conde de Ballobar. The American consul was an ordinary person and he was not really interested in religious issues concerning the Churches in Jerusalem. They did cooperate, as shown by Ballobar's notes, but they never became 'real' friends. There are no records of any diary or collection of papers left by Glazebrook, which perhaps reflects his introspective nature. He had an extensive correspondence, despite the censorship, with Morgenthau and with some American companies eager to invest in Palestine. Of his relationship with Morgenthau, it is apparent that there was mutual respect, and that Glazebrook was eager to act upon requests asking for intervention in favour of the Jews. His attitude was, however, quite different towards the American business community which, during the war, continued to petition the consul asking for his perspective on business in the region. He politely explained to a misinformed public that as Palestine was involved in a war, business was suspended.¹¹⁵ His Christian values and charitable activities always prevailed over business.

Overall, humanitarian activities, as suggested throughout the previous discussion, were often closely linked to politics. Indeed, the relief of the Jewish population was at the centre of strong political activity in all the countries involved in the war. Throughout the war, the Jews of Palestine received constant help, and the Zionist Commission toured Europe to gather support for the establishment of Jewish colonies in Palestine. Zionists in Europe eventually found a receptive audience in the British Government, and it is arguable that the Zionist lobby played a strong role in the issuance of the Balfour Declaration.¹¹⁶

Consuls, besides relief and aid, also had to deal with questions related to prisoners, the economy, and local religious institutions.

Consuls became, in some way, responsible for the fate of prisoners of war, as well as of local political prisoners.[117] On the eve of the British occupation of Jerusalem, Ballobar raised concerns he had in relation to several Jewish leaders detained by Ottoman authorities because of their Zionist activities, and he succeeded in getting these people released on bail.[118] During the war, attempts at foreign economic penetration in Palestine and Jerusalem did not halt. As Europeans were busy with the war, American firms expressed their interest in possible investments, with some extraordinary developments in 1916. The American Film Company, seemingly impervious to the fact that a war was raging in the region, asked Glazebrook to investigate whether it would be possible to invest in the film/theatre business. It appears that the war, at least in America, was felt to be very distant and not significant enough to interfere with trade and business. This perception changed, of course, in 1917, when the United States joined the war, leaving the Spanish consul the only foreign representative not involved in the war, holding and protecting the interests of the Allied countries.[119]

Consuls themselves were also affected by the war, just as the population was; particularly by the shortage of money and other commodities. The American consul was in possession of some gold, which was left under the care of the Franciscans since it was almost impossible to use or even to exchange it.[120] The Spanish consul himself started to run out of money towards the end of the war. With great bitterness, Ballobar recorded his belief that the Ottomans had committed theft by seizing the small quantity of food and medicines left.[121]

Consular activity during the war became instrumental to the situation created by the war itself. The few diplomats left were no longer able to influence the local administration, which was tightly controlled by the military and, in particular, by the wishes of Cemal Paşa. In wartime Jerusalem consuls renegotiated their authority, power, ideology and objectives. The parable of this change can be better studied and appreciated through the study of the Spanish consul in Jerusalem, Conde de Ballobar.

Consul of War: Conde de Ballobar

In September 1914, a young Spanish diplomat, still in his twenties, who had arrived in Jerusalem a few months earlier, began to record in his diary his experiences in Jerusalem. Antonio de la Cierva y Lewita, later Conde de Ballobar and Duque de Terranova, was born in Vienna in 1885. His mother was Austrian, of Jewish origin, but converted to the Catholic faith. His father was a Spanish military attaché to the Spanish embassy in the Austrian capital.[122] In 1911, Ballobar entered the Spanish consular service and was sent as vice-consul to Cuba. In May 1913, Ballobar was appointed consul in Jerusalem; according to his personnel file he took possession of the consulate in August 1913 and remained until the end of 1919.[123] When Ballobar reached Jerusalem, his task was limited to the protection of Spanish interests, mainly religious in nature, and re-establishing 'diplomatic' and more friendly relations with the Custody of the Holy Land.[124] By the time of the British occupation of Jerusalem in 1917, he found himself the only consul in the city, in charge of the protection of the interests of all countries involved in the war. He became a crucial personality but as will be shown later, this character rapidly faded away.

In January 1920, Ballobar took charge of the Spanish consulate in Damascus; however, in November of the same year he moved to Tangiers, where he served for a few months.[125] Also in 1920, he married Rafaela Osorio de Moscoso, Duchess of Terranova. On 24 June 1921, Ballobar resigned his commission as consul and moved back to Spain.[126] Ballobar was commissioned in 1925 to carry out a report on the Spanish convents and hospitals in Palestine, but until 1936 he withdrew from diplomatic service as 'excedente voluntario'; in fact, he took an extended leave of absence. In August 1936 Ballobar publicly supported Francisco Franco and his 'Junta de Denfensa Nacional de España' against the left-wing Popular Front, which had won the election a few months earlier. There had been some aggression against the Church after the elections, so unsurprisingly the pious Ballobar threw in his lot with Franco. From August 1936, Ballobar was first appointed to the Diplomatic Cabinet of the 'Junta', then became Secretary of the

External Relations for Franco's Foreign Office. In the 1940s, Ballobar worked mainly at the Spanish Foreign Office, with a particular interest in relations with the Holy See.[127] In the same period, Ballobar was offered important consular positions around the world, such as Canada and the United States, but he did not accept these appointments. On the contrary, he asked for short leaves of absence, which he alternated with short periods at the Spanish Foreign Office.[128] It is not clear what reasons he had for these, although it is possible to speculate that he did not want to be too involved with public activities or be too exposed, preferring to manage family business enterprises. In May 1949, Ballobar was named, once again, consul to Jerusalem, where he served until 1952. Ballobar eventually died in Madrid in 1971, aged 86.[129]

During his first stay in Jerusalem, the Conde de Ballobar wrote a diary which, together with archival material available, sheds light on Jerusalem during the First World War, particularly regarding social aspects. Local politics was the most important issue to the young consul, as it had a direct impact on Spanish interests; however, considering his isolation from the rest of the world, whilst attending social events he always tried to gather as much information as possible on what was happening outside the microcosm of Jerusalem.[130]

As a source Ballobar has only been mentioned in scholarly written works by Tom Segev and in passing by others, despite the fact that, when the British occupied Jerusalem, the Spanish consul was a well-known figure. It is clear, however, that Ballobar's importance within the city faded quite rapidly after the British capture of Jerusalem for several reasons, including the fact that Spain was not a crucial actor in the Middle East; that Ballobar had a limited knowledge of English; and, lastly, because events excluded him from the main political stream. Segev only partially captured the importance of Ballobar, reporting some of the entries of his diary, but tending to dismiss the young consul as a 'socialite'.[131] Ballobar played a major role in wartime Jerusalem, and his 'socialite' attitude was not an obstacle; in fact, it provides a fresh perspective on the city and its politics.

Ballobar's diary is the testimony of an individual within a specific context, and it would be reductive to see it simply as a personal account. As consul, churchgoer, and local resident, Ballobar had a good, albeit sometimes slightly naive, grasp of the local socio-political context. His narrative is a reflection of a particular historical period and, as long as the problems associated with this type of source are acknowledged, his personal views are still valuable for socio-political history. The advantages of this particular source are in the new information available for this period, and comparing this source with others raises a number of questions. However, there are also disadvantages to working with this type of material, as its very nature raises methodological issues and problems concerning bias and partial views of a clearly complex situation. It is crucial to understand the constructed nature of the source itself, and extract the genuine experience from the ritualised memory of the experience even if written down soon after the event.[132]

Ballobar was a man who cared about his appearance and his social life: even in times of crisis, he always took care to dress appropriately according to the social occasion, wearing suits and elegant garments; he also worried a great deal about his personal residence, seeing this as a reflection of his status, and would change houses when other foreign officials left the city due to the war.[133] He was famous for the luxurious meals he served at his residence, particularly when he entertained local political and military elites: Cemal Paşa, for instance, was a regular guest. Nevertheless, to define him as a socialite is to present a very superficial picture of the consul.

Ballobar was indeed a classical orientalist, in Saidian terms, as he possessed an ideological misperception, latent and manifest, of the 'Orient'.[134] Ballobar's judgement was shaped by classical stereotypes and clichés in relation to the Middle East and its inhabitants; therefore it is not surprising that in his diary and reports he either did not pay much attention to the local population or he discussed them in negative terms. Ballobar did not often differentiate between the different communities living in Jerusalem unless discussing particular cases; therefore, on some occasions he used the term 'Arabs' when referring to the whole of the local population. The first reference in the diary concerning the local population is a note on 16 February 1915, in which he reports the

Arab frustration with the Turks, who sent them to fight a war they did not want to fight.[135] In this case he – ungenerously – states that the Arabs had no sense of nation and national spirit. I believe his comments arise from their lack of knowledge of the local environment. It took fully three months from the outbreak of the war for Ballobar to comment on the locals, a reflection of his lack of attention to the local inhabitants, at least in the first stages of his consular mission in the city; however, it was also a reflection of his consular mission, which concerned religious institutions rather than people. This was quite the opposite to the American consular mission as carried out by Glazebrook, who cared much for the local population and reported quite frequently, and at length, about them. In June 1915 Ballobar was informed of Arab current political activity against the Turks; however, he maintained his negative opinion, and claimed that the Arabs would not be able to achieve anything against the Turks.[136] Ballobar did later take some interest in the condition of the Ottoman army – quite distinct from local Arab activities – and the development of the Palestinian front, as well as the living conditions of the Jerusalemites, primarily towards the end of the war. At the time of the invasion of the locusts in 1915, Ballobar continued to dine with the other foreign officials in the city, as well as with the German commanders, enjoying cognac, wine, cigars and large meals with them, a sign that the war was, indeed, very far from his mind. He did, however, become quite concerned with the price of wheat, which had increased as a consequence of the invasion of locusts.[137] Ballobar was aware of his low-profile role, and continued this way until 1917, when the pressure of the war made itself felt fully in Jerusalem and he had to deal personally with a shortage of resources, and with his new and unexpected role of 'universal' consul. Still, he remained detached from the local population, concentrating on issues such as the devaluation of Turkish paper money and the rising cost of living, albeit less in terms of its impact on the population than on the money available to him.[138]

Despite his low-profile role, Ballobar enjoyed being at centre stage, and Jerusalem under war conditions gave him this opportunity. In April 1917, with the impending British conquest of Jaffa, even though they had been defeated at Gaza on 26 March, the Ottoman authorities ordered the evacuation of this city, with a specific focus on deporting the Jewish population.[139] News of the evacuation of the Jewish population of Jaffa reached Europe and beyond, thanks to the network of the Nili spies and the Aaronsohn group. On 11 April 1917, Ballobar wrote: 'the Jews of Jaffa have left the city for the Jewish colonies in Galilee'. However this was reported as a massacre of Jews and a pogrom in press around the world.[140] The *Revue Israelite d'Egypte* wrote that Jews had been deported, and would be condemned to death, while the *New York Times* ran an article entitled: 'Plea for the Jews of Jaffa; driven out by Turks, they are wandering in increasing misery'.[141] Hardly any mainstream paper in the world failed to report the news, and to state that the Turks were ready to deport and starve to death the Jews of Palestine.[142] The Vatican also expressed its concern in relation to the evacuation of Jaffa and the fate of the Jews. The Apostolic Delegate in Istanbul interviewed the German ambassador in the Ottoman capital and reported to Cardinal Gasparri, Secretary of State at the Vatican, that the deportation had been ordered for military reasons and claims of a massacre were not supported by solid evidence.[143] However, it is clear that the deportation of Jews from Jaffa became a significant topic in both Ottoman and German circles. For Germans, it was crucial not to alienate those German Jews supporting the Reich, as suggested by a campaign led by the press supporting the adoption of a German pro-Zionist stance.[144] The Germans made it clear they believed it was Cemal Paşa's will to evacuate Jaffa, and not a necessity of war.[145] As a result, in June 1917 the German ambassador in Istanbul and Cemal Paşa himself asked the Spanish consul to investigate. Ballobar interviewed some Ottoman and German officials but he also managed to interview local Jews and eventually Ballobar concluded that no massacre had taken place and that the Jewish residents of Jaffa had simply moved towards Galilee, with some going to Jerusalem.[146] However, the evacuation was far from painless, and many died en route; it was only German intervention which prevented this from becoming a humanitarian disaster. The results of Ballobar's work were sent to the various Foreign Offices around the world, but it was not reported in the press until later that year. A similar case occurred after the British occupation of Jerusalem. Rumours reached Europe that the British had sentenced to death some German subjects, including civilians, and Ballobar was urged by the Spanish Foreign Office to investigate.[147] The consul reported that the British had not shot anyone in this affair, but had deported some German subjects for security reasons.[148]

The war, as suggested earlier, provided Ballobar with a chance to become a prominent social actor and to increase his prestige. During the war, Ballobar was charged with the distribution of aid and relief, principally from the United States. This job was handled mainly by Otis Glazebrook, but when, in April 1917, the United States joined the war and broke diplomatic relations with the Ottoman Empire, Ballobar was asked to continue the work. On 17 April 1917, Ballobar met Glazebrook and they agreed on the procedures to adopt in case the United States severed diplomatic relations with the Ottoman Empire.[149] After this in fact happened, Ballobar took charge of the distribution of aid, mainly to the Jewish population of the city, but also to the other communities of Jerusalem.[150] Ballobar complained that this work took up most of his time, as he had to keep a record of all the money which arrived, and make sure it reached the right people. He also worried that this work, and all his social activities, would eventually be detrimental to his health.[151] After the arrival of the British, the consul was the victim of a light neurasthenic attack, due, according to him, to stress caused by work overload.[152]

Although Ballobar was busy with the distribution of relief and other duties, he was also often busy with social events. Dining out in Jerusalem during the war was not an unusual activity. Dinners took place mainly at the residences of foreign consuls, Ottoman officials and local notables. Meals were not the only social gatherings: tea, coffee, poker and lunch were also very popular amongst the elites of the city. It seems that these events were very fashionable and well-known amongst the local inhabitants: other local residents, like Ihsan Tourjman and Wasif Jawhariyyeh also discussed these social events (albeit with different focus and opinions).[153]

Dinners and other gatherings have been discussed at length by social scientists, anthropologists and archaeologists.[154] It has been suggested that food can be used as a system of communication; the way food and activities are organised is a reflection of a particular message, a body of images and a protocol of usages and behaviours.[155] It has also been argued that the way people use food and drink is a metaphor for the character of the relationship between the participants.[156] Food consumption, according to some scholars, is a reflection of the way social classes display their place in a hierarchical system of social distinction, which also implies, occasionally, the adoption of food strategies in an attempt to underline the presentation of self.[157] The dinners and other social events described by Ballobar are indeed a reflection of the historical situation, the status of the relationships between the different actors mentioned in the diary, and personal strategies adopted by the consul to present himself *vis-à-vis* the residents of the city. These gatherings took place during a war, the role of which must not be overlooked. In this context, food is also charged with signifying the situation in which it is used.[158] Before discussing some of the events portrayed by Ballobar, the same category of events as portrayed by Tourjman and Jawhariyyeh should be scrutinised. It is clear from Abigail Jacobson's analysis of Tourjman's diary that he was dissatisfied and angry with the Ottoman government which, according to him, was neglecting the local population in time of crisis. Tourjman was also very critical of public celebrations and parties, which he considered 'decadent and immoral especially in a time of war'.[159] Meanwhile, Jawhariyyeh, as a musician, was often part of these social events which he mentioned as part of his account of music, art and social life in the late Ottoman period in Jerusalem. His account was less critical and more descriptive.[160]

Discussing the diary chronologically, on 25 November 1914 Ballobar dined at his residence with the civil governor, Macid Bey. Ballobar gave a detailed description of the dinner and he praised his Arab chef, who prepared excellent stuffed courgette.[161] The consul was interested in becoming more acquainted with the local establishment; they did not discuss particular topics, or, at least, none were reported, suggesting that the Spanish consul was interested mainly in getting to know the governor, and gathering more information on the ongoing process of mobilisation which had started in Jerusalem in August 1914 with the proclamation of martial law, in preparation for a possible war.[162] This event indeed reveals a particular system of communication, whether intentional or not, put in place through the social consumption of food.

A different example of social activity is represented by a billiards game, followed by dinner, on 23 February 1915. Ballobar played against the Greek consul Raphaël; the two were quite close friends. After the game, they decided to pay a visit to the new military governor, Ali Riza Bey, who was depicted by Ballobar as a pleasant person. Both diplomats were eager to get to know their new counterpart. They enjoyed the night out discussing war news, above all the Dardanelles campaign and the question of the prisoners of war.[163]

Later, in May 1915, Ballobar was informed that Italy had joined the war. An official dinner was scheduled that night, 26 May, at the United States consular residence. The Italian, German and Austrian consuls did not attend the dinner, all sending notes of apology to the American representative, but they could clearly not attend given the circumstances. Nevertheless, the dinner was no less animated; in fact, guest of honour Cemal Paşa entertained the other guests, talking about the CUP and Lord Kitchener, the British Minister of War. Cemal reported that Kitchener had attempted to engage a professional killer, apparently Cemal himself, in order to murder Talat – minister of the interior – as the British believed that eliminating Talat would have removed the Ottoman Empire from the conflict. During the dinner, Raphaël and Cemal discussed the role of Greece in the war. Eventually the discussion was downplayed when the small crowd moved to a cinema, where a party was organised by the local Jewish notable Antebi, and where the ice-cream served helped to cool down the heated Turco-Greek relations.[164] In this case the war is not relevant in terms of dietary change as discussed by some scholars but it is influential in the behaviour of the people sitting around the table.[165]

In a long entry on 9 July 1916, Ballobar described several events that took place from 29 June, when the Spanish consul received a late visit from Cemal Paşa. Ballobar called Raphaël and, with Cemal, discussed the possibility of Greece and Spain joining the war, but according to Ballobar the situation was not tense: in fact, it was quite friendly. Cemal then began to discuss urban plans for Jerusalem, such as the construction of a park on Mount Zion and a new road between the Franciscan school and Damascus Gate. A few days later, on a Friday, Ballobar again met Cemal for a short visit. They discussed the Armenians and the question of whether it was true that these people had to convert to Islam: Cemal denied it. Sitting around the table, Ballobar commented upon a book by the leading Zionist Dr Arthur Ruppin, leading to Cemal yelling: 'He is a swine!'[166] On 6 July Cemal visited Ballobar's residence where they were served a dazzling meal; Ballobar wanted to impress his guest, and the menu included Turkish soup, fish, fillets, meat pies and stuffed turkey; as desserts, vanilla ice-cream, pineapple and fruit were served. After dinner, they played poker and discussed news coming from Europe. It was as if the war was light years away from both them and Jerusalem.[167] Ballobar went to great lengths to serve this meal, considering the scarcity of resources; however, he used this event as a metaphor to demonstrate that he still had power, and to convey the importance he accorded to his guests.

On 9 September 1916, during a dinner hosted by the governor of the city and held at the convent of Artas, Cemal suddenly attacked the Greek consul, accusing the Greeks of being revolutionaries paid by the Entente powers, showing how the tension caused by the war could enter any kind of environment. Cemal, talking about the Greeks, quoted 'Ali Fuad Bey, former ambassador to St Petersburg and then commander of the Western Front against the Greeks: 'We will treat them (the Greeks) worse than the Armenians'.[168] It is clear that Cemal mistrusted the Greeks, but he was also concerned about the rumours of an impending British crossing of the Suez Canal, also mentioned by Ballobar a few days earlier, quoting a German newspaper.[169]

On 4 May 1917, it was clear that the situation in Palestine was to change and it was only a matter of time before the British engaged in a battle for Jerusalem. Ballobar dined at Zaki Bey's home, where German consul Brode confirmed that Jerusalem would not be evacuated, to the great satisfaction of the Spanish consul, who feared tremendously the possibility of a sudden evacuation. They played poker and discussed the question of typhus and America joining the war against Germany, but not against the Ottoman Empire. Typhus was becoming an urgent issue according to Ballobar, as members of the various consular missions in the

Ottoman Empire had also been affected.[170] From the narrative in Ballobar's diaries, it seems that amongst the commanding elites in Jerusalem, there was some sense of foreboding: they were waiting for something to happen.

A few months later the wait was over. On 8 December 1917, Ballobar dined for the last time in the company of German officials. During the dinner, Perfall, a German officer, made an official announcement: 'the 20th Corps of the Army will defend the surrounds of Jerusalem and it will withdraw during the night, leaving only three regiments which then will take the road to Jericho'.[171] Food and war once again went hand in hand. Ballobar described his surprise; however, he had been waiting for this day to come. By mid-November, Ballobar had already written to the Ministry of State informing his superiors of the impeding Ottoman-German withdrawal.[172] After the dinner Ballobar returned to the Spanish consulate. Confusion reigned due to the battle around the city and panic spread amongst the population as well as amongst the troops. That evening he was visited by an Ottoman official, Arif Bey, who asked the consul to surrender the Jews hidden in the consulate: banker Siegfried Eliezer Hoofien and his associate Jacob Thon. Ballobar promised him that he would hand these people over to the Ottomans the following day, clearly aware that by then the city would have been evacuated; he also knew that the Ottomans were in no position to make such a demand.[173] It is difficult to say whether Ballobar was for or against Zionism, with all sources available suggesting a neutral approach towards this particular subject; he was keen to help the Jews, as he did on many occasions, but he never clearly expressed any opinion in relation to Zionism *per se*. Interestingly, not only is Zionism missing from Ballobar's diary and other sources; as soon as the British arrived, references to the previous regime and his 'old friends', Cemal Paşa and others, disappeared.

After the British arrived many things changed in the city; however, not only did social gatherings maintain their important status, they actually became even more important, and, indeed, fashionable due to the influx of new people and new resources. A few months after the British occupation of the city, on 8 April 1918, Ballobar attended an official dinner which was served in a buffet style. He had never seen anything like it; he said it looked practical, although he could not understand how a Lord could enjoy such a system. Music was played, and a short theatrical show performed. He discussed the military and political situation in Jerusalem with several British officials, including General Allenby, who was quite effective in not saying very much at all.

In July, Ballobar dined with the new military governor Ronald Storrs, who claimed that the best solution for Jerusalem was to leave the city to the Americans. Ballobar did not agree, believing that British rule was the best solution given the alternative possibility of a Palestine ruled by the French or even the Italians, the strongest competitors of Spain in the Holy Land.[174] Interestingly, Storrs reported the dinner with Ballobar in his memoirs, although he focused mainly on some comments made by Ballobar on the German and Ottoman authorities in the city: 'Jemal was *sale type* but *bon garçon*, and Enver *aimait beaucoup la boisson*: Falkenhayn and Kress *sympathiques*'.[175]

Ballobar lived in a microcosm which reflected the larger context of the war in the Middle East. The diary and related material have proved to be a valuable and unique historical source, which shed light on several corners: socio-political life in Jerusalem, Ottoman policies, and religious institutions. There is also information on typhus and cholera epidemics in Jerusalem and Palestine, a good picture of the British military administration in Jerusalem, and data, figures and information on the war and its effects in the region.

Consular missions in the aftermath of the War

Once British military authority was established in December 1917, all foreign residents, but mainly Germans and Austrians, were put under surveillance.[176] There were only ten German civilians in the city, as the others had been evacuated earlier. Nearly all religious clergymen of Austrian and German citizenship had also left, while German and Austrian Jews were recognised as Jews, and therefore treated as such: religious identity, in this particular case, took precedence over national one.[177] Austro-German properties were confiscated and converted to accommodate British needs. The American Colony promptly offered its services to the British military authority, while the Spanish consul, as the only diplomat left in the city, was charged with the hard task of representing all countries involved in the conflict.[178]

Allenby, as supreme military authority, had to face pressing political and administrative issues. Italy and France wanted to be represented in Jerusalem in future talks regarding the status of Palestine and of the city itself. Apart from Ballobar, who was an anomaly since he also represented British interests, diplomatic and consular missions were not allowed to enter the city, though travelling permits had been granted *ad personam*.[179] The Italian government was quite anxious to send a diplomat to Jerusalem to counterbalance the influence of the French representative, Georges Picot, the High Commissioner for Syria and Palestine. The Italians, aware of the Anglo-French agreements over the Middle East, were suspicious that the British would allow some French activity in the Holy Land, but did not know how much the British would support Italian aspirations. Confirming Italian anxiety in 1917, Allenby appointed a small French contingent to guard the church of the Holy Sepulchre.[180] Nevertheless, it is also arguable that Italian influence in Palestine before the war was both modest and very recent, and they could not ask for more than the internationalisation of the city. Once again the battle over the religious protectorate broke out; however, the British, and Allenby in particular, were not interested in finding a lasting solution to this internal conflict while the war was still on.[181] Although British military authorities were more concerned with the maintenance of the status quo than with dealing with political issues, at this point they also realised that this was a chance to reduce French influence in Palestine. In view of this, it is not surprising that French clergy, as well as pilgrims, were not immediately allowed to return.[182] The question of the religious protectorate over the Catholics was only part of the quarrel, however, as political and economic concerns, as well as that of prestige were at stake.[183] Furthermore, the British did not reinstate the Capitulations abolished unilaterally by the Ottomans in 1914, *de facto* rejecting any French claim. Only in the spring of 1919 was the question partly resolved: the Italians were at least able to reopen the consulate, which gave them better control over their interests in the Holy Land. Once the Italian Government confirmed the acceptance of the abolition of the capitulations and acknowledged the political status quo, Alberto Tuozzi was appointed to Jerusalem as Italian consul.[184] Picot, meanwhile, moved to Beirut in September 1918, with a delegate left in Jerusalem: Pierre Durieux and then Louis Raïs fulfilled this role.[185] Louis Raïs was also named Consul General in Jerusalem, becoming the last French outpost in British Palestine.[186] True, the French obtained control of Syria and Lebanon, but they lost any claim to Palestine. A note of the French Foreign Office of November 1917 suggests that the French and British were going to administer the former Ottoman Arab territories jointly; however, the not-so-secret internal battle amongst the Allies was clearly won by the British.[187] Nicault suggests that the French, and Picot in particular, had to accept a 'variable' *status quo* due to the *faits accomplis* achieved by the British; as a result both the French and the Italians simply disappeared from the scene of Jerusalem and Palestine.[188]

Later in 1919, the Americans were allowed to reopen their consulate in Jerusalem. Slowly, consular life in Jerusalem began to revive, albeit with some restrictions.[189] National flags could not be flown until 1920, and, with the prior abolition of the Capitulations, privileges were curtailed. The main work of the consuls involved lobbying the British, issuing passports and travel documents to foreign nationals travelling to Palestine, who were primarily of Jewish origin, and the protection of religious institutions; however, this was all done on different terms than in Ottoman times. The Italians, besides a consul, also sought to send a political officer to look after Italian institutions that had been damaged during the war.[190]

The status of the consular corps in Jerusalem was radically different after British occupation of the city. Under Ottoman rule, consuls were part of a restricted but varied elite ruling Jerusalem; under the British they became mere agents of their governments, with defined and limited powers. The age of consuls as part of the decision-making process in relation to Jerusalem was over. In a way, the redefinition of the consular role also had an impact on the local population. Jerusalemites were accustomed to a variety of centres of power under Ottoman rule, providing various routes to political access. However, although the British maintained part of the administrative structure established by the Ottomans, and gave the notables some visibility, they were the real masters in Palestine and Jerusalem: the sole source of any real power. Consulates became the recipients of petitions and complaints, but could no longer influence the local administration. The British successfully transformed Jerusalem from a consular city, a centre of conspiracies and rivalries, into a modern administrative centre, and in the process, redefined the centres of power. The only players now were the British administration, the Zionist Commission and the Arab Nationalist Associations.

4

THE WAR AND THE BRITISH CONQUEST OF JERUSALEM

> For the love of God, let not so free a gift
> Be squandered or recalled for our misuse!
> Let our work's thread and finish correspond
> With the noble design which set our course.
> Now that the way is clear of obstacles,
> Now that the season is favourable to us,
> What shall prevent our racing to the aim
> Of all our triumphs – to Jerusalem!
> Torquato Tasso
> (Jerusalem Delivered, Canto I, St. 27)[1]

In December 1917, the focal point of the transition from Ottoman to British rule of Jerusalem was the military occupation of the city by British troops. This was not simply the replacement of a regime, but represented the entire renegotiation of political and economic values, alliances, cultures and expectations both in Jerusalem and abroad. The British conquest of Jerusalem began well before its actual occupation, as discussed in literature which sometimes highlights the use of propaganda, or simply discusses aspects of military history. The same literature has seldom mentioned the Jerusalemites, their war experiences and their impressions in relation to the British occupation and the process of mobilisation for war, apart from some generalised statements.

There is still a great deal of work to carry out in terms of sources available in investigating the local response to the war and the British occupation of the city. Scholars like Salim Tamari, Issam Nassar and Abigail Jacobson are leading the way on the discovery and discussion of diaries and memoirs of local residents, thereby effectively highlighting the necessity of criticising the previous narratives written in relation to this period, so they would now include the local population in the picture, and move away from traditional and stereotypical historical accounts. In this challenge, I have tried to rely on the sources presented by the scholars mentioned above as well as introducing new material, such as that discussed in previous chapters. The main challenge is to write a history of Jerusalem in transition without necessarily focusing too extensively on the British. It is difficult to fully exclude the British from the picture and it would also be unwise to do so considering the importance of their role; however, it is possible to integrate the two narratives – that of the conquerors and that of the residents.

The very last phase of Ottoman rule in Jerusalem corresponds with the establishment of a military administration in the city, following the outbreak of hostilities between the Central Powers (Germany and Austro-Hungarian Empire) and the Entente (Britain and France) in 1914. In the summer of that year, the Ottoman Empire was not ready for the conflict: Ottomans were not mobilised for a war effort and the CUP declared armed neutrality. At the beginning of the war, the British did not consider the Eastern front of military operations to be of any value. The Palestine campaign and the following conquest of Jerusalem, in the early days of the war, were not planned in advance by British policy-makers, so what then led the British army to occupy Jerusalem? How did they prepare the military and propaganda campaign to support the occupation of the city? What was the value of Jerusalem in British eyes, or in the eyes of their Allies? And how did the local population and international actors react to the occupation? These questions only partially consider the larger picture of the transition of Jerusalem from Ottoman to British rulers, and it is crucial to also consider some aspects of the social and political life in the city during the war. In this case, particular attention will be paid to religious and local political institutions.

Last, but not least, the capture of Jerusalem generated a popular theme among the British public after the occupation of Jerusalem: the conquest of Jerusalem as the final chapter of the Crusades. The British press began to portray the conquest of the Holy City as the fulfilment of the Crusades; Allenby had conquered the city that the English hero Richard Coeur de Lion had not managed to enter. However, the explosion of 'crusading mania' was the logical outcome of a carefully staged campaign, an artificial product of the war propaganda.[2] This romanticised image of the city collided with the reality of the actual situation, but shows the complexity of the narratives representing the politics and desire to control Jerusalem.

Preparing for war: mobilisation of human, material and ideological resources

War is a condition of belligerency between actors that usually begins some time before the process of mobilisation, except in cases of pre-emptive strikes. In modern times, this process entails not only the mobilisation of the military, but also that of material and ideological resources. As part of the mobilisation process every country involved in the First World War also created agencies to control the flow of information, and monitor public opinion.[3] The Ottoman Empire had been under military mobilisation for almost the entire decade of the Young Turks and CUP rule. As a result of the war with Italy in 1911-1912 and the Balkan Wars of 1912-1913, the Ottoman government lost a great portion of its territories. Yet it survived and in order to avoid isolation the Ottomans sought allies in Europe. When the First World War broke out in 1914 Istanbul remained neutral, but by November the Empire was forced to enter the war alongside its German ally.[4] One of the main flaws of the Ottoman Empire was its heavy military and economic dependence on the Western European powers. As soon as the war broke out, the economy of the Empire was completely paralysed. As the Ottoman Bank ran short of cash, the main cities of the Empire experienced a shortage of commodities, soaring prices and a general increase in the cost of living.[5] Protectionism was strengthened to favour domestic producers, but also virtually isolated the Ottoman economy. Nevertheless, internal production dropped drastically as the majority of the male population was mobilised in the army.[6]

Although the Ottoman Empire did not possess a proper institution to deal with intelligence and propaganda, symbolism was exploited in the process of mobilisation, mainly with the purpose of justifying the war.[7] The Ottoman state, however, was not able to organise an efficient propaganda effort, as much of this activity fell victim to the CUP and the strict censorship enforced to avoid dissent.[8] Sacred images and words were going to be exploited by all European countries; the British, for instance, appealed to the image of the crusade against the evil German enemy and her allies; so too did the Ottoman Empire when it openly declared a *jihad* (holy war) on 11 November 1914. The German General Liman von Sanders, responsible for improving the efficiency of the Turkish army, was ordered by German Headquarters to stay in Istanbul and promote anti-British sentiment. Furthermore, a special team working in alliance with German Zionists was formed under the command of Max von Oppenheim, a German intelligence officer, to organise rebellions in Muslim countries loyal to the British.[9] With the CUP coup of 1913 the Ottoman Empire underwent a process of 'Turkification' of the administration and the educational system although, in previous years, Abdülhamid II had attempted to integrate the Arab subjects of the Empire. Despite antagonistic policies against the Arabs, such as the mandatory use of the Turkish language for official messages sent throughout the Empire, the general resentment felt by the local Arab population towards the foreign powers before the breakout of the war was stronger than their dislike of the Turkish officials. This resentment was exploited for political and military ends. On 9 September 1914, the CUP unilaterally abolished the Capitulations, the very symbol of Ottoman submission to European powers. At last the Empire had become a sovereign state.[10] If on the one hand the Arabs disliked the foreign presence, they were also suspicious of the *jihad* called by the Ottoman Sultan Mehmet V in November 1914.

The population in Jerusalem, mainly out of fear of the effectiveness of Ottoman policies, showed support for the CUP government. However, the situation was far more complex than a simple acceptance or rejection of CUP decisions and propaganda. An intelligence report written by a resident of Jerusalem, Anis el-Gamal, who left the city for Egypt in the first weeks of mobilisation, stated that the inhabitants of Jerusalem had a strong desire *for* British occupation.[11] Meanwhile many locals conscripted into the Ottoman army viewed this war as an occasion to disrupt the plans of the Zionists, who had started to establish Jewish colonies and settlements in Palestine. This kind of newcomer had begun to settle in Palestine at the end of the nineteenth century. They were different from the Jewish population of Jerusalem: they were *halutzim* (pioneers).[12] Arab opposition to these newcomers grew in strength at the beginning of the war.[13] In August 1914 the *mutasarrıf*, aware of local feelings towards the Zionists, wrote to the Ministry of Interior about 'the necessity of the strict application of the rules on the Jewish immigrants and watching all their moves carefully'.[14]

The focus on the process of mobilisation taking place in Palestine and Jerusalem will show how this process took place and affected the region in political, economic and demographic terms. Palestine was far from the core of the Empire, but it became strategically important because of the border with Egypt which was regarded by the Ottomans and Germans as enemy territory, as it had been under British control since 1882. A few days after the start of hostilities in Europe in August 1914, the process of mobilisation which had started throughout the Empire began to affect Palestine. Movements of supplies and military equipment began as early as May 1914. Since internal communications were slow and very difficult, the Ottomans moved most of their resources through the sea ports while still a neutral power. This advantage, however, lasted a very short time. In fact, as soon as the Ottomans became one of the warring factions, the British naval fleet prevented the Ottoman navy from operating along the coast. In May 1914, the American consular agent in Jaffa was requested by the consul in Jerusalem to investigate a shipment of munitions from Istanbul, apparently delivered to the city.[15] The American official replied that there were rumours that munitions had been delivered to the port of Jaffa and then moved to Ramleh or Jerusalem.[16] The consular agent questioned the customs at Jaffa and reported that: 'cases were found containing altogether about 4,000 empty cartridges for three different kinds of rifles, Martini, Mauser and so called Montenegro rifles. The cartridges were seized by the custom authorities and the matter reported to Constantinople by wire.'[17] It is clear that the Ottomans were trying to cover up the movement of military equipment towards the extremely sensitive imperial border with British-occupied Egypt.

From August 1914, the mobilisation of material and ideological resources started to affect Jerusalem, and involved the active civilian population. Officially, the Empire was still neutral in the conflict, but the CUP government knew that this situation would not last. The first step the Ottomans took to establish the framework for mobilisation was to declare martial law. On 3 August 1914, the Governor of Jerusalem Macid Şevket issued the following instructions:

> 1. Martial law has been declared in the district of Jerusalem, owing to the proposed mobilisation of troops.
> 2. The military authorities have undertaken to preserve peace from now on.
> 3. Whoever disobeys the orders of the Government or disturbs the peace will be court martialed.
> 4. Carriage of arms and firing inside the town is forbidden.
> 5. Whoever hides in his house deserters or animals or does not give information of their whereabouts, if it is known, will be court martialed.
> 6. Those who wish to go away must apply to the military bureaus where they are registered and obtain a permit. Whoever attempts to travel away without permit will be conducted to the court martial, even if he is not subject to military service.[18]

The enforcement of public security was obviously paramount, but it is also clear that the imposition of martial law was conceived as a first step towards enforcing conscription. On 8 August 1914, the Governor of Jerusalem made a general call to arms for all men born between 1872 and 1893, including Ottoman subjects employed by foreign consulates. Besides the Muslim subjects of the Empire, Jews and Christians who were Ottoman citizens were called to arms too. By the order of the Minister of War, Jews and Christians up to 45 years of age were called for military service. In theory, they could pay an exemption tax (*bedel-i askeri*) of 30 Turkish liras and an extra tax of ten Turkish liras for munitions. In practice, the sum requested was too high, and almost impossible to pay considering the economic conditions of the urban population.[19] It seems, however, that Christians not willing to fight alongside the Ottomans were making strenuous efforts to pay for the exemption.[20] The enlistment of the troops was carried out by the local gendarmerie, under the control of the municipality. In the first stages of the conscription process, recruits were sent to Damascus, where the Headquarters of the 4th Army Corps was stationed.[21] The Ottoman authorities did what they could to track down those who evaded military service, and military police searched for deserters in public and private premises. Some people managed to hide throughout the entire war, reappearing only once it had ended. The punishment for those caught was flogging.[22]

The mobilisation process meant that not only were men conscripted, but strict measures were put in place to control the local civilian population, including foreign citizens. In late August 1914, it seems that the military authorities were relatively successful in their efforts to gain momentum for conscription: apparently, 16,000 new recruits gathered at Nablus.[23] At the beginning the Islamic appeal to fight alongside the Caliph's army elicited positive responses from the Muslim population; army service was a sign of loyalty to the Empire.[24] In August 1914, it was not only Muslim conscripts, however, that reported to the military commander: Ottoman Jewish subjects also paraded, and expressed their pride in serving the Empire.[25] Interestingly, this patriotism expressed by the Jews of Palestine is quite similar to that of American Jewry who, in time of conflict, try to prove their patriotism and loyalty to the state.[26] However, things changed with the arrival of Cemal Paşa in the city in 1915, and with the intensification of conscription. It no longer gave a sense of pride to be part of the Ottoman army: often Christians and Jews were employed in labour battalions (*tawabeer al-amaleh*) and many died during their service, carrying out back-breaking jobs.[27]

The finances of the Empire were in poor shape. The outbreak of the war in Europe brought serious disruption to trade, causing state revenue to fall sharply, and the army eventually faced a shortage of funds and provisions.[28] Because of this, the military authorities in Jerusalem began to requisition food for the war effort. Food was rationed; in the prisons, for instance, inmates received only water and three small loaves of bread each day.[29] It could also be argued that, as the majority of the population in 1914 was not Muslim, the Ottoman authorities tried to capitalise on non-Muslim Ottoman subjects through taxation and confiscation of commodities.[30] To an extent, the Ottomans showed a measure of leniency towards some subjects, as suggested by the sixth point of the declaration of martial law. Yet this apparent goodwill concealed an intention to raise as much money as possible from the exemption tax paid by non-Muslim subjects.

In August 1914 the Governor of Jerusalem addressed the foreign consuls, informing them that, according to orders received from the Ministry of War, military equipment such as weapons and gunpowder would be confiscated from foreign subjects. The Governor stressed that these orders also applied to animals which were crucial as a means of transport, and in case of need, could also provide additional food supplies.[31] The Italian consul, Senni, reported that the *mutasarrıf* was asking the consulates of the neutral countries to help the authorities carry out the orders, but this request was disregarded by them.[32] Indeed, the consulates were concerned with the protection of their interests and those of their subjects. A few days after the proclamation of martial law, the Italian consul noted that the economic crisis was worsening by the day. Furthermore, he reported that commerce had completely halted and, at the same time, the cost of living was increasing at a very fast rate.[33] The prices of all commodities, then, began to rise. Basic foodstuffs like rice and beans increased by 40% and 50% respectively, and coal for domestic use also increased by 50%.

Table 6: Increase in the cost of living 1914.

Article	Price before War	Price in November 1914	Increase
Meat	0.74	0.96	30%
Rice	0.177	0.247	40%
Sugar	0.247	0.389	57%
Beans	0.265	0.43	50%
Petroleum 10 gallons	1.52	2.23	46%
Coffee	1.16	2.05	84%
Potatoes	0.124	0.212	70%
Italian pasta	0.398	0.637	60%
Alcohol	0.627	1.06	66%
Coal per ton	15.44	23.015	50%

(Prices in US dollars)[34]

Local traders, who were mainly Christians and Jews specialising in the sale of soap, oil and tourist souvenirs, were suffering a great deal of distress. However, Muslim traders, mainly involved in the sale of agricultural products and general foodstuffs, fared the worst. Not only had many been dispossessed of their goods, but they were also conscripted.[35]

The military authorities also seized buildings and open spaces, mainly for military purposes. As accommodation was needed for troops, many schools, guesthouses for pilgrims and hospitals, were converted into barracks or military infirmaries. The Franciscans of the Custody of the Holy Land reported in September 1914 that local authorities had seized convents and hospices. Furthermore, they had ordered the closure of the Franciscan schools, both in Jerusalem and across the Holy Land.[36] With the arrival of about 40 cannons in the same month, the urban landscape changed drastically as war machinery required space for manoeuvres.[37] The seizure of buildings belonging to foreigners was also part of a policy adopted by Cemal Paşa, military governor of Syria, aiming at the urban 'refurbishment' of Syria.[38] A building belonging to the Greek-Catholic Church of St Anne in the Old City of Jerusalem was turned into an Islamic school, to show that there was a restored Ottoman authority over the city; Notre Dame de France was turned into a resting station for Ottoman troops, while local monuments were placed under renovation and restoration.[39]

Part of the process of mobilisation was the imposition of censorship, to prevent the circulation of anti-Ottoman and anti-Turkish propaganda. Local newspapers, such as the Arabic *al-Karmil* and the Hebrew *ha-Ahdut* were closed and their publishers arrested, accused of publishing anti-Ottoman articles.[40] Ottoman authorities also shut down the post offices run by European countries such as France and Britain, but also those of Ottoman allies Austria and Germany, which were serving both the local population and the foreign visitors.[41] The only postal service left was that run by the Ottomans themselves. The Ottoman intention was to centralise the service, so that they could control it completely. In September 1914, Macid Şevket complained in writing to the Ministry of the Interior in Istanbul that the British were distributing, in closed envelopes, notices informing the population 'that Muslims in India and Egypt are satisfied with British rule and that they are Anglophiles'.[42] Propaganda of this kind became commonplace, and censorship was increased throughout the conflict. The military and civil authorities also required all foreigners and their families to register their names in police stations.[43]

The Ottomans entered the war in November 1914 in an atmosphere of considerable uncertainty regarding the future. After the great celebrations staged by the Ottoman regime, both in Istanbul and Jerusalem, which followed the declaration of *jihad* against the infidels of France and Great Britain, people went back to their daily activities in an atmosphere of pessimism and anxiety.[44] Mobilisation was over: the war was now coming.

The real value of Jerusalem at the beginning of the war

Besides the process of mobilisation, involving real people in a real city, Jerusalem was also the object of political and propaganda discussions in distant circles, particularly towards the end of the hostilities. There are at least two aspects to consider regarding the political and strategic significance of Jerusalem in the context of the First World War. First, the reasons why Jerusalem became a specific focus in the last stages of the conflict. Secondly, it is necessary to discuss how Jerusalem was involved in the overall military effort which engaged British troops in the Middle East. Jerusalem was not strategically important, as the city lay on hills of no military value and it did not possess any key resources.[45] In view of this it is necessary to put aside the map of the Middle Eastern front and look elsewhere to understand the increasing importance of the city in British military thinking, as well as in other circles: the political and strategic significance of Jerusalem had its origins in the European front. In 1917 some major events took place in the war in Europe: the disastrous defeat of the Italians by the Austrians and Germans at Caporetto, the Russian revolution (which forced the Russians to abandon the conflict) and the mutinies in the French army following the failure of plans by Robert Nivelle, the French military commander, to launch a new offensive on the Western Front.[46]

Despite the failed offensive proposed by Nivelle, the military potential of the Entente was still intact in 1917. Yet, according to John Keegan and Keith Robbins, leading scholars in First World War studies, these events brought doubt and uncertainty to the British, French and Italian commands regarding the outcome of the war.[47] Furthermore, on the British side there was a change in leadership which was the outcome of some indecisive policies towards the war. In December 1916, David Lloyd George, who belonged to the Liberal Party, took over as Prime Minister. Lloyd George was looking for a personal victory and a moral reward for his country, which had been involved in the conflict since the beginning. The Prime Minister was a supporter of the Eastern Front. He believed that a strong effort in Palestine and

Mesopotamia would change the course of the war.[48] Like-minded individuals in the Cabinet believed it was possible to achieve a faster and more decisive victory in Europe once the Middle East had been tackled. Lloyd George was unable to set a comprehensive war strategy to this effect because of his struggle with William Robertson, Chief of the Imperial General Staff (CIGS), as well as some of the senior members of the military establishment.[49] Once it was decided to proceed with the military campaign in the Middle East, further disagreements rose in relation to the targets and tasks to achieve by the Expeditionary commander, General Allenby.[50] Lloyd George wanted Jerusalem to boost the morale of a nation at war. Without exaggeration, Matthew Hughes notes that 'in the space of a month […] Allenby pushed forward over forty miles and took a biblical city that eluded the West for over seven hundred years; in almost four months of fighting […] General Haig advanced five miles and captured an unknown, ruined Belgian village'.[51] What Allenby achieved was less important in the grand scheme of the war against Germany, but produced a tremendous effect in terms of propaganda and morale.

The material cost of the operation, in terms of men and resources, may also aid understanding of the significance of Jerusalem. In early 1917 the Middle Eastern front, as well as other fronts, was in a stalemate. On 28 June General Allenby assumed command of the Egyptian Expeditionary Force, with instructions to prepare for an offensive campaign during the autumn and winter.[52] Lloyd George personally ordered the newly appointed chief of the Expeditionary Force to make Jerusalem a 'Christmas present for the British nation'.[53] As far as the Prime Minister was concerned, Jerusalem was to be taken no matter the cost. The symbolic value of the city was the main reason it became the object of such intense military scrutiny. The conquest of Jerusalem was planned and staged in order to enhance the nation's morale.[54] How to conquer Jerusalem was left in the hands of Allenby, who proved to be the right man for the job. The British had only very broad and generic strategic plans for the future of the region. Wartime agreements and declarations, like the Sykes-Picot agreement (1916), the Husayn-McMahon correspondence (1915-1916) and the Balfour Declaration (1917), proved to be generic as to the future administration of the region and, indeed, contradicted one another. But it can be argued that, in late 1917, the focus of British policy-making in the Eastern front was Jerusalem.

Jerusalem was also used as an ideological tool. Evidence suggests that the case for Jerusalem in the Foreign and War offices was built as early as the spring of 1917. Although the Eastern Front was debated among British officials, Jerusalem was still mainly a personal concern of the Prime Minister; it was only in late 1917 and early 1918 that Jerusalem became a topic in the News Department of the War and Foreign offices. Under the supervision of Mark Sykes since November 1917, this department capitalised on the conquest of the city. From the early stages of the planning of possible military operations in Palestine, the news that Jerusalem, sooner or later, was to be conquered by the British began to spread across Europe, thanks to a strong propaganda campaign promoted by the Foreign Office.

The British Government was creating so much expectation that the Anglican Bishop in Jerusalem became over-excited. Genuinely convinced of fulfilling a sort of Christian 'reconquista', in May 1917 Rennie MacInnes wrote to the High Commissioner of Egypt discussing 'the desirability of taking official possession of every building erected originally as a Christian church [in Jerusalem], which is now used as a Mohammedan mosque'.[55] Although this was MacInnes' personal opinion, it reflected feelings shared by some representatives of the Anglican Communion at that time.

The British, however, were much more concerned with another issue of religious and political character. The Ottoman Sultan claimed to be the spiritual leader of the Muslims, the Caliph of Islam, inside and outside Ottoman lands. Early in the Middle East campaign there had been a great effort by the British to not displease the Muslim subjects of their Empire, particularly Indian Muslims, in any way. The British looked for Muslim support in the war against the Islamic Ottoman Empire; Britain also knew that the Muslims would never forgive any damage or disruption to the Muslim shrines located in Ottoman territories.[56] A note issued a few weeks before the conquest of Jerusalem by the News Department of the Foreign Office, addressed to the press, clarifies how carefully British intelligence moved in the Muslim world:

> The attention of the press is again drawn to the undesirability of publishing any article, paragraph or picture suggesting that military operations against Turkey are in any sense a Holy War, a modern Crusade, or have anything whatever to do with religious questions. The British Empire is said to contain a hundred million of Mohammedan subjects of the King and it is obviously mischievous to suggest that our quarrel with Turkey is one between Islam and Christianity.[57]

As clearly stated in the last line, the purpose of this note was to ensure that Muslim subjects of the Empire would not consider the war as a Christian-Muslim conflict.[58] Clearly, British officials were well aware that using Jerusalem as a symbolic and ideological tool was extremely hazardous, and would only be successful if done properly. Retrospectively, it can be argued that Jerusalem in the short term proved to be a winning bet. The conquest of the Holy City helped gather momentum for the Allies, and played a crucial role in boosting the morale of the troops employed on other fronts of the war. However, looking at the long term, the occupation of the city created more complex disputes rather than solving existent ones.[59] Once the British took over its administration, the inconsistency of the wartime agreements, promises made to Arabs and Jews, and the extreme romanticisation of the city came to the fore.

The British conquest of Jerusalem: 9 December 1917

The transition between the Ottomans and the British, when the city 'changed hands', is also the moment when the attention of much of the literature available shifts away from the city itself, focusing on the new conquerors and then on the emergent communal conflict, reshaping the city once again.[60]

The conquest of Jerusalem and Palestine did not prove easy; the British attempted twice to take Gaza, under the command of General Archibald Murray, but he failed to achieve the goal. At the end of April 1917, Lloyd George offered the command to General Edmund 'The Bull' Allenby and the Palestine campaign entered a new phase which led eventually to the capture of Jerusalem.[61]

Edmund Allenby was born in 1861 in Nottinghamshire. After failing two attempts at entering the Indian Civil Service he turned to a military career, serving in South Africa during the Boer War (1899-1902) where he was able to demonstrate his qualities as field commander.[62] Allenby was a religious man, so attached to the Bible that he chose the name Megiddo (the biblical site of the Armageddon) as part of his honorary titles when he was made Viscount in 1919. Known for a violent temper and a very strong character, his nickname is somewhat unsurprising. At the outbreak of the First World War he was made commander of a cavalry division on the Western Front. He took part in the second battle of Ypres, and in October 1915, took over the British Third Army. However at the battle of Arras in 1917 he failed and he was replaced. As mentioned above, Allenby was appointed commander of the EEF in 1917; he made his name with the conquest of Jerusalem in 1917 and Damascus in 1918, and with the Battle of Megiddo, which was fought in September 1918. Turning out to be the modern 'crusader' par excellence, he was an impressive and dramatic figure who benefited personally from being the conqueror of the lands of the Bible.[63] Allenby remained in the Middle East as High Commissioner of Egypt and Sudan until 1925 when he retired. He then travelled the world extensively, and after a brief return to England, was appointed rector of Edinburgh University. He died in London in 1936.[64]

What General Allenby brought to the Middle Eastern front was a new strategy. When Allenby reached Egypt from London, it was still not clear how far he should go into Palestine, but he prepared himself for a third strike on Gaza after General Murray had attempted to take the city twice.[65] Allenby was to change the strategy employed by his predecessor. Rather than a direct attack against the city of Gaza, he struck the village of Beersheba first. The plan was to outflank the Ottomans in Gaza, so that the British army could attack on two fronts, as well as secure water supplies.[66] Allenby was very careful about supplies and logistics, particularly about water, a precious commodity in the Palestinian desert. Allenby's strategy was one of mobile warfare. He relocated the headquarters from Cairo to the battlefield near Rafah, a border crossing between Egypt and Palestine close to Gaza.[67] The Gaza breakthrough, which began on 30 October 1917, consisted of an elaborate plan employing cavalry, infantry and artillery. The original plan was that, once Beersheba had been taken, the British would then take Gaza on the flank. However, because of a shortage of water supplies the attack was delayed, giving time for the Ottoman army to escape.[68] Ottoman soldiers were not able to cope with the new style of warfare adopted by Allenby's army and did not deploy the flexible defence system suggested by German military advisers. This proved disastrous for the Ottoman forces.[69]

Transport was another crucial factor. At first Allenby relied on the cavalry but it proved to be unsuitable as horses needed large amounts of water and were not designed for the uneven terrain of Palestine.[70] Hughes states that the cavalry was caught between Gaza and Beersheba, unable to pursue the retreating Turks as they lacked water for the horses.[71] Eventually, the British turned to rail transport. Rather than building new rail tracks, the British exploited the existing Ottoman railway lines.

At home, the Prime Minister pushed for a decisive advance towards Jerusalem, but on the ground Allenby wanted to ensure he could be in a position to support his army in the advance with water, weapons and other supplies.[72] By mid-November 1917, the British were moving towards Jerusalem. When planning the capture of the city, Allenby attempted to avoid fighting in its proximity as he was fearful of damaging sacred buildings in Jerusalem, and being labelled forever as the person who destroyed the Holy City.

In parallel with Allenby's operations in Palestine, the Foreign and War offices in London were discussing the future asset of Jerusalem. A few weeks before the occupation of the city, debates among the members of the different Governmental offices were frequent and, indeed, full of conflicting ideas. Most of the policies adopted in relation to Jerusalem were a reflection of the wartime agreements mentioned earlier. Mark Sykes was the key policy-maker, who consistently attempted to connect policy in relation to Jerusalem with policy in the wider Middle East. The debate in Government circles also shows that British policy-makers were aware of and sensitive to the tensions between the different religious communities in Jerusalem. Their primary aim was therefore to avoid any clashes between the Christians and Muslims, as well as between the different Christian denominations. To this effect, in July 1917 the Archbishop of Canterbury, under the suggestion of the Foreign Office, wrote to the Bishop in Jerusalem, Rennie MacInnes, who had been living in Cairo since 1914, about the desirability of sending formal greetings to the other Christian denominations represented in the city in the case of British conquest of Jerusalem.[73]

A few days after Allenby's army took Gaza in early November 1917, the Prisoner of War Department in London questioned whether any of General Allenby's staff were aware of the religious complications surrounding the holy places.[74] In November 1917 Mark Sykes, now adviser to the Cabinet on Middle Eastern affairs, acknowledged that problems might have occurred; however, he said 'I believe myself that rows about the holy places are usually of Turkish origin, and I do not apprehend people will desire to indulge in immediate fights'.[75] In this document Sykes advocated some of the main policies which were to be enforced after Jerusalem was captured. Two spheres, according to this report, were crucial to bear in mind: the local dimension and the international one. Sykes proposed that the Christian places were to be guarded by men accustomed to police work, and that a British political officer, with executive military authority, should supervise the maintenance of order in the city. Regarding the Muslim shrines, Sykes proposed that the Aqsa Mosque be handed to a representative of the King of Hejaz, Sharif Husayn, and a military cordon established around the perimeter. Furthermore, non-Muslims would not be allowed to enter the area of the Temple without a proper pass, released by the political officers and countersigned by the King's representatives.[76]

Using the justification that 'agents provocateurs may be left behind', Sykes proposed to purge the city of any enemy influence, mainly represented by Christian clerics of German and Austrian citizenship, and to give the French and Italian governments a degree of control over religious institutions.[77] Sykes also proposed that the city be placed under military administration and martial law, so as to avoid Franco-Italian complaints. Under martial law, France and Italy would not be able to compete for the control of religious and educational institutions, but they had been given the right to take charge of those institutions where the majority of the clergy were French or Italian. Lastly, Sykes suggested the compilation of a register of clerics left in Jerusalem from countries on the opposite side in the war, with the purpose of expelling Austrian and German priests, monks and friars belonging to religious institutions in the city.

Soon after, the Foreign Office sent Sykes's remarks to Reginald Wingate, the British High Commissioner of Egypt, but added another clause: in the doorway of the Holy Sepulchre there was a Muslim *waqf*, a small religious endowment, which housed the Muslim family of Nuseibeh, responsible for the key of the Church of the Holy Sepulchre. In the event of the conquest of Jerusalem, the Foreign Office wished the Muslim *waqf* be maintained in order to respect the Status Quo, and to not upset the Muslim subjects of the Empire.[78] Wingate, as requested, discussed the document with Allenby. The joint document produced by these two was sent to the Foreign Office a few days later, and is remarkably different from the Sykes's original.[79] Wingate and Allenby noted that there would be no representatives of the King of Hejaz in Jerusalem; more importantly, the appointment of a representative of the King of Hejaz in an official position in Jerusalem could give rise to aspirations which were in contrast with the provision of the Sykes-Picot agreement, according to which Jerusalem was to be placed under an international administration. Therefore, Allenby and Wingate proposed that the Mosque of Omar and the other Muslim holy places should come under the control of Muslim troops, namely Indians. Secondly, Allenby proposed the appointment of Colonel Borton Pasha, former Postmaster-General of the Egyptian Postal Service, as military governor of Jerusalem. It was this proposal that revamped French claims: the French representative in Egypt, Defrance, was supposed to travel to Jerusalem and to attend Allenby's official parade. He was refused permission to attend the ceremony, but Georges Picot was eventually admitted. The French were clearly not satisfied with the British military administration in Jerusalem.[80]

The debate surrounding the occupation of Jerusalem came to a close three weeks before the actual occupation of the city, when the War Office formalised the main policies to be adopted for its administration.[81] This was in the form of a note prepared by the

War Office, as guidelines for how the announcement of British entry into Jerusalem should be made by the Prime Minister. In this note, the suggestions made by Wingate and Allenby with regard to the Muslim holy places were taken into consideration. Non-Muslims would not be permitted to pass the cordon established around the Mosque of Omar without permission from the political officer and the Muslim official in charge of the Mosque. Internal security was to be the primary task of the new occupying force. Although the question of the presence of a representative of the King of Hejaz was dropped completely, policy-makers in London felt that they had to go to extra lengths to strengthen their position regarding the Muslims of Jerusalem, as they could not afford to upset the many Indian Muslim subjects of the Empire. In view of this, the Tomb of the Patriarchs at Hebron, Rachael's tomb, and other holy shrines were to be placed under Muslim control.[82]

In London, in mid-November 1917, the occupation of Jerusalem was considered merely a question of time. At the same moment, the divergences between the War Office and the Foreign Office became more apparent. The former advocated military occupation of the city as, at that time, the future of Palestine and the war as a whole was unclear. In contrast, the Foreign Office was already working towards the consolidation of strong civilian rule. Moreover, the commitments made in the Balfour Declaration meant that a military occupation could be only a transitional administration. In early January 1918, the Foreign Office pressed Wingate for more propaganda material to be sent to London, as it was necessary to create support for a lasting British presence in Palestine and Jerusalem.[83]

'Gerusalemme Liberata'

Between 1565 and 1575, the medieval Italian poet Torquato Tasso wrote the epic poem 'Gerusalemme Liberata' (Jerusalem Delivered). Tasso related the adventures of Godfrey de Bouillon and other crusader knights who fought the first crusade, which ended with the capture of Jerusalem in July 1099. Godfrey of Bouillon became a popular hero, the protagonist of many *chansons de geste* written since the twelfth century.[84] Little more than 800 years later General Allenby was portrayed as the heir of Godfrey. The title of a short film made during the official entry of Allenby into Jerusalem was highly symbolic: 'With the Crusaders in the Holy Land. Allenby the Conqueror.'[85] *The Times* defined the occupation of Jerusalem as the 'most memorable event in the history of Christendom'. Both Allenby and Godfrey de Bouillon entered popular imagery as the conquerors of Jerusalem, the heroes who had defeated 'the infidels'.[86]

Jerusalem was conquered by Godfrey de Bouillon after a siege with the help of a movable tower, placed under the walls; Allenby also brought with him a new strategy of mobile warfare. The two also share a common fate as Christian conquerors of Jerusalem. Godfrey entered the city and immediately faced the internal divisions among the Christians, while Allenby also had to face rising tension among the different ethnic and religious communities of Jerusalem.[87]

Some scholars have depicted the conquest of Jerusalem as a personal enterprise of Allenby; others have pointed out that London pushed for a quick advance. Cyril Falls, in his recollection of the military operations in Egypt and Palestine, and the Marquess of Anglesey's history of the British cavalry, gave Allenby total credit for the conquest of Jerusalem, stressing Allenby's determination.[88] However, Anthony Bruce suggests how political pressure played a crucial role in pursuing military operations on the Palestine front.[89] It was the political establishment of the Foreign Office and the Prime Minister who planned and pushed for the final advance which led to the capture of Jerusalem. Allenby's troops halted their march towards Jerusalem after Gaza and Jaffa had been secured, as they were tired and fresh supplies were urgently needed, water in particular. However, Allenby noted the apparent disorganisation of the enemy and decided to press on to Jerusalem.[90] Wishing to avoid fighting close to the city, unlike his medieval predecessor Godfrey de Bouillon, Allenby planned an elaborate siege which proved to be a more difficult tactic than a direct attack.[91] The XXI Corps were to advance through the main road from Jaffa to Jerusalem, while the 52nd Division and the Yeomanry Mounted Division advanced north of Jerusalem. The 75th Division was to join them as it approached Jerusalem, in order to sever the Nablus-Jerusalem road.

The operation started on 19 November, but the following day it was delayed by a heavy rainstorm which increased the already difficult task of the troops. They were equipped with summer uniforms and not prepared for the cold and wet weather; the winter clothing was not yet available.[92] The Ottoman troops, on the other hand, were scattered across the hills surrounding Jerusalem. In the meantime the German General Erich von Falkenhayn, who had replaced General Friederich Kress von Kressenstein on 5 November 1917, adopted a strategy of survival. He left a few contingents as rear guards on the hills surrounding the city, with the purpose of delaying the British advance to give the Ottoman Seventh Army time to organise a proper defence of the city.[93] On 24 November, Allenby halted the operation as it was necessary to move supplies from Gaza to the front and to provide some respite to the troops; he replaced the XXI Corps with the XX Corps, which was stationed on the coast under the command of Lieutenant General Philip Chetwode. Von Falkenhayn seized this opportunity and organised a counter offensive, based on a 'shock tactic'. His troops began to strike the British forces on 27 November, but by 3 December the Ottoman-German troops were forced to halt their offensive due to a clear military inferiority and lack of resources.[94]

The deployment of the XX Corps became pivotal in the final battle for Jerusalem. On 3 December, under the command of Chetwode, high-ranking British officials met in the Judean Hills and planned the capture of Jerusalem. The plan was to cut the main roads which connected the city of Hebron to Bethlehem and to Nablus, using the Jaffa road to deploy the artillery. The Ottoman army was left with only one possible route of escape from the city – to the south. Between 3 and 7 December, the units involved in the attack took position, while the Ottoman Seventh Army was entrenched in the hills west of Jerusalem. Von Falkenhayn knew that the fate of Jerusalem was just a matter of time.

On 7 December everything was ready on the British side for the second assault on Jerusalem and despite the cold and the heavy rain the British were able to surround Jerusalem. On 8 December the Ottomans began to withdraw from the city, more out of fear of the encroaching British troops than as a result of British military operations. The Ottoman governor and the German and Austrian consuls also fled during the night.[95] No one was left; the governor of the city, Izzet Paşa, was the last civil official to leave before dawn, with the help of Mr Frederick Vester of the American Colony.

In the meantime, the 60th and 74th Divisions were operating on the Jaffa-Jerusalem road; the 53rd Division was not far from Bethlehem, whilst the Worcestershire Yeomanry and the 10th Australian Light Horse Regiment were expected to be the liaison of the 60th and the 53rd Divisions; and the 179th Brigade of the 60th Division began the advance towards Jerusalem on the night of 7 December.[96] They were not aware of the Ottoman retreat, and were perhaps more concerned with the bad weather conditions and the prospect of a battle the following day.

No fighting took place inside the city, and by 9 December Jerusalem was free of Ottoman and German troops. The last Ottoman soldier is said to have left Jerusalem early in the morning through St Stephens or Lion's Gate.[97] The battle for Jerusalem was over.

'A dramatic incident of war'[98]: the surrender of Jerusalem

It took until late December for the British army to secure Jerusalem from Turkish counterattacks. Once Jerusalem had been occupied, its surrender became an ideological tool in British hands and, not surprisingly, this is reflected in the different accounts of the occupation of the city. The narrative of the surrender of Jerusalem was to be exploited as propaganda, and it was necessary for this narrative to be dramatic and glorious: Jerusalemites simply disappeared, merely becoming secondary characters in what was an entirely British theatrical production. The ceremonial entrance staged by Sykes was meant to underline British humility: they had respect for the Holy City, and Jerusalem was being liberated rather than occupied. It is therefore not a surprise that the narratives reporting the actual events of the numerous surrenders of the city vanished; these were not worthy accounts of the liberation of the Holy City.

The slow surrender of Jerusalem began on the morning of 9 December when, before leaving the city alongside the withdrawing Ottoman-German troops, Governor of Jerusalem Izzet Paşa met Mayor al-Husayni and handed him the decree of surrender, addressed to the British commander, which stated:

> To the English Command. Since two days howitzer shells are falling on some places in Jerusalem which (city) is sacred to all nations. (Therefore) The Ottoman Government, for the sole purpose of protecting the religious places, has withdrawn her soldiers from the city. And she installed officials to protect the Holy Place such as the Holy Sepulchre and the Aqsa Mosque with the hope that the same treatment (of the place) will also continue from your side. I am sending this letter to you by the acting Mayor.[99]

The mayor decided to keep the document, deciding to simply read it to the British. Husayn al-Husayni, alongside the other notables of the city, feared that if the Ottoman army returned they would be branded traitors.[100] For their part, the Ottoman authorities saw to it that holy places were left guarded, a course of action which underlined the religious value of the city. The Ottomans wanted to rescue their religious credentials in terms of both Sultanate and Caliphate, which had not been yet abolished. Germany and Austria were Christian countries, and had an international image to protect at home as well. Their troops left the city quietly and without unnecessary destruction. *Realpolitik* and religious concerns played a major role in these decisions.

Early on 9 December the mayor of Jerusalem, delegated by the governor to surrender the city, went to the American Colony, located outside the city walls to the East, and knocked at the door of the Spaffords, the founder family and managers of the Colony. As the American Colony was active in the relief of the local population, the mayor had become a close friend of the family and told them he was going to deliver the letter of surrender left to him by the Governor of Jerusalem to the English troops. Bertha Spafford, although excited by the news, warned him not to go without a white flag as a symbol of truce.[101] It is not clear whether this was a genuine suggestion in order to avoid incident, or simply Bertha Spafford, in classical orientalist mode, believing that the mayor had no understanding of the rules of military surrender.

This was the first step in one of the several surrenders that took place on that day as the military and civilian authorities collapsed. Although public order was maintained by the municipal police, it was difficult to control the movements of the population. Civilians left Jerusalem to look for supplies and sought help from the invading army as soon as residents realised that the city had been abandoned by the German-Ottoman troops. Wasif Jawhariyyeh, a local resident, reported that some people were cutting down the Ottoman telephone lines and taking them home.[102] According to the Conde de Ballobar, Jerusalemites were looking for food, water, clothes and animals. Furthermore he noted that, along Jaffa Road outside the walls, pillage was the main activity of the Jerusalemites: 'everything suitable to be taken was stolen'. The Spanish diplomat also reported that municipal police were rather helpless and did not intervene, but they were also aware that, as soon as the British took over, the pillaging would stop.[103]

Whilst wandering around the city, it was one of these civilian groups who first met two British soldiers, Privates Church and Andrews, who, as cooks, were looking for 'some heggs for their hofficers'.[104] They had been sent by their superiors to look for some fresh supplies of milk or eggs, and had apparently lost their way.[105] The mayor, accompanied by a small party, attempted to deliver the keys to the city to them, but they refused and returned to their battalion. Apparently, on their way back, other civilians met the two privates and also informed them that the city desired to surrender.[106]

This episode may have been considered amusing, rather than heroic or at least reasonably epic enough to be officially reported. The wanderings of the official surrendering party and the civilians around the city bordered on the bizarre. While the crowds of Jerusalem were busy looking for any suitable supplies left outside the walls, the mayor, with the decree of surrender in his hands, was still looking for British troops, in order to surrender the city officially. Following the first, informal, meeting with the two British soldiers, al-Husayni and his party met Sergeant Hurcomb and

Sergeant Sedgewick of the 219th Battalion London Regiment on outpost duty, who again refused to accept the surrender of the city. Not only were the soldiers not of the proper rank to accept the surrender, but they were unsure whether the mayor was genuine. The third meeting between al-Husayni and British soldiers was with Major Barry and Major Beck, who contacted their superiors and the commander of the 303rd Royal Field Artillery, Lieut.-Colonel Bayley, who met the party of notables.[107] This meeting was also somewhat bizarre: as Bayley walked towards al-Husayni, 'there he was with three chairs in a row on the road'.[108] Bayley sat down, with the mayor on one side and the chief of the municipal police on the other, and the mayor was finally able to read the act of surrender. Lieut.-Colonel Bayley telegraphed Major-General Shea, and then arranged for the occupation of some of the key buildings inside the city.

At the same time, Brigadier General Watson, commander of the 180th Brigade, arrived at the spot and also accepted the surrender of Jerusalem from al-Husayni. However, details of this particular event, in the same way as the 'other' surrenders, were culled from official reports. An order was issued to the effect that evidence should be destroyed, including photographs and negatives, of Brigadier General Watson's acceptance; only evidence regarding General Allenby was to be recorded.[109] Around noon, Major-General Shea was ordered by General Chetwode, commander of the XX Corps, to take over the city. After a short surrender ceremony, he did so in the name of General Allenby, commander of the EEF.[110] After 400 years of Ottoman rule, Jerusalem was delivered to British forces.

In comparison with the development of the events discussed earlier, the British Government issued only one, short, official document on the circumstances of the surrender of the city, which detailed the involvement of a *parlementaire* sent by the enemy on 9 December.[111] It is difficult to quote a specific official narrative of the takeover, as Jerusalem was won with no actual fight due to the abandonment of the city by the Ottoman-German troops. The occupation of Jerusalem was, however, a powerful political symbol to be exploited at home. The fact that there are no official reports on the early attempts of the mayor to deliver the city perhaps also demonstrates the high symbolic value attached to the city by the British: the surrender needed to be glorious.

General Allenby made his formal entry into Jerusalem following plans which had been carefully devised by Sykes. He entered the city through Jaffa Gate on foot, in contrast to the German Emperor Wilhelm II who in 1898 had entered the city riding a horse. The *Daily Mail* noted the difference with pride: 'As a conqueror General Allenby entered Jerusalem on December 11 with more simplicity and true dignity than Kaiser Wilhelm did when he presented himself as a blend of Cook's tourist and *Envoy of Allah*'.[112] Allenby was followed by a procession of British military officials, two small Italian and French contingents and representatives of the religious communities. He then read, in English, French, Italian, Arabic and Hebrew, the proclamation of martial law, stressing that the British would maintain the existing customs in relation to the holy places.[113] Even though the text read was vague and *de facto* promised religious freedom, the Jerusalemites were generally just happy that the war was over; paradoxes and inconsistencies in the British policy were yet to become apparent.

Jerusalem conquered: local, British and international reactions

The occupation of Jerusalem had important local, regional and international repercussions, and elicited responses across the world. Inside the city, the inhabitants of Jerusalem endeavoured to come to terms with foreign occupation. Far from Palestine, the reactions of British policy-makers were consistent with the agenda they had put forward before the occupation, yet the British troops and public opinion in the United Kingdom responded in a variety of ways. The question of the reaction of the international community to the British occupation is also extremely important considering that, in accordance with the agreement negotiated during the war, Jerusalem was to be placed under international administration.

Regardless of their background, Jerusalemites generally welcomed the British army as ultimately the regime of the CUP was over. The process of 'Turkification' which had started before the war, the mobilisation of resources for the military effort, and the state of war itself had strained the relationship between local residents, both indigenous and foreigners, and their Ottoman rulers.[114] The streets of the city became crowded, packed with joyful people; people who, at least in the first stages of the British occupation, genuinely and warmly welcomed the British troops.[115] According to the Conde de Ballobar: 'the popular enthusiasm was spontaneous and terrific. Every British soldier was followed by an unbelievable crowd that touched them and their horses, they admired them as heroes.'[116] Major Vivian Gilbert, walking through the old city, was impressed by the warm welcome of the locals: 'the narrow streets were packed with towns-people, old men and women and children, all wild with delight and dressed in their best to greet the victorious army'.[117] Wasif Jawhariyyeh celebrated the arrival of the British in the streets with his friends.[118] Although jubilant, the Arab population, Muslim and Christian alike, were looking for justification to support a new foreign occupation. Although the imagery of the Crusades was almost forgotten in Muslim memory, they were nonetheless forced to confront the mounting 'crusading-mania' spreading through the press in Britain and the local Christian churches.[119]

In the aftermath of the occupation, British propaganda endeavoured to make the new rulers acceptable to the Arab Muslim population. The Foreign Office also sought to stage the British entry in Jerusalem in keeping with a Muslim story, which claimed that a prophet would enter the city in order to end Turkish rule while the waters of the river Nile would flow into Palestine; in fact the British planned to carry water from Egypt to Palestine through a pipeline which eventually proved not to be feasible. As for the Prophet's story, an anagram was made, with Allenby's name miraculously transformed into *al-Nabi* (the Prophet).[120] In Britain, Allenby was also presented as a conquering Muslim, as suggested by a headline of *The Times* 'Saladin entered [Jerusalem] in triumph as General Allenby enters it to-day'.[121] Another connection between ancient prophecies and the British conquest of Jerusalem was found in the Bible as the Book of Daniel (Ch. 12, verse 12) states: 'Blessed is he that waiteth and cometh to the thousand three hundred and five [1335] and thirty days'. This passage was promptly understood by some Christians, and also some Muslims, as the fulfilment of a prophecy, as the year 1335 of the Muslim era (*hijira*) corresponded to the year 1917 of the Gregorian calendar.[122]

In 1917 there were great expectations among the local population, and Christians in particular hoped to enjoy more freedom under the aegis of a Christian power. The Arabs envisaged a possible inclusion in an Arab state, following the awakening of Arab sentiment after the Arab rebellion led by Sharif Husayn of the Hejaz in 1916. The Jewish population was also hoping for more tolerant rule, while the Zionists expected to profit from the change of regime as, a few weeks before the British occupation of Jerusalem, the British Government had issued the Balfour Declaration which had raised hopes for the creation of a National Jewish Home in Palestine.

Despite popular furore and expectations, the Catholic clergy were sceptical about the British occupation. The Franciscans, for instance, feared that the city rather than being liberated was simply passing to Anglican rule; they had hoped for a Catholic power to take over the administration of the city.[123] Wasif Jawhariyyeh provides an interesting perspective on the changing attitude of Arab residents who had some nationalist inclination. He noted in his diary: 'I remember this day [of the British occupation] to have been a very happy one for the people. You could see them dancing for joy in the streets, congratulating each other on this happy occasion.'[124] As far as Wasif was concerned, however, the 'honeymoon' did not last long. As the diary was written later, in the 1940s, there is no doubt that his narrative was affected by the clashes of the 1920s and 1930s between Arabs and Jews; in the same diary, Wasif summed up the British occupation with the following words: 'We did not realize then that this damned occupation would be a curse, not a blessing, for our dear homeland'.[125]

The first reaction of British troops as they entered the city was one of strong emotion; some of them felt part of a great mission, others felt like modern-day crusaders. W.T. Massey, official correspondent of the London newspapers with the EEF, noted that 'not a great proportion would claim to be really devout men, but they all behaved like Christian gentlemen'.[126] Nevertheless, it was necessary to stress, both to the population and to the troops themselves, that British troops were not conquerors but liberators, as had been intended in the general planning of the occupation of the city. Due to this, a notice was posted on the city walls soon after its conquest:

> The British troops have entered Jerusalem not as conquerors but as liberators, and their advent has been joyfully welcomed alike by Moslems, by Christians and by Jews. By this historic stroke, Jerusalem has been freed from the shadow of an age-long tyranny, and a prosperous future has been opened up for the virile and intelligent races who inhabit the soil of Palestine.[127]

The Military did not yet know that they were to stay for a long period, eventually becoming a long-lasting occupying force.

In Britain, Jerusalem represented the biblical focus of Christian life. Furthermore, Jerusalem was the city that had been precluded centuries earlier to the national hero Richard Coeur de Lion (the Lionheart) who failed in his attempt to retake it from Salah al-Din in 1192. The popular press hailed the news of the conquest of Jerusalem with celebratory headlines such as one in the *Daily Telegraph* which praised Allenby for accomplishing the feat which 'Richard Coeur de Lion, our Crusader King, just failed to achieve'.[128]

The Foreign Office aimed to strengthen the effects of this event in terms of propaganda, while the War Office was concerned with the continuation of the military campaign in Syria and Palestine. Sykes wrote to the British headquarters in Cairo from the Foreign Office: 'If we have full and detailed information [on the occupation of Jerusalem] we can get much atmospheric advantage wherever these influences [propaganda on Vatican, Zionist, Orthodox] have effect'.[129] The idea was to create a 'mediatic' effect in Britain. Early in 1918, Sykes invited the News Department to send correspondents to Palestine in order to write articles on the history, politics and society of Jerusalem. Through these articles Sykes proposed to 'spice up' the case for the capture of Jerusalem, thereby supporting the British cause. The conquest of Jerusalem was also important as it boosted the morale of British troops deployed on all war fronts, as well as all military and civilians involved in the allied war effort. W.T. Massey claimed that 'the capture of the Holy City by British arms gave more satisfaction to countless of millions of people than did the winning back for France of any big town on the Western Front'.[130]

British Jews also rejoiced, as highlighted by *The Jewish Chronicle* in London: 'The capture of Jerusalem illumines with the picturesque grim battlefields of the world'.[131] Vladimir Jabotinsky, a leading Zionist and future leader of a prominent paramilitary organisation (*Haganah*) which operated during the Mandate period, published many articles in the British press suggesting a close involvement between the British Foreign Office and the Zionist leadership.[132] His first article was published in *The Times* in February 1918, and dealt with the last days of Jerusalem under the Ottomans, stressing the positive effect of the British occupation in comparison with the weak and inefficient Turkish rule. This article left religious issues aside, and refrained from mentioning words such as 'crusade' or 'crusaders' in order not to alarm Muslim public opinion in the British Empire.[133] In another article, published few months later, Jabotinsky poured scorn on the old Jewish communities of Jerusalem for contributing, in his view, to the lowering of 'Jewish prestige in the eyes of the British' and for resisting the activity of the Zionist Commission, which handed out the funds available as war relief.[134] Jabotinsky openly criticised those Jews belonging to the old Jewish communities who lived off alms known as *halukka*. He was also critical of those Jews whose only function was to say prayers before the Wailing Wall. This article also tells us of the mounting tension among the Zionist Commission and the '*halukka* Jews'. The Zionist Commission wanted to show that Jews were different from these stereotypes and that the new Jewish style was represented by the Zionist settlers in Tel Aviv and Rehovoth.[135]

The Christian Churches, and the Christian powers that had interests in Jerusalem, officially welcomed British rule. In December 1917 the Greek Orthodox Church in London wrote to the Archbishop of Canterbury, praising 'the great achievement of the fall of Jerusalem [which] fills [...] the glory and honour [of] the brave British army fighting for the liberty of Nations and of Justice'.[136] In many European countries church bells rang to celebrate the return of the city to Christian hands, while the Italian and French governments began a campaign to secure control of the Catholic institutions of Jerusalem and Palestine.[137] The British occupation of the city raised the issue of the traditional protection over the Catholic population exercised by the French Government, and the Italians were keen to extend their influence as much as possible. In December 1917, the Italian Ambassador in Paris wrote to the Italian Ministry of Foreign Affairs that 'The British occupation of Jerusalem has given new strength to the question of the French protection of the Catholics in the Middle East. [...] We should be ready to defend our rights when times will come.'[138] In a speech delivered to the Parliament, Italian Prime Minister Vittorio Emanuele Orlando underlined the desirability of Italian and French cooperation, in order to define mutual rights in the future assets of Palestine and Jerusalem.[139] Nevertheless, French and Italian interests had different emphases; as well as controlling the Christian institutions, the French were also interested in the future of the Middle East, as France was one of the powers that had territorial ambitions in the region, in accordance with the Sykes-Picot agreement of 1916. On the other hand, Italy had not yet expressed a colonial interest in the region.[140]

In Paris, a *Te Deum* was sung in Notre Dame cathedral and a thanksgiving prayer was recited in the Mosque of Nogent de Marne in the suburbs of the French capital, in order to praise the deliverance of the city from Turkish rule. The Bishop of Arras delivered a sermon which expressed perfectly the kind of sentiments that were shared in the aftermath of the deliverance of Jerusalem: 'We have seen during the war remarkable victories, thanks to great manoeuvres and strategies. However, none has been able to seize universal attention. [...] In the end, everything we think, everything we believe, everything we hope, become nearly irrelevant in front of such event, that more and better than a military victory, is in fact the dawn of a new era.'[141] The French Government supported these public celebrations, but, like the British Government, it was determined to not give the impression that the occupation of Jerusalem was a Christian victory over the Muslims. For this reason the Quay d'Orsay, the French Foreign Office, issued a letter stating that Jerusalem had not been conquered but freed from Turkish misrule. Eventually, some French Muslim troops were employed as guardians of the Muslim holy places in Jerusalem.[142]

Similar celebrations took place in Italy, although due to the unstable military situation of the country, and the shadowy presence of the Vatican, there was not the same level of enthusiasm. In Italy, posters were published in the press and in public spaces celebrating the capture of Jerusalem, highlighting the Italian presence in the military contingent fighting in Palestine, despite the fact that no more than 1,000 men were part of the EEF.[143]

Following his strict policy of neutrality in the conflict, Pope Benedict XV forbade celebrations in Vatican City. The Secretary of State Cardinal Gasparri explained that this course of action was necessary in order to keep strong ties with all belligerents; it was clearly a strategy which aimed to ensure a prominent position for the Vatican in any post-war settlement.[144] The *Osservatore Romano*, the Vatican newspaper, was allowed to express deeper sentiments, however, and it published an article stressing the importance of the city falling to Christian power; it also expressed gratitude towards Divine Providence, as the Russians had not been part of the mission.[145] At this time, the attention paid to Jerusalem was also the result of the position taken by some Catholic clerics resident in the city. As the Latin Patriarch of Jerusalem, Camassei, had been deported to Damascus by Ottoman authorities earlier in 1917, the Congregation of the Propaganda Fide (the Catholic institution dealing with the Catholics around the world) informed the Vatican that Cardinal Dolci, the Apostolic Delegate in Turkey, was working to free the Latin Patriarch, and for the Catholic community in Jerusalem as a whole.[146] Other Christian non-Catholic communities, such as the Abyssinians, appealed directly to the Foreign Office. They expressed their delight at the British conquest of Jerusalem, but voiced their anxiety with regard to their co-religionists still in the city.[147]

Among the most prominent players on the international stage was the Zionist movement. In December 1917 Chaim Weizmann, President of the British Zionist Federation since February of the same year, wrote to Herbert Samuel, a member of the British

Cabinet who would become the first British High Commissioner for Palestine in 1920, refuting rumours that the Zionists had decided to relinquish any claim on Jerusalem.[148] In the same letter, it is clear that Zionist claims over the city relied on the numerical strength of its Jewish inhabitants, who constituted the majority of the urban population.[149]

The reactions on the German and Austrian side reflected their position in war. In Germany, the popular press presented the British victory as a moral, rather than a military achievement. As the *Kölinsche Volkszeitung*, published in Cologne, emphasised: 'for the British the capture of Jerusalem is undoubtedly a success, but it is more of a moral than of a military significance'.[150] The *Frankfurter Zeitung* stressed the undeniable political value underpinning the military achievements of the British army.[151] The Austrian *Neue Freie Presse*, meanwhile, showed a degree of optimism when it published an article which stated that 'though regrettable in itself it [the loss of Jerusalem] will bring no change into the main lines of struggle'.[152] In reality, the British conquest of Jerusalem had serious military repercussions, as it allowed the British army to march towards Syria in the following months, eventually removing the Ottoman Empire from the war.

The end of the last Crusade?

In Britain, the idea of the war as 'holy war' appears to have originated in the Church. It was the sermons of Anglican Bishop Winnington-Ingram in London, and the articles of William Robertson Nicholl (a close friend of Lloyd George) who edited the nonconformist paper the *British Weekly*, that labelled the conflict as a holy crusade from the outset.[153] Considering defeat as a punishment for sin, victory in the war was to come with the redemption of the combatants: the crusading spirit was the means to obtain redemption.[154] It would be an exaggeration to consider the notion of a crusade as the main image portrayed in this aspect of the war; however, following the successes of the Palestine campaign and the capture of Jerusalem, to the idea of a 'new' or 'last' crusade became widespread among the British public.[155] First-hand accounts of the campaign were published in the form of diaries, and the feeling spread of being party to something important: of the fulfilment of an eschatological project. Most of those diaries bore titles referring directly to the Crusades: *The Aussie Crusaders, Khaki Crusaders, The Great Crusade, The Modern Crusaders*. None of these books, however, resembled the diary of a crusader; of someone fighting in the name of God. Rather, they were more like chronicles of war.[156] Captain Adams, once it was announced that Jerusalem had been occupied, reported that a bottle of wine had been opened in order to celebrate the occasion suitably.[157]

The use of the word 'crusade', as synonymous with holy war, comes from the Latin word 'cruciare', which means to mark with a cross, and has a particular Christian connotation; holy war, on the other hand, is not unique to Christianity, as both Islam and Judaism have forms of holy war.[158] Both crusade and holy war are also different from the idea of 'just' wars, as a just war requires a set of conditions to be satisfied, whereas holy wars have their own justification: 'Deus Vult' (God wills it) was the cry of the first crusaders.[159] Some Englishmen became convinced that the Great War was a struggle between the Christian civilisations opposing the German Teutonic savagery. It has been suggested by Bar-Yosef that the theme of the crusade was only mused upon by the upper classes, as a consequence of their higher level of education.[160] Lower classes possessed a stronger knowledge of the Bible and the Holy Land was more associated with vernacular Bible culture than with memories of medieval conquest of Palestine.[161] However, sermons, press and propaganda made the crusade theme more popular and accessible to the public. Poems and songs talking of the war as the last crusade became normalised. One example is the collection of *Songs of the Last Crusade*, written by Ella McFayden in 1917. It is interesting to note that, in a poem she wrote in 1915, well before the Palestine campaign, even the members of the Saint John ambulance service, based in England and part of the Red Cross, were defined as Crusaders:

> Among the shifting chances / of intake, siege and fray;
> Time's ever green romances / Can never pass away;
> Where desert foes are halted / And bared the Turkish blade
> Today the Cross, exalted / Leads out the Last Crusade.

Of old the Hermit pleaded / By market-square and street;
The humble ploughman heeded / the seigneur left his seat;
Then Antioch was shaken / Edessa fell our gain,
Jerusalem lay taken / by Godfrey of Lorraine.
Now 'gainst the Unbeliever / old paynim fields upon,
The Red Cross of Geneva / leads out thy knights, Saint John!
Our manhood holds thy measure / thy work goes forward yet;
Rest well and take thy leisure / great soul of Jean Valette!
From treacherous invader / from scathe in field or fight,
God guard my young crusader / Geneva's swordless knight.
The hospitallers' daring / was worthy all men's cheers,
But what of these men faring / unarmed among the spears?
They chase no proud ambition / no gilded, glad emprise;
Their consecrated mission / among the stricken lies;
'Mid Bedouin or Dervish / or that more hated foe,
Where'er men need their service / the Knights of mercy go.
The prayers of those that love them / be more than shield or blade
Spread Thou Thy might above them: / God bless the Last Crusade![162]

If indeed knowledge of the Crusades was reserved for a small section of society, the war and the media disseminated this idea to the public at large who, in times of crisis, turned to mystical, prophetical and miraculous beliefs.[163]

As shown, the origins of the crusading theme are to be found alongside the genesis of the war itself; however, the Palestine campaign acted as a catalyst for the expansion of the crusading theme. This theme then came to be exploited and feared simultaneously: exploited as part of the official propaganda, but feared as it may have damaged the relations with the Muslim component of the British Empire. Although the notion of a crusade was very strong during the conflict, it appears that it then faded away quite rapidly. The British soldier Cecil Sommers, writing his memoirs, distanced himself from the numerous other war diaries which were talking explicitly of the crusade. Sommers wrote to his daughter: 'Your Grandmother, who is apt to sentimentalize, will tell you that Daddy was a crusader'.[164] Sommers recognised that the crusader comparison was quite impossible in reality, but he did acknowledge the power of this particular idea. Sommers also went further, claiming that, in idealistic terms, every soldier, who was a butcher or a baker before the war, became a temporary crusader, regardless of being employed in France or Palestine or any other theatre.[165] Sommers, having reached Palestine, wrote: 'this morning I woke up to the old familiar sound of the guns. So far I have been on a Cook's tour. Now, I suppose I become a Crusader.'[166] The crusading metaphor was deeply rooted in education, imagery and even genealogy, as some scoured their family histories looking for crusading ancestors. It is therefore not surprising that a myth was eventually born.[167]

Looking at the literature of the time, it appears that the Crusade theme was mainly a feature of British belief and propaganda: 'crusading-mania' was almost entirely unheard of in other countries, the only exception being the collection of letters written by a French officer, later translated into English under the title *A Crusader of France*.[168] In the United States it was the press that spread the theme. The main newspapers, such as the *New York Times*, the *Chicago Tribune*, the *Washington Post* and the *Los Angeles Times*, published articles on Palestine and Jerusalem after the British conquest of the region. The American press *de facto* aimed to stress the Christian nature of Palestine as most of the knowledge available to the readers was limited to biblical references.[169] There are also examples of crusading literature among the Anzac and South African forces, like the South African *Khaki Crusaders* and the Australian *The Aussie Crusaders*.[170] Depicting the success of Allenby as the final victory of Christianity over Islam proved too strong a temptation for chroniclers and the military establishment, even though it was out of touch with the real context of the war.[171] An actual contentious Christian-Muslim context was never present in the battlefield; Allenby himself underlined many times the crucial role played by Muslim members of the British army in the Palestine campaign, such as the Egyptian Camel Corps.[172] Nevertheless, he also often turned to Bible images when advancing into Palestine, and as previously stated he added the name of Megiddo to his title of Field Marshal Viscount Allenby of Felixstowe following his military success at place of the same name.[173]

5

BRITISH MILITARY RULE 1917-1920 AND THE CASE OF THE NEBI MUSA RIOTS

Urbs beata Jerusalem dicta pacis visio,
Quae construitir in coelis vivis ex lapidibus
(7th Century)

Following the conquest of the city, the British established military rule which lasted until 1 July 1920. From the perspective of the local population the government of the city had passed from Ottoman rule to that of a new foreign power. However, the British were not only European Christian rulers: they had also shown their support for Jewish immigration and settlement in Palestine by issuing the Balfour Declaration. By observing the main features of the British military in Jerusalem, and in particular the administrative structure, it may be possible to note the main continuities and changes between the Ottoman and British administrations, as well as discuss the role of the military in relation to the local elites and the Zionist Commission. Although the civil administration of the city after 1920 has been studied extensively, the military administration has been reviewed as a transitional period.[1] Irrespective of poor academic attention, this was a rather formative period. Indeed, military rule forced the renegotiation of several aspects of Jerusalem: politics, urban geography, language and the economy, amongst other things, were all reshaped according to the requirements and values of the new rulers. The military establishment was generally reluctant to engage with the complexities of high politics, so how did their rule affect the city of

Jerusalem?[2] To answer this question, attention should be paid to one of the key characters of the British administration: the military governor Ronald Storrs. Military rule did not create a complex structure of government in Jerusalem, but was based upon a high concentration of power in the hands of Storrs. As military governor Storrs ruled the city almost undisturbed between 1917 and 1920, *de facto* reshaping the city according to his sense of aesthetics and his own values.

Despite the military's dislike of politics, in the 30 months of military rule Jerusalem was the centre of great political activity: the British were preoccupied with defining their role in the region, while the local population was more concerned with the reshuffling of the local political milieu and the emergence of a complex Arab-Zionist struggle. Eventually, the Nebi Musa riots of April 1920 proved to have a, generally underestimated, impact on local politics and British policy-making. Jerusalem, as the new capital of the region, became the locus of the tripartite political struggle involving Arabs, Zionists and British, with the occasional external intervention of actors such as religious institutions and other foreign governments.

Military rule: 1917-1920

The actual establishment of military rule in Jerusalem took place the day Allenby entered the city, 11 December 1917. The first military governor of the city was General Bill Borton, who was Postmaster General of Alexandria and had been involved in the Sudan campaign, later serving as governor of Khartoum.[3] The military administration of the region was left to Allenby and then to the OETA (Occupied Enemy Territory Administration). Eventually, a Chief Administrator, who was also in charge of appointing the military governors of the five districts into which the country was divided, ruled Palestine in Allenby's name.[4] Three Chief Administrators held office in this period: Major General Arthur Money, General H.D. Watson and Major General Louis Bols.[5] The execution of policy was left to the War Office, although it was acting under instruction from the Foreign Office.[6] The leading principles of the military administration were drawn in the *Manual of*

Military Law, compiled at the Hague Conference in 1907, which imposed on the occupying army adherence to the principle of the *status quo ante bellum*.[7]

According to international law the military administration of occupied territories had to preserve the *status quo* in order to avoid the introduction of changes, in both procedures and legislation.[8] The Governor of Jerusalem Ronald Storrs, who replaced Borton after few weeks of governorship, confirmed previous administrative arrangements, and the former mayor of Jerusalem, al-Husayni, retained his privileges. Yet the Jerusalem municipality was deprived of any real power and the mayor became a figurehead; the municipal administration was simply charged with the task of liaising between the local population and the British. Significantly, the military administration could not radically change the system of taxation.[9] The military regime established by Allenby was supposed to be temporary and last only as long as military needs prevailed, but it eventually lasted two and half years.[10] The length of the military administration mirrored the uncertainty in London regarding the future of the Middle East, and particularly of Palestine. The strict maintenance of the *status quo* was also meant to avoid French-Italian antagonism especially considering that Picot immediately began to pressure Storrs to increase French visibility in the military administration, whilst the Italians began to protest against the liturgical honours given to the French.[11]

At the conclusion of the military operations, the former Arab territories of the Ottoman Empire were divided into three military administrations. Palestine was part of the OETA South, ruled solely by the British. Technically, the administration was acting under a Chief Administrator, as mentioned earlier, who received orders from Allenby, who was responsible for creating the laws in the occupied territories.[12] Besides the Chief Administrator, a Chief Political Officer (CPO) was appointed, attached to the Expeditionary Force of Allenby.[13] General Gilbert Clayton as CPO received orders directly from the Foreign Office and the relationship between the Chief Administrator and the CPO was never clearly defined, creating a sense that the Foreign Office was effectively in charge despite the fact that the military government was part of the Egyptian Expeditionary Force and therefore theoretically under control of the War Office.[14] In this context, it is because of the supremacy of the Foreign Office over the War Office that, in line with the Balfour Declaration, the British Government allowed a Zionist Commission to travel to Palestine to work as an advisory body to the British authorities.[15]

The first task of the military administration was to cope with the general lack of food, medicine and fuel; in other words, it had to cater for the needs of the army and the civilian population. The army re-established a railway connection to the city through the reconstruction of the line between Jaffa and Jerusalem, and food was brought from Egypt. Like Borton, Storrs had to face the immediate necessity of obtaining supplies for the city, and decided that the distribution should be placed in the hands of the municipality. The activity was to be supervised by representatives of all three religious communities (Muslim, Christian and Jewish).[16]

Within the boundaries and limitations of the *status quo ante bellum*, the military administration, in order to administer the occupied territories, established departments of health, law, finance and commerce.[17] Health was a priority, and the Health Department started to operate in 1918 with the purpose of fighting an outbreak of cholera and typhoid, and to deal with widespread diseases like malaria and trachoma.[18] In restoring essential services, the OETA was assisted by the American Red Cross, the Hadassah Zionist Organisation of America, and the Syria and Palestine Relief Committee, established by the Anglican Bishop Rennie MacInnes.[19] Their main purpose was to re-organise the hospitals, improve the sanitation of the city and provide relief, which, in the final stages of Ottoman control, was done mainly by the American Colony through a soup kitchen and direct help to the inhabitants.[20] Veterinary measures were also taken in order to eliminate cattle diseases.[21] The shortage of water and the lack of a proper drainage system at the beginning of the occupation, however, impeded the implementation of the full sanitation works needed as it was also found necessary to restrict the water supply.[22] Because of this, the Royal Engineers started to pump water to Jerusalem from several reservoirs around the city, but the problem of water was not solved satisfactorily until the 1920s.

In the legal sphere, the British appointed a Senior Judicial Officer, who exercised control over the courts and land registers, and eventually also worked as legal adviser to the Chief Administrator.[23] Ottoman criminal and civil law was largely maintained. Although Arabic remained the official language of plea in the courts, the business of the courts was carried out in English with simultaneous translation into Arabic and Hebrew.[24] A court under the authority of the municipality was also established, dealing with minor criminal offences. Religious courts were maintained, but they had jurisdiction only in matters regarding personal status such as registration of marriages, birth and deaths, and also solved disputes concerning Muslim *waqfs*.[25] Overall, the military administration preserved the Ottoman system of courts but reduced their personnel. The only court of appeal in the region was established in Jerusalem, composed of two British and five local officials.[26]

Former Ottoman state schools were slowly re-opened and the first measure taken was to replace Turkish with Arabic as the medium of instruction. Hebrew was used only in private Jewish schools such as the Jewish educational institution Alliance Israélite Universelle. In 1917, the military administration appointed Major Williams of the India Civil Service in order to rebuild the educational system; he was replaced by Major Tadman of the Egyptian Ministry of Education in October 1918.[27] Non-governmental schools continued to function, offering religious and technical education. According to a report of the Palestine Zionist Office (the name of the Zionist Commission during the Mandate), at the end of 1919 there were 94 Jewish educational institutions: 32 kindergartens, 45 primary schools, 8 secondary schools, 4 business schools and 1 school of music.[28] Government schools were mainly attended by Arabs as these classes were taught in Arabic, though in some Christian schools Arabic was also used as language of education.[29] The Zionists established a school system which paralleled public education, though the schools were attended only by Jewish students.[30]

Funds were needed to carry out the reconstruction of basic infrastructures. According to C.R. Ashbee, the civic adviser of the military administration, the first works of reconstruction carried out in Jerusalem were sanitation, health service, engineering and scavenging; attention would then turn to the preservation of the Holy City.[31] Nevertheless, the military administration was not entitled to change the system of taxation and it proved quite difficult to collect revenues from a starving population to pay for the reconstruction works. As noted by Storrs, the immediate liabilities of Jerusalem far exceeded its assets.[32] The principal sources of revenue were still customs duties, house and land tax, tithes, animal tax, fees of court and the surplus from the post office.[33] The British administration modified the method of collection and abolished the most vexatious and oppressive imposts like the *temettü* (a professional tax imposed mainly on merchants and artisans), a number of licensing fees and, lastly, the tax to avoid forced road labour.[34] Apart from the budget, the military administration introduced the Egyptian currency as the Turkish lira had lost all its value; it was also declared illegal.[35] The new currency did not win public confidence, however, as some locals expected Ottomans to return. Later in 1918, in concert with the Treasury, the Foreign Office ordered a removal of the restrictions on the Turkish currency;[36] however, people were no longer interested in the old money as the Egyptian pound had slowly gained the confidence of the public. This, to an extent, implied that people had understood the Ottomans would never come back to Jerusalem, and that the British were likely to be there for a while.

The military administration also worked towards the re-establishment of commerce and industry. After six months of British rule, commerce was lively thanks to financial grants by the British military administration to local entrepreneurs.[37] Ronald Storrs personally endeavoured to support the establishment of local industries. The British administration developed a legal and economic framework in which business could expand; however, investments belonged mainly to the private sector. In the process of establishing a framework for commerce and industry, in 1918 Storrs renewed the Jerusalem Chamber of Commerce, which he actually claimed he founded; meanwhile, the military administration temporarily prohibited the import of articles such as salt, printed matter, cotton, copper and other materials, in order to promote local industries.[38] Licences for the import of these goods were eventually issued by the administration in Jerusalem, after payment of the necessary fees.³⁹ Once the foreign consuls were permitted to return in 1919, their role as promoters and intermediaries of their own countries' industries restarted. In responding to a request for information from an American firm about the transport situation in Jerusalem in 1919, the American consul Glazebrook stated that there were no private cars in the city, and only a few bicycles, but he predicted large commercial possibilities in the future.⁴⁰ That year Glazebrook also replied to an American enterprise interested in the cinema business, although this time the consul was more pessimistic, telling the firm that there were three cinemas in Jerusalem, but that they could not afford to buy films at the moment.⁴¹

The question of the local police force was one of great importance, as the different religious groups wanted to be represented within it. The force for the Jerusalem region was re-organised and reduced as, in the opinion of the military, it was necessary first to improve the quality of the corps.⁴² Towards the end of Ottoman rule there were two police systems in Palestine and Syria. In Jerusalem there was a municipal police force composed of trained policemen, and regular army troops under the command of Ottoman senior officers. The second force was a gendarmerie, composed of irregulars, called to reinforce the local police force in times of trouble such as riots.⁴³ In the early stages of the British occupation of the city, responsibility for policing fell on the Military Police; however a city police force was re-established soon after and, by January 1918, one British and several Arab officers led a total of 340 men engaged in police work.⁴⁴ By July 1920, with the establishment of the civil administration, the Palestine Police Force was born. The force was composed of 18 British officers, 55 Palestinian officers and 1,144 ranks, mainly local Arabs.⁴⁵ Some Indian Muslims were employed in the police force, in order to serve in the corps protecting the Muslim holy places. During the Nebi Musa riots in 1920, Storrs claimed that the local police force was only partially trained, and lacked tradition.⁴⁶ Storrs was referring to the fact that local Palestinian officers continued to enforce the so-called 'Turkish System' of policing, which meant obtaining confession and gathering information by using physical violence.⁴⁷

Zionists, meanwhile, requested that the military administration recruit more Jewish police officers for Jerusalem, but also that the selection of the officers be controlled by the Zionist Commission.[48] The military were ambiguous in their response, as they did not want to be involved in political games despite strong pressure from the Zionist Commission.[49]

Although the military government was closely involved with local issues, officers carefully avoided direct involvement with the Foreign and War offices regarding the future of Palestine. With the establishment of the military administration, the Foreign Office decided to postpone crucial decisions in relation to Palestine and Jerusalem, and left to the military the business of local politics.[50] On Christmas Eve, Borton Pasha, as first military governor of Jerusalem, attended mass at Bethlehem and he found himself involved in a clash between the French and Italian representatives.[51] A few days later Borton resigned as governor, overwhelmed by the duties of the role; this was possibly due to a breakdown in his health, but also, perhaps, because he was unable to deal with the religious and political issues that had emerged amongst the various communities of Jerusalem. On 28 December 1918, Ronald Storrs was appointed Lieutenant-Colonel Governor of Jerusalem.

Storrs had no military experience; he had previously served as Oriental Secretary to the Residency in Cairo. He was meant to act as a bridge between the military, which disliked (or did not understand) politics, and the political establishment in London.[52] Groups such as the Zionist Commission and the Arab-Christian associations, as well as the internal questions among the religious groups, forced the military to face the inevitable issue of politics.[53] The military had to deal with local politics as it was charged with enforcing the *status quo* while waiting for events to develop, but the arrival of the Zionist Commission was considered contrary to the principle of the *status quo* and its work interfered with that of the military administration.[54] According to the Foreign Office, the Zionist Commission was to be entrusted to a British officer under General Allenby's command, but with a direct link to London.[55] In the Foreign Office's plans, the Commission was to represent the Zionist Organisation, and act as an advisory body. The main objectives of the Commission were to form a link between British authorities and the Jewish population in Palestine; to coordinate relief work directed towards the Jewish community; to develop Jewish colonies; to assist Jewish organisations; and, lastly to establish friendly relations with the Arabs and other non-Jewish communities.[56] However, the Commission and its members *de facto* tried to 'sell' Zionism as an acceptable ideology and to paint European Jews as 'non-foreigners' to Palestine. Indeed, through this project of the Foreign Office, it is possible to understand why the military thought of the Zionist Commission as a competing, parallel governmental institution. To an extent the military permitted the peaceful coexistence of the people in Jerusalem, albeit at the high cost of limiting the freedom of the population; the main concern of the military administration was public security and distribution of basic services, which were dispensed under martial law.[57]

In the spirit of the *status quo ante bellum*, the British did not distance themselves from the 'politics of the notables', but continued the Ottoman practice of relying on the main families of Jerusalem.[58] Once again, the local notables were to play their role as intermediaries between the local population and the administration. The mayor appointed before the war by the Ottomans, Husayn Salim al-Husayni, remained in office. He did not hold any effective power unless it was specifically granted by the British, as in the case of the distribution of the relief after the occupation.[59] When the mayor died, early in 1918, Storrs appointed the most prominent member of the Husayni family, Musa Kazim, to replace Husayn.[60] He was a political activist who, once in charge of the mayoral office, was initially tactful in his opposition to the British; however, he was dismissed after the Nebi Musa riots.[61] Notable Arab families were able to maintain their power base, and by opposing Zionism they in fact managed to increase it. The leaders and the young cadres of the notable families were ready to deal with the new rulers, as well as support their own political causes with a stronger voice as suggested by the creation of the Muslim-Christian associations and other political organisations.[62] Following the arrival of the Zionists, Muslim and Christian Arabs found a common ground that unified them in both ideological and political terms. This unity was then transformed into political action controlled by the notables; nevertheless, it has been noted that, though Palestinians possessed a strong elite, they did not possess a charismatic leader.[63] The lack of a charismatic leadership, however, did not prevent the rapid development of a political consciousness which increased steadily in strength.

Despite the growing Arab nationalist movement, the most complex relationship of the military administration was with the Zionist Commission. When Chaim Weizmann arrived in the region as head of the Zionist Commission in 1918, members of the military administration expressed their disappointment and surprise.[64] General Money, Chief Administrator, was highly critical of Zionism, and of British support to the Zionist cause, although his opinions might also have reflected a strong feeling of anti-Semitism: '[Jews] were as a class inferior morally and intellectually to the bulk of the Muslim and Christian inhabitants of the country'.[65] Following the occupation of Jerusalem, the Chief Political Officer, Gilbert Clayton, expressed to Sykes his concerns in relation to British support for Zionism, as he feared it might alienate Arab support in the region.[66] Louis Bols, the last Chief military Administrator, became disillusioned with Zionism after the Nebi Musa riots in April 1920; in fact, he acknowledged that the Zionists were not ultimately claiming a 'National Home' but a Jewish state.[67] The only pro-Zionist member of the military administration was Colonel Richard Meinertzhagen, the Chief Political Officer who held the office from March 1919.[68] He supported the Zionists as he claimed they would be the most loyal friends to the British in the Middle East, and he added that the administration should have been purged of anti-Zionist elements.[69] Although the members of the military establishment were concerned with the political situation, they never publicly expressed opinions about it. The military proved to be more concerned with practicalities than politics. They saw the Zionist Commission as a threat to their legitimacy, as the bureaucratic apparatus of the Zionist Commission was running almost in parallel with the British administrative one.[70] The Commission was officially charged by the Foreign Office to carry out, under Allenby's authority, the steps necessary to establish in Palestine a Jewish National Home, through the formation of a link between the British authorities and the

Jewish population of Palestine, assistance to Jewish organisations and population, and the collection of information with a view to the further development of Jewish settlements.[71] It would not be surprising, then, if the military administration considered the Zionist Commission as an arrogant newcomer; furthermore some British army officers believed during the war that the Ottoman government was controlled by a group of Jewish freemasons who had infiltrated the CUP.[72]

The second relationship of the military administration was with the religious groups of the city, primarily Christians. The British military administration, particularly the governorate of the city, was ordered by the Foreign Office to settle matters between the religious denominations regarding the holy places directly rather than through intermediaries. The Chief Administrator was also ordered to allow for the return of those religious leaders who had left Jerusalem at the beginning of the war.[73] A careful eye was placed on the Greek Orthodox Church, as it had been the most disrupted after the conflict due to financial constraints.[74] Ronald Storrs, who had power over the Status Quo, often moved physically from one church to another in order to control and prevent breaches of the Status Quo by clergy and believers of the different Christian confessions.[75] He also tried to involve the Churches in public discussions regarding the future of Jerusalem. When Storrs founded the Pro-Jerusalem Society in 1918, in order to develop various projects on Jerusalem, he brought together the Franciscans, the Dominicans, the Orthodox, the Armenians and the Anglican Bishop.[76] Members of the different denominations were quite sceptical with regard to the British military administration, with the most sceptical being the Anglican Bishop in Jerusalem, Rennie MacInnes, who continued to blame his fellow countrymen for allowing the establishment of the Zionists in Palestine.[77] Bishop MacInnes became quite disillusioned and in early January 1918 said he believed that the British authorities were very afraid of the political difficulties in Jerusalem but preferred to delay any serious political discussion on the future of the city and Palestine.[78]

The 'despot' ruler of Jerusalem: Ronald Storrs

While Otis Glazebrook and Conde de Ballobar were the leading foreign representatives during the war period, Ronald Storrs rose in prominence in Jerusalem under military rule. A proper study on Storrs as governor of Jerusalem has never been published, but scholars have dealt with this figure through studying the beginning of the British mandatory government in Palestine. Storrs has been portrayed as a despot and autocrat by several scholars, as well as some of his contemporaries, and Storrs played the part well, claiming in 1920 to rule the Jerusalem district like his 'predecessor' Pontius Pilate.[79]

Ronald Storrs was born in 1881 in Bury St Edmunds in Suffolk; he was the eldest son of Reverend John Storrs, a vicar in London and then Dean of Rochester.[80] Storrs was interested in languages, culture and the arts, and read classical studies at Pembroke College in Cambridge. He entered the civil service in 1904 and was appointed to the Egyptian Civil Service in the Ministry of Finance until 1909. He was then appointed Oriental secretary to the British Agency in Cairo. It was with this appointment that Storrs had the chance to show his skill with the Arabic language, and was able to prove his abilities with Middle Eastern affairs. With the outbreak of the war, Storrs was appointed assistant political officer to the Anglo-French Expeditionary Force in order to deal with Sharif Husayn and Thomas Eliot Lawrence, who led the Arab Revolt against the Ottoman regime, and in 1917 he was briefly appointed to the secretariat of the War Cabinet. Following the capture of Jerusalem and the resignation of the first military governor of the city, Storrs was appointed governor of Jerusalem. He served until 1920 as military governor of the city and then, from 1920 to 1926, as civil governor of Jerusalem.[81]

As governor of Jerusalem, Storrs' main concern was to rebuild the city after the war, and harmonise relations between the different religious and ethnic communities.[82] As sources are contradictory, it is difficult to say whether Storrs was pro- or anti-Zionist. He did, however pay, special attention to Christian matters, as shown in his memoirs, and especially by his two meetings with the Pope in

Rome in 1919 and 1921.[83] In a note by the French Foreign Office, in January 1918, Ronald Storrs is portrayed as being against French interests in the Middle East. It was claimed that it was Storrs who censored all Egyptian press articles discussing French achievements in the war, in order to diminish French appeal to the local population.[84] A few weeks later, following an investigation of the French chargé d'affaires in Cairo, French opinion of Storrs became more conciliatory. He was no longer considered a 'gallophobe', but rather a great enthusiast for French culture and literature.[85] Nevertheless Storrs was never fully appreciated by the French authorities. In April 1920, following the Nebi Musa riots, Storrs was accused by the British Court of Enquiry, as well as by general public opinion, of having been negligent. In 1926, Storrs' career in Jerusalem came to an end as he was appointed governor and commander in chief of Cyprus. In Cyprus he found a similar situation to Jerusalem, as the island was divided between the Turkish and Greek communities. Although he proved to be balanced, Storrs could not avoid clashes. During the riots of October 1931, the Government House was burned and his private art and antiquities collections destroyed.[86] Twice in his career Storrs faced the outbreak of violent riots and it appears that, in both cases, he could not have predicted, nor prevented, them.

After the Cyprus experience, Storrs was appointed as governor of Northern Rhodesia. He was clearly out of his environment as he had little knowledge of sub-Saharan Africa. During his time there Storrs suffered from tropical diseases, and in 1934 he retired from the civil service and went back to Britain. He then dedicated himself to local government for Islington council in London, and was active in social life promoting cultural and music societies. Ronald Storrs died in 1955, survived by his wife but no children.[87] Interestingly, there are no traces of Storrs in twenty-first century Jerusalem: there are no memorials, plaques or statues, despite the fact that some of the decrees issued during his rule had a huge impact on setting the character of modern Jerusalem.

Ronald Storrs unequivocally intertwined imperial interests and his personal views in his style of government. Aesthetics, a very high civic and religious sense, and a feeling that the communities of the city should be involved, led Storrs towards the creation of the

Pro-Jerusalem Society in 1918: a non-governmental association designed to assist the military governor in the 'preservation and advancement of the interests of Jerusalem, its districts and inhabitants'.[88] The Pro-Jerusalem Society as a non-governmental institution, was a transitional organisation which was able to avoid the restrictions imposed on the military administration by the customs of the *status quo ante bellum*. The Society was composed of the mayor of Jerusalem, the consular corps, the chiefs of the Christian denominations, and other leading members of the British, Arab and Jewish communities. According to its statute, the main purposes of the Pro-Jerusalem Society were the preservation and advancement of the interests of Jerusalem; the provision and maintenance of parks, gardens and open spaces; the establishment of libraries, museums, music centres and dramatic theatre; and the protection and preservation of antiquities.[89] Charles Robert Ashbee, a member of the arts and crafts movement, was appointed as civic adviser and secretary to the Pro-Jerusalem Society. As such, he was involved in all aspects of the planning of Jerusalem and was regarded by the administration as the resident professional planner.[90] However, Ashbee was neither a government nor a municipal employee; he was, in fact, paid directly by the Pro-Jerusalem Society.[91] The Society did not receive funds from the local government, only private donors. The Society also worked towards the encouragement of the establishment of arts and handicrafts industries, under the sponsorship of Ashbee.[92]

The members of the Pro-Jerusalem Society gathered on a regular basis; they met 58 times between its first meeting on 6 September 1918 and 1924.[93] The voices of Ashbee and Storrs were often the strongest, as suggested by the operation of re-naming the streets.[94] The question of street naming was a sensitive one, as it carried strong ideological value.[95] Storrs followed only minimally the familiar British colonial pattern in street naming; indeed, the majority of the names chosen were not linked to the British Empire as he chose to link street naming to the history of Jerusalem, perhaps in an attempt to achieve some sort of sectarian harmony.[96] Storrs chose saints, prophets, scholars and kings, supposedly belonging to the three religious camps, to be the new street names, and personally named St Francis Street, St Paul's Road, Coeur de

Lion Street, Saladin's Road, Streets of the Prophets, and also Queen Melisende Road, the only one dedicated to a woman.[97] These names were indeed linked to the history of the city, although none of them symbolised the unity of Jerusalem; on the contrary, they suggested a clear division of the city according to a religious cleavage. In this sense, Storrs and the Pro-Jerusalem campaign failed to promote some unity, or at least a common sense of citizenship, amongst the Jerusalemites. Local residents and the new rulers possessed a different idea of physical space: for Jerusalemites, streets did not represent the same values as in the British mentality. Anonymity in Jerusalem was almost unknown: every person was easily located. In Ottoman Jerusalem streets were known by more than one name, but this did not mean mail could not be delivered.[98]

The Pro-Jerusalem Society was generally efficient, although criticism from the local population was frequent, and they did not always appreciate the reforming zeal of Storrs and Ashbee.[99] This is crucial: most of the scholarship on Jerusalem has been quite sympathetic to Storrs, as there has been appreciation of his vision to preserve the beauty of Jerusalem and to re-establish the holiness of the city, which had been lost under Ottoman rule.[100] The personal decrees of Storrs, in the form of Public Notices, and the suggestions of the Pro-Jerusalem Society, were the basis of the conservation process promoted by the British, which was going in the opposite direction of the one promoted by local elites until the outbreak of the war; that is, modernisation.[101] As experienced colonial rulers, the British were trying to establish their means of control; therefore, it is not a surprise that local participation in processes such as town planning and street naming was nominal. However, much of the literature discussing these events has deliberately portrayed the local population as neutral recipients of 'enlightened' British rule, *de facto* perpetuating colonial rule over Jerusalem.

Looking at some of the decrees issued by Storrs, the extent of administrative and ideological control established by the British administration becomes apparent. In April 1918, Storrs issued a statement with a long-lasting impact upon the city: 'No person shall demolish, erect, alter or repair the structure of any building in the City of Jerusalem or its environs within a radius of 2,500 meters from the Damascus Gate until he has obtained a written permit from the military governor'.[102] The necessity to establish basic rules in relation to town planning was in keeping with the conservative attitude of Storrs, as he was trying to protect the traditional aspect of the city by avoiding any stylistic corruption in the architecture. Storrs projected his own British and Victorian ideals onto the reconstruction of the city: he always aimed to preserve the 'celestial' character of Jerusalem. Because of this he also prohibited commercial advertisements, unless they were out of sight of the walls of the city. A sense of the aesthetic prevailed even when it came to business.[103]

> The limitation of advertisement is an urgent need. The promiscuous placarding and profanation of every conspicuous wall-surface must at all hazards be stopped. The Society, therefore, drew up for and in conjunction with the municipal authorities the series of regulations which are given in Appendix VII, an appropriation was made for them in the municipal budget of 1920, and they have since been incorporated in the legislation of the country.[104]

Storrs not only worked towards the amelioration of Jerusalem's built environment, but he also made efforts to restore the city's 'moral image'. Non-licensed public bars within the walls were closed, and distilling was prohibited except in private homes. In licensed bars, alcohol was not served between 2 pm and 6 pm, and between 8 pm and 5 am.[105] Prostitution was also regulated. It was a very sensitive issue; Jerusalem might have been a 'holy city' but it was, first and foremost, a living city, and likely not a very religious one. Prostitution was common before the war, and increased after the war: the British presence meant that more money was available for this kind of service, so an increasing number of women from poor backgrounds became members of the 'world's oldest profession'.[106] Brothels were forbidden within the walls of the city, and they were allowed only in Feingold Street (a courtyard on Jaffa Road), in the neighbourhoods of Nahalat Shiv'ah, and in the Milner Houses. Women with sexual diseases were liable to imprisonment if caught having sex, due to the possibility of transmitting the disease to members of the military force.¹⁰⁷ This decree was indeed issued because of health reasons and to guarantee the good conduct of the soldiers but, in the eyes of Storrs, prostitution was inconceivable in a city like Jerusalem. He also prohibited hotel dances and cabarets within the walled city.¹⁰⁸ This conservative and puritanical attitude was undermined by the lifestyle of the British military officials, who often attended parties and dances, despite the criticism of the religious institutions. The Latin Patriarch of Jerusalem did not hesitate in condemning Storrs as a 'disaster' as he permitted fancy balls, which were strictly forbidden in Ottoman times.¹⁰⁹

The most difficult task faced by Storrs was the political issue of Zionism, and the politics of the various religious institutions. Storrs never gained the full support of these bodies of Jerusalem; the Arabs (both Muslims and Christians) thought Storrs was pro-Zionist, as he was part of the British establishment that supported Zionism and Jewish immigration to Palestine; Zionists thought Storrs was pro-Arab; and non-local Christians such as the Italian and French clergy never fully trusted him as he was seen as an agent of the Anglican Church.¹¹⁰ In the years of the military administration, Storrs was genuinely convinced that he could have controlled the local population, and the quarrels between the different communities, as an enlightened ruler, without realising that he had become a despotic agent of British *mission civilisatrice*.

Planning Jerusalem

With the British occupation of Jerusalem, planning in colonial and non-local terms for Jerusalem began. The local notion of space was to be reshaped, and the traditional geographical units of the old city, like the courtyards, the clusters of houses, and small squares, were to be replaced by the concept of segregated quarters.¹¹¹ Regardless of what the local inhabitants might have desired for their city, Ronald Storrs initiated the planning of the city following, according to him, the basic policy of the *status quo*. Storrs never transferred the activity of planning to the Pro-Jerusalem Society; the minutes of the Society's meetings prove that the planning of the city was never even discussed.¹¹² Storrs was a preservationist; he used the *status quo* to protect the old city and its environs, rather than promoting changes and particular developments. When asked to grant a concession to run street-car lines to Bethlehem and the Mount of Olives, he is reported to have said that 'the first rail section would have to be laid over the dead body of the military governor'.[113] Another example of this conservationist zealousness was the removal in 1922 of the Clock Tower built by the Ottomans in 1902 above the Jaffa Gate as, in the minds of the British planners, and Storrs in particular, the clock tower represented an alien element in the old city: ugly and not in keeping with the ancient walls.[114] Interestingly, following the reunification of the city after the Six Days war in 1967, plans were made to remove the very same walls that Storrs regarded as a symbol of Jerusalem: Ben-Gurion did not consider the walls of Jerusalem as Jewish.[115]

In 1918 William McLean was called to Jerusalem by the military administration, where he prepared the first town planning scheme.[116] He was a civil engineer with experience in the Sudan Civil Service and a former municipal engineer of Khartoum and Alexandria in Egypt. He arrived in March and by July of the same year he completed the plan, which was approved by Allenby later that month.[117] The plan was simple, designed to preserve the old city and surround the walls with a green belt, whilst the modern city was to be developed to the west.[118] McLean's scheme, however, was short lived; it was opposed by Ashbee, whose duty was to implement the plan, by the city engineer Guini, and also by the Zionists, who suspected the plan could have been contrary to Jewish interests.[119] Although the plan had been signed by Allenby, it was not legally binding. Public Notices were merely intended to regulate and not to initiate developments, as suggested by the rule of the *status quo*.[120]

The strongest critic of McLean was Patrick Geddes, a professor of Botany at St Andrew's University, but also a well known urban planner.[121] Geddes persuaded the Zionist Commission to contest McLean's plan; they responded by hiring Geddes, whose arrival in Palestine in 1919 was well publicised by the *Jewish Chronicle* and the *New York Times*.[122] Geddes was asked to work on different projects, such as the Hebrew University and a general plan for the urban development of Jerusalem.[123] The military administration also hired Geddes to report on McLean's plan, which obviously raises a question. Geddes was paid by administration to comment on the plan, and hired at the same time by the Zionist Organisation to present an alternative plan: it is clear that McLean's scheme was to be short lived. Geddes prepared a new town plan by 1919; however, as there was no central town planning until 1921 in Palestine (Town Planning Ordinance), the military administration, and Storrs in particular, worked mainly towards the conservation of the city, both helped and constrained by the policy of the *status quo*.[124]

According to Hyman, British planners and administrators were agents of culture transfer. These people, however, did not only want to transfer their own culture to Jerusalem; they also wanted to reshape the city according to their specific purpose as in the case of Geddes, who followed Zionist principles, or Ashbee and Storrs, who looked at the city as something ethereal, to be preserved in its original configuration no matter the cost. The emblem of Pro-Jerusalem showed four small Christian Crosses drawn inside a Jewish Star of David, outflanked by a Muslim Crescent. The idea was to show that harmony between the inhabitants, and those who cared about the city, was possible. Despite this declared interest, it is clear that the real absentees from all these activities of planning were the Jerusalemites themselves. As any symbolic city, Jerusalem was often, if not always, appropriated and therefore transformed by the new rulers. From King David, who reunited the kingdom of Israel and made Jerusalem his new capital, through to the Romans and the Muslim and crusading conquerors, everyone adapted the city according to their purposes and visions. The British, enlightened rulers of the *mission civilisatrice*, did not escape this pattern and, once in power, started to plan their Jerusalem.

April 1920: Nebi Musa Riots

The military administration had to deal with several episodes of inter-communal violence, for example on the first anniversary of the issuing of the Balfour Declaration when, during a Jewish procession, there was a scuffle with some Arab bystanders.[125] However, the riot of April 1920, known as Nebi Musa, proved to be crucial for the fate of the administration; it produced a strong reaction in the Foreign Office and among the political establishment in London. The military administration was accused by Jewish and non-Jewish Zionists of being anti-Zionist and, eventually, David Lloyd George and Arthur Balfour became convinced that time had come to establish a civil administration.[126] Not only were the Nebi Musa riots fatal for the military administration, but after them it was clear that something had changed in the city. These riots were not local scuffles between neighbours, fighting over the possession of a small piece of land. These riots, in my view, radically changed the political aspect of Jerusalem. Jerusalemites were no longer the inhabitants of a peripheral town of the Ottoman and then British empires, but were the main actors of a larger and more politicised struggle. A variety of sources is available; however, none is really decisive enough to provide a local answer to these events, regardless of communal affiliation.

Surprisingly, in my opinion, the Nebi Musa riots have not attracted much academic attention in English-speaking literature. Historians have considered these events to be of secondary importance, mostly overshadowed by clashes between Arabs and Jews like the Wailing Wall riots in 1929, or the revolts of 1936-1939. Firstly, they have failed to grasp the catalysing dynamic of the riots in the change of the nature of the administration from military to civilian. Secondly, they have failed to discern any sign of a patterned and organised conflict in the structure of the riots.

Some of the existing literature available covers this event briefly, highlighting the emergence of two clear opposing sides – Jews and Arabs, and also discusses the role played by the military administration, mainly in relation to Zionism. Bernard Wasserstein, in his seminal work on the British in Palestine, in fact emphasises the deteriorating relations between the military administration and the Zionist Commission, due to the apparent anti-Zionism of members of the military administration. Wasserstein, therefore, understands the riots more in terms of outcomes, as they were the catalyst for the change from military to civil administration.[127]

Rashid Khalidi, Louis Fishman and Yehoshua Porath discuss the Nebi Musa riots as part of a process in the creation of a Palestinian identity that transcended the Jerusalem region; nevertheless, the actual events seem not to have attracted much attention.[128] Tom Segev has also written on the riots; however, he fell into the trap of discussing the incidents that triggered the riots, looking for those responsible rather than looking for the political, social and historical roots which led to the event.[129] Segev stresses that the replacement of the military administration with a civil one was an achievement of Chaim Weizmann, who managed to exploit the riots in favour of the Zionist cause.[130] Benny Morris highlights British responsibility, but suggests the possibility of the involvement of an undefined Damascus-based Arab-nationalist group.[131] Both Segev and Morris come to the conclusion that this clash was effectively a pogrom, a persecution directed against the Jews. Radically different is the view taken by Ilan Pappe, who claims that it is not actually necessary to look at the riots as a demarcation indicating the beginning of the Arab-Jewish conflict. He suggests that the Nebi Musa riots were part of a larger ideological battle between two emerging nationalist ideologies.[132]

A completely different perspective emerges from the account by the Jewish scholar Yehuda Benari.[133] Benari clearly defines the riots as a pogrom against the Jewish population of Jerusalem, and accuses the British military administration as having sole responsibility for the 'pogrom'. Benari considers the military officers were anti-Semitic and scared of the Jews, as rumours from Russia depicted the Jews as promoters of the Communist revolution. He also claims that the head of the military administration had secret meetings with Arab leaders in order to assist them in fighting the Zionists.[134] Nevertheless, Benari fails to provide convincing evidence for his arguments.

Most of the arguments discussed in the literature reviewed are valid, and based on reliable sources; however, I believe that the riots also suggest the possibility that the two emerging national movements were testing each other's strength. The British, the only real obstacle to the development of the riots, misunderstood or ignored the signs preceding these events, thereby allowing the movements to organise themselves and be ready to fight. There are no signs on either side which allow us to think they wanted to avoid direct confrontation. The notion that it was inevitable is particularly controversial and likely does not reflect the reality on the ground. However, considering the socio-political situation and the presence of a distracted third party, it seems to me the Nebi Musa riots turned out to be the first organised test of national struggle.

Nebi Musa was an Islamic religious festival which included processions from different towns around Jerusalem, leading into the city; they celebrated the prophet Moses during the same period as the Christian Orthodox Easter and the Jewish Passover. The central celebration was the long pilgrimage to the traditional burial site of Moses, along the Jericho road from Jerusalem; the celebrations lasted a week.[135] According to local memory, this festival was established by Salah al-Din in the twelfth century, to counterbalance the presence of Christians and Jews flocking to Jerusalem for the Easter celebrations.[136] Though it is not certain when the festival was first celebrated, the Nebi Musa festival was never a fully religious event. This celebration served as an opportunity for the Muslim political and religious leaders to demonstrate their power vis-à-vis the Christian and Jewish communities. The celebrations had the power to create a bond between people from various parts of the country, which were usually divided and had poor communications, who gathered in a single place because of the festival.[137] Leaders of the Arab political parties and associations exploited the excitement and enthusiasm aroused by the festival in order to make sure their petitions would be heard.[138]

To discuss and assess the Nebi Musa riots, I have chosen to use some of the defining criteria for a 'riot' as discussed in the political and anthropological academic literature. The reason for this choice is to try to support a different reading of these events, and to show their relevance in both international and local contexts. In the literature, a riot is generally understood to be an intense and sudden, though not necessarily unplanned, attack between the members of two or more communities.[139] A riot has been considered a patterned event, as opposed to a spontaneous outbreak of violence.[140] It has been noted that before most riotous events, it is possible to perceive a particular kind of 'atmosphere' which corresponds to a particular socio-political context.[141] In the case of the Nebi Musa riots, before the explosion of violence two political parties and one paramilitary organisation emerged as opposing one another. The Arab Muslim-Christian associations emerged in support of the incorporation of Palestine into Syria and with anti-Zionist petitions addressed to British authorities with the aim of stopping Jewish immigration.[142] In March 1920, the Syrian Congress declared Faysal king of Syria and Palestine; Arabs who had hoped to be incorporated into his kingdom fuelled large nationalist demonstrations in Jerusalem, which also took on an anti-Zionist nature.[143] At the same time, on the Jewish side, leading Zionist Vladimir Jabotinsky started to recruit people in order to form a paramilitary Jewish self-defence organisation, then known as *Haganah*, composed of some 200 troops; however, by the end of March there were 600 men performing military drills on daily basis.[144]

At the beginning of 1920, the political context in Palestine was becoming complex and, in Jerusalem, the Zionist Commission felt that they were the victims of the British military administration.[145] In late March 1920 Weizmann wrote:

> Many intelligent Arabs hate us because they genuinely believe we are tools of the English, who have come in now to grab the whole of the Near East. I shall go further and say that if not for the English, who are at present taking great care that we should not get into direct touch with the Arabs, we could comparatively easily make friends with the Arabs.[146]

However, the Zionists were quite scared of Faysal and the possible consequences of his attempt to gain control of Syria. Zionists felt that, due to Arab pressure, the Balfour Declaration could be evaded and the establishment of a 'National Home' delayed, if not forgotten; on the other hand, Arab elites were alarmed by the increasing Jewish immigration to the country, which could lead to the eventual dispossession of Arab properties and lands.[147] Arab elites were also afraid of the Zionist Commission, as it was seen as a government within the government, as mentioned earlier, and a sign of the will to establish a Jewish state. In 1920, once the implications of the Balfour Declaration began to become clear to the Arab elites and the population at large, attitudes towards the

Jews changed radically – assuming a more confrontational tone.¹⁴⁸ A local Arab Palestinian identity was already developing during late Ottoman rule, as shown by the publication of papers such as *al-Filastin* and *al-Carmel*; they expressed Palestinian aspirations of Arab unity and ending Ottoman-Turkish rule as well as attracting attention to Jewish immigration.¹⁴⁹ *Al-Filastin*, whose name clearly shows the emergence of a local sentiment, became the strongest opponent of Zionism, but also the voice of the Arab Greek Orthodox, who were attempting to free themselves from the domination of the Greek Orthodox hierarchy.¹⁵⁰ It is therefore apparent that a local patriotism was already present and that Zionism acted as catalyst for the development of this local sentiment into a larger ideological framework.

In late March 1920, Chaim Weizmann, the president of the Zionist Commission in Palestine, wrote to the Zionist Commission in London:

> Relations between the Jews and the Administration have gone from bad to worse. [...] In view of possible outbreaks of hostility against us, the Military Authorities have found it necessary to take measures, but the order which has been issued to the troops is in my opinion almost a direct provocation not to do anything in case outbreaks do take place.¹⁵¹

Weizmann, according to his own definition, was actually predicting a pogrom. Zionists were quite concerned at the benevolent treatment that the military administration reserved for Arab nationalists, as in the case of the limited British military intervention after the Arab nationalist demonstration in March 1920.¹⁵² After these demonstrations, and with the Nebi Musa festival approaching, a delegation of the Jewish Self-Defence Force asked Storrs for the right to carry weapons during the festival in order to protect the Jewish population of Jerusalem; Storrs rejected the request on the basis that 'every precaution will be [...] taken by the Authorities to ensure public security'.¹⁵³

Colonel Meinertzhagen, the Chief political officer of the military administration, and an open Zionist supporter, wrote to Lord

Curzon (the Minister of Foreign Affairs) expressing his concern: 'though I do not anticipate any immediate trouble in Palestine, there is always the risk of isolated cases of Jews being killed, of reprisal by the Jews, or of extensive Arab raids along the Palestine border'.[154] The atmosphere depicted was not idyllic. Vladimir Jabotinsky, meanwhile, wrote to Weizmann on 12 March predicting that a pogrom was liable to break out any day.[155] Considering the tone of a letter from the Arab Club to Allenby, it is possible to see how early signs of a riot were clearly visible: 'we declare that we cannot accept the Jews in our country. Should they be permitted to do what they intend doing, we shall fight against them till death.'[156] Nevertheless, there were those who thought differently. Having prohibited the carrying of weapons by the Jewish Self-Defence Force, Storrs wrote to Allenby suggesting that, as far as he could gather, information from preliminary signs and reports showed that tensions were no greater than the previous year, and saying that he thought nothing serious would happened.[157] The question, therefore, is whether this was lack of judgement or premeditated negligence.

Moving to another criterion in discussing the riots, it is necessary to differentiate from the causalities and the causes of a riot. The causality of the event may be triggered by single, individual episodes, which cannot alone explain the cause for the explosion of violence.[158] The newly appointed Spanish consul, Pedro Marrades, in his report to the Spanish Foreign Office, did not focus at all on the causalities as he thought the riots were just the result of ambiguous British policy-making and the arrogance of Zionist activists.[159] Although the causalities cannot explain what was behind the outbreak of violence, discussions on single episodes can highlight the degree of existing tension, and the readiness to move from rhetoric to action. On Friday 2 April the first ceremony of the Nebi Musa festival passed without incident and it seems that the small police force dealing with the procession was successful.[160] On Sunday 4 April, the day of the main pilgrimage from the shrine of the prophet Moses to Jerusalem, the procession stopped on the Jaffa road just opposite the Jaffa Gate and notables and religious leaders started to deliver inflammatory political speeches, contrary to the usual protocol.[161] Among the people who proclaimed speeches, two are particularly of note. Aref al-Aref, the editor of the popular nationalist newspaper *al-Suriyya al-Janubiyya* (The Southern Syria), published since 1919, declared: 'if we don't use force against the Jews, we will never be rid of them'. In response the crowd chanted 'Nashrab dam al Yahud' (We will drink the blood of the Jews).[162] From a balcony, Musa Kazim al-Husayni also spoke, and after his speech the crowd roared: 'Palestine is our land, the Jews are our dogs!' Pictures of Faysal were also displayed, and he was acclaimed as King of Syria and Palestine.[163]

At this point, the riot began just inside Jaffa Gate. Although it is not clear what the exact trigger was, according to the sources available, it is arguable that there was more than one.[164] In the vicinity of the Arab rally, some Zionists were listening to the speeches. Some evidence suggests that these Jewish spectators were quite provocative. Allegedly, a Jew pushed an Arab carrying a nationalist flag, similar to the one used by Faysal in Syria, and he tried to spit on the banner and on the Arab crowd.[165] Another incident, reported as the trigger of the riot, suggests that a Muslim pilgrim was attacked by a Jewish soldier.[166] According to a testimony gathered by the French consul, some young Jews standing near the Jaffa Gate attacked some Arabs after the speech delivered by Mohammed Derweesh of the Arab Club.[167] All of these reports suggest only Jewish provocation; however, although not reported, it is likely that Arab activities also triggered the riots.

Shops were looted, and spectators were beaten with stones.[168] Some Jews involved carried weapons, as in the case of two men who fired from a house which overlooked the procession route. Both were then shot by the British-Indian police deployed by Storrs.[169] The incidents started at 10 am, and it was practically over by midday. During the night, everything appeared to be quiet. Early on Monday morning the pilgrims from Hebron, who had been confined for the night in the Police barracks for their own protection, were escorted out of the city through St Stephen's Gate. Disorder broke out again early in the morning and lasted until 3 pm, when martial law was declared.[170] The following day the looting and violence continued, albeit on a smaller scale, though two cases of rape against Jewish women were reported. A number of Jews entered the city through the Arab quarter, where they had been accommodated in a synagogue, and by the evening the situation was under control.[171] The reported casualties amounted to 251, of whom 9 died and 22 were critically wounded. Five Jews and 4 Muslims had been killed; the great difference was in the number of wounded: 211 Jews were reported wounded, as opposed to 21 Muslims and 3 Christians. Seven British soldiers were also wounded; however, it appears that the police were never the target of the attackers whether Arabs or Jews.[172]

Through the definition of targets or victims, riots can also be defined by highlighting the perception of the riots itself according to different actors.[173] The term 'target' has been used by those who see riotous crowds as organised and motivated, acting purposefully rather than randomly. The term 'victims', on the other hand, has been used by those who see crowds as chaotic, disorganised, leaderless and aimless.[174] However, riots involve both targets and victims. When in a fight, the people involved define the casualties of the struggle itself as targets, which generally means that one or more groups acted as structured entities. These groups can also possess a strong identification, particularly in terms of values, and their attack is not random but directed towards a specific objective. If the casualties of incidents, on the other hand, are defined as victims, it is arguable that the actors did not belong to any organised structure, and they are moved more by passion rather than a clear purpose. 'Victims' are often the by-product of turmoil, whilst targets of a more patterned event like a riot.[175]

The term 'victims' also bears a secondary meaning, quite problematic, when used by one side to describe their own casualties, for then the 'victims' may also have been 'assailants'.[176] This second meaning is crucial in the interpretation and analyses of the events, as it may indicate which side has been taken by the people involved or the scholars studying the event. Besides 'victims' and 'targets' in a riot, there may also be 'innocent' casualties: passers-by, mere onlookers or people simply present in the crowd, who are injured or even killed. Nonetheless, 'innocent' can also be problematic as one side may define its own casualties as 'innocent'.[177] I would suggest that the term 'neutral' casualties be used instead, as these particular players did not take any side in the riot itself.

The structural development of the riots, and the dynamics discussed, suggest that it is indeed more accurate to use the definition of 'target' rather than 'victims'. The riots saw two competing nationalist aspirations, Arab and Zionist, with a strong national and religious identity, following rational and specific political purposes: to promote Arab nationalism and the opposition to Zionism on the one hand and, on the other, the creation of a Jewish national home that, in Zionist ideology, meant the creation of a Jewish state. Neither crowd was leaderless; both looked organised. Arabs were led by notables and nationalists whilst Zionists were led by Jabotinsky, as leader of the *Haganah*, who took part directly in the fight; he was then arrested and charged for illegal possession of weapons, and sentenced to 15 years' imprisonment. The sentence was revoked in 1920.[178] Although in their own statements Arabs and Zionists described the casualties as 'victims', they had been targets of a conflict planned by both sides. The Zionist Commission defined the Jewish casualties of the riots as victims of a pogrom.[179] In contrast, the Muslim-Christian Society, writing to Storrs in the aftermath of the riots, accused the Jews of disturbing the peace of Jerusalem which led to the 'massacre of a number of innocent Muslims and Christians'.[180] Arabs systematically looted Jewish shops, while Jews fired upon Arabs with illegally owned guns. The difference in the number of casualties may be explained by the number of Arabs in the city. On an average day the Jews were the majority in Jerusalem, but the number of Muslims in the city had soared due to the celebrations.[181]

Eventually, the two crowds were composed primarily of committed people interested in fighting for their own cause; however, among the casualties were 'neutrals' such as a few Orthodox Jews not politically interested in the fighting, as they did not support Zionism but were suspicious of the new Muslim-Christian alliance. Also a Muslim girl fell victim to random shooting.[182]

There were also two external criteria in relation to the development of the riots. A riot may often have the presence of 'specialists': people who are ready to be called out on riotous occasions, who profit from it, and whose activities profit others who may or may not be actually paying for the violence carried out, similar to mercenaries.¹⁸³ Some 'specialists' are sometimes employed in order to escalate the nature of a fight, from an initial incident to more serious riots. 'Specialists' may also include journalists and pamphleteers, who deliberately spread rumours and propaganda against a particular group.¹⁸⁴ Another external criterion to be discussed in defining the Nebi Musa riots is that of the 'third party'. Aside from two fighting parties, there may be a third side which should be neutral, and could possibly bring order and safety. Nevertheless, the third party may decide to support one of the sides involved, in order to protect its own interests; support given to one of the side is generally secretive and may, although not exclusively, consist of financial or technological support. A third party may also be interested in supporting all the sides fighting following the classical principle of *divide et impera*. Academic literature tends to consider the 'third party' as the state or public institutions.¹⁸⁵

In relation to the presence of specialists, according to the reports available it is arguable that amongst the Arabs gathered outside Jaffa Gate there were agents provocateurs, who are likely to have belonged to some associations, whose purpose was to ensure that the inflammatory speeches would be followed by direct action.¹⁸⁶ However, considering the already present high degree of tension between the parties, and a simple lack of evidence concerning agents provocateurs, it may be argued that these agents did not play a decisive role in the riots. No evidence has been found to support the idea of the presence of specialists amongst the Zionists.

Regarding third parties, it is necessary to underline that this is likely the most complex issue in any analysis of the Nebi Musa riots, as there are a number of questions which need to be addressed: What role did the British military administration play? Did they support one of the sides involved, or did they try to simply restore order as quickly as possible? Were there any divisions among the British military officers?

From the reports available in late April, and from the Commission of Inquiry established by High Commissioner of Egypt and Commander-in-Chief Allenby in April 1920, Storrs seems to have ignored early warnings of impending troubles.¹⁸⁷ The local police force had been accused by Zionists of being inadequate, and having a clear Arab majority.[188] Storrs deployed only a fraction of the force available in the old city at the beginning of the Nebi Musa festival, as he did not believe more troops were necessary to keep order.[189] On Friday, the day before the outbreak, the ceremony passed without incident, as noted earlier; this led Storrs to think, or at least to claim, that the small local police force, composed mainly of Arabs, could cope with the main procession. After the first day of riots, Storrs decided to withdraw the main bulk of the troops from the old city in order to enable business to proceed as usual. Storrs believed that showing that normality had been restored could prevent more violence from breaking out. However, the Court of Inquiry stated that the 'removal of the inner pickets proved to be a very serious error in judgement'.[190] The report of the Court did not claim that the military administrators favoured one side over the other, but did note that the military administration was indeed divided, with the majority being pro-Arab and the rest being pro-Zionist. The prime minister's secretary, Philip Kerr, wrote to the Foreign Office asking for more details in relation to the alleged anti-Zionist attitude of members of the military administration, as the matter was no longer self-contained in Palestine: and it was becoming an issue which required the attention of the prime minister.[191]

The Chief Political Officer, Col. Meinertzhagen, openly claimed that the administration was warned of pending troubles in Jerusalem, but that the military took inadequate steps to prevent it, and failed to keep order in the city when trouble arose. Meinertzhagen was shocked when he found out that officers of the British administration were actively implicated, and plotting against their own government. He warned both Allenby and Bols but, according to him, they preferred silence to exposure.[192] As evidence Meinertzhagen claimed that, on the day of the rioting, a notice was displayed all over Jerusalem stating: 'the Government is with us, Allenby is with us kill the Jews; there is no punishment for killing Jews'.[193] Looking at the developments of the events, it is difficult not to think that Meinertzhagen was partly right; however, the lack of more substantial evidence leads us to think that while the military administration was likely to have been anti-Zionist, it was far from supporting open conflict.[194]

The Jewish definition of the riots has been equated with that of a pogrom. 'Pogrom' is a Russian word which has been used to refer to an organised massacre since the beginning of the twentieth century. In the English-speaking world, the definition of pogrom has been applied chiefly to those who organised slaughter directed against the Jews.[195] Furthermore, the term pogrom also connotes collusion between the official power and those perpetrating the violence.[196] My point is that a pogrom is a subcategory of the riot, as this concept has ended up defining only attacks on Jews.[197]

Zionists did not hesitate in defining the Nebi Musa riots as a pogrom; Meinertzhagen also considered these events as a miniature version.[198] According to the narrow definition of pogrom, as an attack against persons and properties of a particular group, the April riots were indeed a pogrom. Arabs, as a distinctive ethnic group, fought against the Zionists, who represented another distinct ethnic and religious group. However, if one considers the pogrom as a riot with the participation of the state and/or its agents, the question becomes more complex. There is evidence suggesting that the military administration was at odds with the Zionists; the military felt uncomfortable with the presence of the Zionist Commission, and some of the officials were openly anti-Semitic. Nevertheless, to state that the British were actively involved in the Nebi Musa riots is to jump to an uncritical conclusion. The *Jewish Chronicle*, the popular Jewish paper published in London, was reluctant to believe that there was a British manoeuvre against the Zionists.[199]

To summarise, the dynamics of this riot show how the military administration dealt with this event, which was a representation of the emerging Arab-Zionist conflict. The military apparatus allowed the demonstrations to take place, and they adopted a sort of 'wait and see' policy. Only when incidents became evident and events unstoppable did the military intervene to bring the riots to a halt. The apparent British failure to prevent and to deal with the riots has shown the political limits of the military administration, which proved to be openly anti-Zionist and supportive of the Arab cause. The military was clearly distant from the Foreign Office, which was indeed supportive of the Zionist cause. The riots took place a few weeks before the San Remo Conference, which sanctioned the allocation of the mandates for the administration of the former Ottoman Arab lands. The riots became a strong argument for the Foreign Office to speed up the process of transfer from a military to a civil administration in Palestine. This shift was not only a cosmetic change; it represented the primacy of politics over military decisions, and the reallocation of political values. The military rule represented anti-Zionism, the civil administration was to represent pro-Zionism. Despite the fact that the British had not yet signed the peace treaty with Turkey, which was eventually signed at Lausanne in 1923, they decided to dissolve the OETA and establish a civil administration, even though it was contrary to the customs of the *status quo ante bellum*. It is therefore arguable that the Nebi Musa riots catalysed and accelerated the process of change from military to civilian administration, which reflected the re-establishment of the main political aims of the British in Palestine, and a victory for the Zionists. This can be viewed as a double victory for the Zionists and, in particular, for the Zionist Commission. As first High Commissioner for Palestine, the British Government appointed Herbert Samuel: a capable officer, but also a secular Jew, strongly in favour of Zionism.

As for Jerusalem, the riots had a visible impact. The stage was now set for an open tripartite political battle between British, Arabs and Zionists; yet, this does not mean an escalation in the degree of hostility between these actors was inevitable. There was a bitter and a strong political clash, but not yet an open violent conflict. In April 1920, local values and alliances were renegotiated but not radicalised.

EPILOGUE

In some ways, Jerusalem is a holy place for all Abrahamic faiths and people. What is Jerusalem? For Christians it is the *umbilicus mundi*; it is the 'mountain of the Lord' for the Jews; and for the Muslims it is the original *qibla*. While it is difficult to define the political, religious and historical meaning of the city, Jerusalem has proved to be contested throughout history; it is an urban space which, according to the three religions, is the gateway to the divine world. This very nature has made the city the subject of various conflicts over political and religious control. Claims by various groups have been embedded in the production of narratives, which were often designed to support those claims.

It is because of this power that, when the British took over the city in 1917, religion and politics went hand in hand. However, religion was not the main interest of the British: in this respect, Abigail Jacobson rightly argues that the British attempted to underplay the religious symbolism of the occupation, as in the case of the restrictions on publishing articles concerning the Crusades.[1] Engaging in religious issues, clearly, was too complex, even for the world's largest empire. It was merely exploited for internal propaganda, in order to boost the morale of a nation heavily involved in the war effort.

The administrative transformations brought about by the British, and the problematic question of the *status quo ante bellum* – which, according to sections of the military administration and the non-Jewish population of the city, was violated by the Balfour Declaration and the promise of a national home to the Zionists – reshaped the political and demographic structure of Jerusalem. Although the Jews comprised the majority of the city's population during the late Ottoman administration, they did not possess any political power; this was exercised exclusively by Muslim and Christian Arabs, as suggested by the composition of the local administrative councils. The arrival of the British, and the establishment of the Zionist Commission in Jerusalem, meant that the Jews were now able to enter the local political arena and exploit their numerical advantage politically, as well as ensuring that the promises made by the British Government in the form of the Balfour Declaration were kept.

In administrative terms, the military nature of British rule did not constitute a radical rupture with the previous state of affairs. In fact, during the war the city was led by a military Ottoman governor, who ruled alone, albeit in accordance with wartime commitments and with the local notables. Similarly, the British administration of the city was led by the appointed Ronald Storrs who, as military governor of Jerusalem, used a strong and consistent personal approach. This manifested itself through the enforcement of decrees which reflected his personal tastes, as in the case of the art and architecture of the city. Storrs had in mind a Jerusalem which should be British but looking at the biblical past, which resulted in the alienation of both Arabs and Zionists, but also those in the British establishment who disagreed with the central British policy-making.

As mentioned earlier, the occupation by the British changed the political balance amongst the population of Jerusalem in favour of the Zionists. Arabs, both Christians and Muslims, became united against the new common enemy represented by Zionism, as shown by the establishment of the Christian-Muslim associations. The greatest change in the political balance of the city after the arrival of the British was represented by the establishment of the Zionist Commission, which became a parallel *and* competing institution to Britain's military administration. Eventually, the competition between the two administrative institutions erupted in open conflict and direct criticism of one another, as suggested by the frequent exchange of letters, and the administrative obstructionism used by the British military. After Nebi Musa, this conflict was ended by the Foreign Office in favour of the wishes of the Zionist Commission, with the establishment of a civil administration in July 1920 ending over two years of British military rule.

The occupation of the city also brought developments in the urban life, and in the relationship between the city's local inhabitants and its foreign population: the consuls, private citizens, religious authorities, pilgrims and institutions. However, it would be wrong to attribute the role of moderniser of the city solely to the British. Other foreign and local agencies played a major role in this process at the end of the nineteenth century: the presence of foreigners in the city under Ottoman administration – which was often the case in urban areas of the Arab Middle East – was crucial to the modernisation of the city in the late nineteenth and early twentieth centuries. Jerusalem not only acquired new hospitals and schools, but also street lighting and a new railway connection to Jaffa, all built with foreign capital. Foreign presence during the period of the transition from Ottoman to British rule was mainly represented by a few diplomats, religious clergy, and members of the American Colony who were mainly carrying out relief work and supporting the inhabitants of Jerusalem suffering the disruptions caused by the war.

To a degree, the British occupation reshaped the role of foreigners in the city. Pilgrims began to flock there and tourism increased, due to a larger selection of tourist facilities and services. Consuls and businessmen returned to the Holy City with new interests and new commercial activities. Religious institutions, galvanised by a potential freedom never experienced under Ottoman rule, resumed the promotion of their political, religious and economic interests, competing against one another and petitioning the British administrators. After the break caused by the war, Zionists also resumed the multiple activities designed to change their status from foreigners to locals. Zionists of different nationalities aspired to acquire legal residence in Jerusalem and Palestine by lobbying the British, acquiring land from Arabs and promoting their worldwide project to re-establish the Jews in Palestine. Nevertheless, Jerusalem was not the focus of the Zionist activity; the city was the symbol of the old Jewish population. However, for the British, Jerusalem was the natural capital of the region; as a result Zionists were forced to establish the Zionist

Commission in the same city, leading Jerusalem to become the primary scene of the Arab-Zionist struggle, as suggested by the Nebi Musa riots.

In all of this, the local population were not mere pawns in a political conflict. What most of the available literature seem to have forgotten is that Jerusalemites did not simply disappear: there is too much focus on the *conflict* and too little on the context. Jerusalemites experienced the war in the same way as the inhabitants of any village near the Somme or the Marne, but ended up being ignored. With the inclusion of Jerusalem in the British 'Empire', the city itself was anglicised and those local, genuine attempts to reform Jerusalem from within were simply overlooked, with a new set of reforms imposed. Narratives on Jerusalem have been affected, too. Is it then possible to write a history of Jerusalem without including the British? Perhaps it is not feasible, but we should still try to write histories which include all of the 'voices' available, rather than the single 'voice' of the ruling masters. Jerusalem in 1920 was far less divided than general opinion may think; not even the British managed to break certain links between the local population. Political ideology, and the production of political and historical narratives, exacerbated the situation and contributed to the radical division of the city. One inevitable question remains unanswered: is this process reversible?

NOTES

Introduction

1. D. Kushner, *To Be Governor of Jerusalem* (Istanbul: Isis Press, 2005), 179-180.
2. B. Anderson, *Imagined Communities* (London: Verso, 2006), 6.
3. I. Nassar, 'Jerusalem in the Late Ottoman Period', in *Jerusalem Idea and Reality*, eds. T. Mayer and S. Ali Mourad (Abingdon: Routledge, 2008), 206-207.
4. E.H. Carr, *What Is History?* (London: Penguin, 1990), 60.

Chapter 1

1. Quoted in M. Tütüncü, *Turkish Jerusalem 1516-1917* (Harlem: SOTA, 2006), 11.
2. The structure and purposes of the *millet* system are discussed in detail in Chapter 2.
3. A. Singer, *Palestinian Peasants and Ottoman Officials* (Cambridge: Cambridge University Press, 1994), 4-7.
4. *Kudüs* was the name of Jerusalem in Ottoman Turkish; it meant 'the Sacred City'. In Arabic the name of the city is *al-Quds*.
5. Singer, *Palestinian Peasants*, 7; A. Cohen, *Palestine in the 18th Century* (Jerusalem: The Magnes Press, 1973), 169.
6. Y. Ben-Arieh, *Jerusalem in the 19th Century. The Old City* (New York: St Martin's Press, 1984), 104.
7. S. Noja, *Storia dei Popoli dell'Islam. L'Islam Moderno*, vol. 5 (Milan: Oscar Mondadori, 1990), 5.
8. B. Doumani, *Rediscovering Palestine* (London: University of California Press, 1995), 16.

9   Noja, *Storia dei Popoli dell'Islam*, 11-13.
10 T.A. Idinopulos, *Weathered by Miracles* (Chicago: Ivan R. Dee, 1998), 41; A. Hourani, *A History of the Arab Peoples* (London: Faber and Faber, 1991), 273.
11 M. Abir, 'Local Leadership and Early Reforms in Palestine 1800-1834', in *Studies on Palestine During the Ottoman Period*, ed. M. Ma'oz (Jerusalem: The Magnes Press, 1975), 303.
12 J. Dunn, 'Egypt's Nineteenth Century Armaments Industry', *The Journal of Military History* 61, no. 2 (April 1997): 232.
13 Ben-Arieh, *The Old City*, 108. The councils will be discussed in detail in several sections of this chapter.
14 D.R. Divine, *Politics and Society in Ottoman Palestine* (Boulder: Lynne Rienner, 1994), 65-69.
15 Ben-Arieh, *The Old City*, 109.
16 A. Schölch, *Palestine in Transformation 1865-1882* (Washington DC: Institute for Palestine Studies, 2006), 49.
17 Divine, *Politics and Society*, 66; S. Shamir, 'Egyptian Rule (1832-1840) and the Beginning of the Modern Period in the History of Palestine', in *Egypt and Palestine: a Millennium of Association*, eds. G. Baer and A. Cohen (New York: St Martin's Press, 1984), 221.
18 Divine, *Politics and Society*, 66.
19 Idinopulos, *Weathered by Miracles*, 45-46; Divine, *Politics and Society*, 65.
20 Shamir, 'Egyptian Rule', 228; for the economic development of Palestine in the eighteenth century see the seminal work of Schölch, *Palestine in Transformation*.
21 Doumani, *Rediscovering Palestine*, 106.
22 Divine, *Politics and Society*, 72-73; Shamir, 'Egyptian Rule', 228.
23 Idinopulos, *Weathered by Miracles*, 46.
24 H. Laurens, *La Question de Palestine 1799-1922* (Paris: Fayard, 1999), 49.
25 Ben-Arieh, *The Old City*, 107-110; Idinopulos, *Weathered by Miracles*, 46.
26 I. Pappe, 'The Rise and Fall of the Husaynis, 1840-1922', *Jerusalem Quarterly File*, Issue 10 (2000).
27 See Chapter 4.
28 Pappe, 'The Rise and Fall of the Husaynis'.
29 R. Brunelli, *Storia di Gerusalemme* (Milan: Oscar Mondadori, 1990), 258; N. Schwake, 'Le Développement du Réseau Hospitalier en Palestine', in *De Bonaparte à Balfour: La France, l'Europe Occidentale et la Palestine 1799-1917*, eds. D. Trimbour and R. Aaronsohn (Paris: CNRS, 2001), 111-112.
30 Ben-Arieh, *The Old City*, 115.

31 D. Kushner, 'Intercommunal Strife in Palestine During the Late Ottoman Period', *Asia and African Studies*, no. 18 (1984): 191.
32 Literature on the *Tanzimat* is vast. See for instance these contributions: E. Zürcher, *Turkey. A Modern History* (London: I.B.Tauris, 1993), 53. B. Lewis, *The Emergence of Modern Turkey*, 3rd edn (Oxford: Oxford Press University, 2002), 107; R.H. Davison, *Nineteenth Century Ottoman Reforms and Diplomacy* (Istanbul: Isis Press, 1999); M.S. Hanioğlu, *A Brief History of the Late Ottoman Empire* (Princeton: Princeton University Press, 2008).
33 J. McCarthy, *The Ottoman Turks* (London: Longman, 1997); S.J. Shaw and E.K. Shaw, eds., *History of the Ottoman Empire and Modern Turkey*, vol. 2 (Cambridge: Cambridge University Press, 1977), 55.
34 McCarthy, *The Ottoman Turks*, 298-299.
35 See Chapter 2 for details on the Capitulary system.
36 Hanioğlu, *A Brief History*, 106.
37 Divine, *Politics and Society*, 107; McCarthy, *The Ottoman Turks*, 297; S. Deringil, *The Well-Protected Domains* (London: I.B.Tauris, 1999), 11 and 175-176.
38 Zürcher, *Turkey*, 81-85; Hanioğlu, *A Brief History*, 123-129.
39 Zürcher, *Turkey*, 97-100; Hanioğlu, *A Brief History*, 150-151.
40 Shaw and Shaw, *History of the Ottoman Empire*, 89.
41 C. Nicault, 'Retour à la Jérusalem Ottoman', in *Jérusalem 1850-1948*, ed. C. Nicault, 92 (Paris: Éditions Autrement, 1999); in the last five decades of Ottoman rule it is possible to see that the average mandate for a governor was two years.
42 H. Gerber, *Ottoman Rule in Jerusalem* (Berlin: Klaus Schwarz Verlag, 1985), 93; P. Schoenberg, 'Palestine in the Year 1914' (PhD Thesis, New York University, New York 1978), 470. According to Gerber attached to the *sancak* of Jerusalem there was the sub-district of Majdal that was eventually abolished in 1909 and replaced by the sub-district of Beersheba. Using British sources he argues that the sub-district of Nazareth was detached from the province of Nablus and attached to Jerusalem, but because of logistical problems it was abrogated in 1909.
43 Y. Avcı and V. Lemire, 'De la Modernité Administrative à la Modernisation Urbain: une Réévaluation de la Municipalité Ottomane de Jérusalem 1867-1917', in *Municipalités Méditerranéennes*, ed. N. Lafi (Berlin: Klaus Schwarz Verlag, 2005), 73. Divine, *Politics and Society*, 115.
44 R. Kark, 'The Jerusalem Municipality', *Asia and African Studies*, no. 14 (1980): 141.

45 Gerber, *Ottoman Rule in Jerusalem*, 7.
46 N. Libertun de Duren, 'Jerusalem at the Beginning of the Twentieth Century', *City Vision*, MIT (2004): 1; see M. Gilbert, *Jerusalem in the Twentieth Century* (London: Chatto & Windus, 1996).
47 Libertun de Duren, 'Jerusalem at the Beginning of the Twentieth Century', 2-3; see M. Gilbert, *Jerusalem Rebirth of a City* (London: Chatto & Windus, 1985).
48 B. Abu Manneh, 'The Rise of the Sanjak of Jerusalem in the Late Nineteenth Century', in *The Palestinians and the Conflict*, ed. G. Ben Dor (Haifa: Haifa University, 1982), 23-24.
49 Gerber, *Ottoman Rule in Jerusalem*, 96; Kushner, *To Be Governor of Jerusalem*, 119-120.
50 Gerber, *Ottoman Rule in Jerusalem*, 97.
51 Gerber, *Ottoman Rule in Jerusalem*, 100.
52 D. Kushner, 'The Ottoman Governors of Palestine', *Middle Eastern Studies* 23 (July 1987): 280.
53 In relation to Ekrem Bey see Kushner, *To Be Governor of Jerusalem*.
54 Kushner, *To Be Governor of Jerusalem*, 276-278.
55 Laurens, *La Question de Palestine*, 150.
56 Gerber, *Ottoman Rule in Jerusalem*, 100.
57 Gerber, *Ottoman Rule in Jerusalem*, 113. The Encyclopaedia of Islam defines the term *Baladiyya* (Arabic for the Turkish *Belediye*) as a modern institution of European style as against earlier Islamic forms of urban organisation.
58 H. Gerber, 'A New Look at the Tanzimat: The Case of the Province of Jerusalem', in *Palestine in the Late Ottoman Period*, ed. D. Kushner (Leiden: E.J. Brill, 1986), 39; Gerber, *Ottoman Rule in Jerusalem*, 115-116.
59 Gerber, 'The Case of the Province of Jerusalem', 42.
60 Kark, 'The Jerusalem Municipality', 119.
61 Kark, 'The Jerusalem Municipality'; Gerber, *Ottoman Rule in Jerusalem*, 114.
62 Kark, 'The Jerusalem Municipality', 120. Kark quotes a letter addressed by the Governor of Jerusalem Nazif Paşa to the Prussian consul in Jerusalem in November 1867 about the constitution of the Municipal Council and its composition. The letter is conserved at the Israeli State Archives (ISA).
63 See Avcı and Lemire, 'De la Modernité Administrative à la Modernisation Urbain', 94; for a thorough discussion of the administrative reforms of the late eighteenth century affecting Jerusalem see Gerber, *Ottoman Rule in Jerusalem*, Chapter 4.

64 Kark, 'The Jerusalem Municipality', 118-119; Avcı and Lemire, 'De la Modernité Administrative', 97.
65 G. Young, *Corps de Droit Ottoman* (Paris, 1905), Vol. 1, 73.
66 Kark, 'The Jerusalem Municipality', 125; Ben-Arieh, *The Old City*, 123.
67 Kark, 'The Jerusalem Municipality', 131-132.
68 MAE, Nantes, Constantinople Ambassade Série D, Carton 15, Governor of Jerusalem to French Consul, Jerusalem 11 August 1905.
69 NARA, RG 84, Vol. 57, 154, Governor of Jerusalem Cevdet Paşa to American Consul, 26 October 1911.
70 NARA, RG 84, Vol. 72, File 310, Governor of Jerusalem to Glazebrook, 5 August 1915.
71 NARA, RG 84, Vol. 69/A, Vice Consul to Department of State, Jerusalem, 24 January 1914.
72 Kushner, *To Be Governor of Jerusalem*, 112.
73 MAE, Nantes, Jérusalem Série B, Carton 7, Bullettin de la Chambre de Commerce, Jérusalem, July 1909. An excellent article on the question of water has been published by V. Lemire, 'L'Eau, le Consul et l'Ingénieur: Hydropolitique et Concurrences Diplomatique à Jérusalem, 1908-1914', in *France and the Middle East*, ed. M. Abitbol (Jerusalem: Hebrew University Magnes Press, 2004), 125-137.
74 MAE, Nantes, Jérusalem Série B, Carton 7, Public Message of the Municipality, Jerusalem, 7 June 1911.
75 NARA, RG 84, Vol. 69/A, Vice Consul to Department of State, Jerusalem, 24 January 1914: 'From a political point of view the award of concessions of such importance to French interests is in line with the French policy of political domination in Syria and Palestine. [...] From a municipal point of view, there is no doubt that these concessions will be of great benefit to the city. An adequate water supply is one of the most urgent needs of Jerusalem, as the lack of rain for seven months of the year, causes a great deal of suffering in the city. The tramways will be no doubt open up the suburban sections and relieve the overcrowding and unsanitary conditions prevailing in within the walled part of the city.'
76 Kushner, *To Be Governor of Jerusalem*, 122.
77 Schoenberg, 'Palestine in the Year 1914', 499. He also states that according to American sources one Jew and one Christian along with ten Muslims composed this police force. According to Ben-Arieh, *The Old City*, 124, the police force was composed of 14 men, one of them Jewish.
78 Avcı and Lemire, 'De la Modernité Administrative', 111.

79 Gerber, *Ottoman Rule in Jerusalem*, 114-115
80 Avcı and Lemire, 'De la Modernité Administrative', 105.
81 See all documents available in MAE, Nantes, Constantinople Ambassade Série D, Carton 15, August 1905.
82 Ben-Arieh, *The Old City*, 125: 'At the end of the 19th century, elections were held for Jerusalem Municipality […] about 700 Muslims and 300 Christians too part in the voting.'
83 Kark, 'The Jerusalem Municipality', 124: 'In the municipal elections of 1908, for example, votes were cast by 700 Moslems, 300 Christians and 200 Jews'.
84 Kark, 'The Jerusalem Municipality', 122; a law governing the elections of the Municipal Councils was promulgated in 1875, then redefined in 1877, according the taxpayers the right to elect council members.
85 D. Yellin, *Jerusalem of Yesterday* (Hebrew), vol. 1 (Jerusalem, 1972), 192-223. Quoted also in Kark, 'The Jerusalem Municipality', 123; Gerber, *Ottoman Rule in Jerusalem*, 116.
86 Yellin, *The Jerusalem of Yesterday*, 192-193; also in Gerber, *Ottoman Rule in Jerusalem*, 116.
87 M.J. Reimer, 'Becoming Urban: Town Administration in Transjordan', *International Journal Of Middle East Studies*, no. 37 (2005): 191.
88 Gerber, *Ottoman Rule in Jerusalem*, 136.
89 C.V. Findley, 'The Evolution of the System of Provincial Administration as Viewed from the Center', in *Palestine in the Late Ottoman Period*, ed. D. Kushner (Leiden: E.J. Brill, 1986), 21; Gerber, *Ottoman Rule in Jerusalem*, 137. Interesting is a document from the Ottoman Archives in Istanbul that gives us some hints on the structure of the General Council for the *vilayet*. OA, DH.UMUM 62/34, 25 Safer 1333 (11 January 1915), *Mutasarrıf* to Interior Ministry, Jerusalem: 'Because of new elections here, members of the General Assembly were convoked on 15 December 1331. Since the Mayor of Jaffa is also a member of the assembly and he is under investigation by the assembly. It has been asked from the Jaffa administration (*kaimmakanlık*) whether the mayors should be excluded from assembly membership, counting them as government employees. Although the causes for dismemberment for general assembly are defined in the article 109 of the law of administration of the *vilayet*, the situation of the mayors who are later assigned as government employees is not clear and since the mayor of Jaffa has been locally taken from his post, we await for instructions about other mayors who are also members of the general assembly of Jerusalem.'

90 Gerber, *Ottoman Rule in Jerusalem*, 138.
91 Schoenberg, 'Palestine in the Year 1914', 484.
92 NARA, Consular Post, Vol. 69/A, Vice Consul to Department of State, Jerusalem, 9 February 1914.
93 Gerber, *Ottoman Rule in Jerusalem*, 130-131; H. Gerber, 'The Ottoman Administration of the Sanjaq of Jerusalem 1890-1908', *Asia and African Studies* 12, no. 1 (1978): 59; Findley, 'The Evolution of the System of Provincial Administration as Viewed from the Center', 10-11.
94 Schoenberg, 'Palestine in the Year 1914', 485.
95 Gerber, *Ottoman Rule in Jerusalem*, 132. Population statistics are discussed in the second part of this chapter.
96 Gerber, 'The Administration of the Sanjaq of Jerusalem', 55.
97 Gerber, 'The Administration of the Sanjaq of Jerusalem', 55-56.
98 D. Farhi, 'Documents on the Attitude of the Ottoman Government Towards the Jewish Settlement in Palestine After the Revolution of the Young Turks', in *Studies on Palestine During the Ottoman Period*, ed. M. Ma'oz (Jerusalem: Magnes Press, 1975), 190-191.
99 OA, DH. EUM. 4 ŞB 23/5, Mutasarrıf to Ministry of Interior, Jerusalem, 24 Ramazan 1332 (16 August 1914).
100 ASMAE, Italian Embassy in Turkey, 122, Italian Foreign Office to Baron Mayor des Planches (Italian Ambassador in Istanbul), Rome, 22 April 1911.
101 ASMAE, Italian Embassy in Turkey, 122, Italian Consul (Senni) to Italian Foreign Office, Jerusalem, 25 April 1914.
102 ASMAE, Italian Embassy in Turkey, 122, Senni to Italian Embassy in Istanbul, Jerusalem, 6 April 1915.
103 ASMAE, Italian Embassy in Turkey, 122, Senni to Italian Foreign Office, Jerusalem, 9 July 1915.
104 ASMAE, Italian Embassy in Turkey, 122, Italian Foreign Office to Senni, Rome, 28 July 1915.
105 Gerber, *Ottoman Rule in Jerusalem*, 123.
106 ASMAE, Italian Embassy in Turkey, 122, Senni to Italian Embassy in Istanbul, Jerusalem, 6 April 1915.
107 Gerber, *Ottoman Rule in Jerusalem*, 127-128.
108 Khalidi, *Palestinian Identity* (New York: Columbia University Press, 1997), 59.
109 P.S. Khoury, *Urban Notables and Arab Nationalism* (Cambridge: Cambridge University Press, 1983), 10.

110 A. Hourani, 'Ottoman Reform and the Politics of Notables', in *The Modern Middle East*, eds. A. Hourani, P. Khoury and M.C. Wilson (London: I.B.Tauris, 1993), 87.
111 G. Baer, 'Jerusalem's Families of Notables and the Wakf in the Early 19th Century', in *Palestine in the Late Ottoman Period*, ed. D. Kushner (Leiden: E.J. Brill, 1986), 109.
112 Hourani, 'Ottoman Reform and the Politics of Notables', 89-90; A. Manna, 'Continuity and Change in the Socio-Political Elite in Palestine During the Late Ottoman Period', in *The Syrian Land in the 18th and 19th Century*, ed. T. Philipp (Stuttgart: Steiner, 1992), 11; Khoury, *Urban Notables*, 11.
113 For a detailed history of this family see B. Glass and R. Kark, *Sephardi Entrepreneurs in Jerusalem: The Valero Family 1800-1948* (Jerusalem: Gefen Publishing House, 2007).
114 Other important families in Jerusalem were the Dajamis, Alamis, Jarallahs and Nusseibehs: C. Nicault, *Une Histoire de Jérusalem 1850-1967* (Paris: CNRS Éditions, 2008), 109-110.
115 Divine, *Politics and Society*, 77.
116 Gerber, *Ottoman Rule in Jerusalem*, 106-109.
117 B. Kimmerling and J.S. Migdal, *Palestinians* (New York: The Free Press, 1993), 71; I. Pappe, *A History of Modern Palestine* (Cambridge: Cambridge University Press, 2004), 19.
118 Khalidi, *Palestinian Identity*, 39.
119 B. Abu-Manneh, 'Jerusalem in the Tanzimat Period: The New Ottoman Administration and the Notables', *Die Welt des Islams* 30 (1990): 40-41.
120 B. Abu-Manneh, 'Jerusalem in the Tanzimat Period:', 42-43; Nicault, *Une Histoire de Jérusalem*, 111.
121 Khalidi, *Palestinian Identity*, 65.
122 Khalidi, *Palestinian Identity*, 80-81.
123 Khoury, *Urban Notables*, 71.
124 I. Pappe, 'The Husayni Family Faces New Challenges', *Jerusalem Quarterly File*, Issue 11-12 (2001); Divine, *Politics and Society*, 146.
125 Pappe, 'The Husayni Family'.
126 Pappe, *A History of Modern Palestine*, 56-57.
127 MAE, Nantes, Constantinople Ambassade Série D, Carton 15, Ligue de la Patrie Arabe, 1905.
128 See the cases of Wasif Jawhariyyeh and Ihsan al-Turjman discussed in Chapter 4.

129 TNA: PRO FO 882/14, The Politics of Jerusalem, Cairo, 29 December 1916.
130 B. Vester Spafford, *Our Jerusalem* (New York: Arno Press, 1977), 252.
131 Khalidi, *Palestinian Identity*, 153.
132 C.V. Findley, *Bureaucratic Reform in the Ottoman Empire* (Princeton NJ: Princeton University Press, 1980), 253-254.
133 U.O. Schmelz, 'Population Characteristics of Jerusalem and Hebron Regions According to Ottoman Census of 1905', in *Ottoman Palestine 1800-1914*, ed. G.G. Gilbar (Leiden: E.J. Brill, 1990), 18.
134 Ibid.
135 The first distinction in the construction of a credible and consistent table representing the population of Jerusalem for the period from 1905 to 1922 is between sources. There are available primary sources as well as secondary sources in terms of reconstructions attempted by scholars and I will combine and analyse these different materials.
136 ASV, *Segr. Stato, Affari Eccl. Straordinari, Africa, Asia, Oceania*, Pos. 102, Fasc. 69, Robinson P. on the situation in Palestine, 1 February 1921.
137 MAE, Nantes, Constantinople Ambassade Série D, Carton 15, French Consul Gueyraud Communiqué au Department, Jerusalem 27 July 1909. The French consul states that from the beginning of the twentieth century the Jewish population of Jerusalem has grown from 35-40,000 to 45-50,000.
138 A. Schölch, 'Jerusalem in the 19th Century', in *Jerusalem in History*, ed. K.J Asali (Essex: Scorpion Publishing, 1989), 18.
139 ISA, RG 123.1, File 790/12, Report on Trade of the Consular District, Jerusalem 1911.
140 British consul Satow stated that in 1911 there were 350 British citizens living in Jerusalem.
141 Luncz, *Eretz Israel Almanac* 19 (1912/1913), 34; see also R. Kark and M. Oren-Nordheim, *Jerusalem and Its Environs* (Jerusalem: The Hebrew University Magnes Press, 2001), 29.
142 G. Biger, *An Empire in the Holy Land* (New York: St Martin's Press, 1994), 29.
143 LP, Davidson 396, Bishop Blyth to Archbishop, London, 20/08/1914.
144 O.G. Matson, *The American Colony Palestine Guide* (Jerusalem: The American Colony, 1913), 8-10.
145 TNA: PRO FO 882, The Politics of Jerusalem, Arab Bureau, Cairo, 29 December 1916. The report is of 1916; however the figures reported relate to the year 1914.

146 TNA: PRO WO 158/986, 1917. The figures reported are for the year 1914.
147 N. Bentwich, *Palestine of the Jews* (London: Kegan Paul, 1919), 106.
148 NARA, Consular Post, Vol. 69 A, Consular Sanitary Report, Jerusalem, 7 February 1914.
149 NARA, Consular Post, Vol. 69 A, Consular Sanitary Report, Jerusalem, 6 January 1915.
150 A. Ruppin, *Syria: An Economic Survey* (New York: Provisional Zionist Committee, 1918), 7-8; see also Kark and Oren-Nordheim, *Jerusalem and Its Environs*, 29.
151 R. Storrs, *The Memoirs of Sir Ronald Storrs* (New York: G.P. Putnam's Sons, 1937), 278-282.
152 Palestine Office of the Zionist Organisation quoted in Kark and Oren-Nordheim, *Jerusalem and Its Environs*, 29.
153 T. Segev, *One Palestine Complete* (New York: Henry Holt, 2001), 59.
154 Biger, *An Empire in the Holy Land*, 29.
155 F.F. Andrews, *The Holy Land Under Mandate*, vol. 2 (Boston: Houghton Mifflin Company, 1931), 29.
156 Ibid. Andrews states that in 1918 there were 300 Bokharans among the Jews and 300 Persians.
157 N. & H. Bentwich, *Mandate Memoirs 1918-1948* (London: The Hogarth Press, 1965), 48-49.
158 Schmelz, 'Population Characteristics of Jerusalem', 26. The figures are for the Jerusalem region (*kaza*).
159 The British census is available in PC, Reel 8, Box III, Jerusalem, 1922.
160 The single 'other' was a Druse; there were no Hindus living within the walls.
161 There were 5 Druses (1 male, 4 females); 489 Hindus (488 males, 1 female).
162 Bentwich, *Palestine of the Jews*, 106.
163 NARA, Consular Post, Vol. 69 A, Consular Sanitary Report, Jerusalem, 6 January 1915; TNA: PRO FO 882, The Politics of Jerusalem, Arab Bureau, Cairo, 29 December 1916.
164 ASV, *Segr. Stato, Affari Eccl. Straordinari, Africa, Asia, Oceania*, Pos. 102, Fasc. 69, Robinson P. on the situation in Palestine, 1 February 1921.
165 Schölch, 'Jerusalem in the 19th Century', 231.
166 Luncz, *Eretz Israel Almanac 19* (1912/1913), 34; LP, Davidson 396, Bishop Blyth to Archbishop, London, 20/08/1914.
167 See Table 1.
168 U.O. Schmelz, 'Population Characteristics of Jerusalem', 25.

169 For more details see the discussion on deportation during the war in Chapter 4.
170 Ben-Arieh, *The Old City*, 131.
171 R. Storrs, *Orientations* (London: Nicholson & Watson, 1943), 401.
172 L. Jacobs, *The Jewish Religion* (Oxford: Oxford University Press, 1995), 36; 'The name Ashkenaz in the Bible (Genesis 10:3) was identified in the Middle Ages with Germany, hence Ashkenazim, "Germans"'.
173 I. Kolatt, 'The Organization of the Jewish Population of Palestine and the Development of its Political Consciousness before World War I', in *Studies on Palestine During the Ottoman Period*, ed. M. Ma'oz (Jerusalem: Magnes Press, 1975), 211-214. See also E. Benbassa and A. Rodrigue, eds., *Sephardi Jewry: a History of the Judeo-Spanish Community 15th to 20th Centuries* (Berkeley: University of California Press, 2000).
174 Storrs, *The Memoirs*, 280-282; Ben-Arieh, *The Old City*, 357.
175 A. Jacobson, 'From Empire to Empire: Jerusalem in the Transition Between Ottoman and British Rule 1912-1920' (PhD thesis, The University of Chicago, Chicago, 2006), 127-130.
176 Jacobson, 'From Empire to Empire', 137-130; D. Friedlander and C. Goldscheider, *The Population of Israel* (New York: Columbia University Press, 1979), 15-18; D. Willner, *Nation-Building and Community in Israel* (Princeton NJ: Princeton University Press, 1969), 30-38.
177 Bukhara is a city in what is now Uzbekistan; most of the Bukharians moved at the beginning of the 20th century, either to the United States or to Palestine.
178 The Bukharian quarter is today populated by Ultra Orthodox Jews. Ben-Arieh, *The Old City*, 278 and 363.
179 Ben-Arieh, *The Old City*, 283.
180 Kolatt, 'The Organisation of the Jewish Population', 214-215.
181 Ben-Arieh, *The Old City*, 292-294.
182 Ben-Arieh, *The Old City*, 351-363.
183 A. O'Mahony, 'The Christian Communities of Jerusalem and the Holy Land: A Historical and Political Survey', in *The Christian Communities of Jerusalem and the Holy Land*, ed. A. O'Mahony, 4 (Cardiff: University of Wales Press, 2003).
184 A. Sanjian, 'The Armenian Church', in *The Christian Communities of Jerusalem and the Holy Land*, ed. A. O'Mahony (Cardiff: University of Wales Press, 2003), 58.
185 See Chapter 4 for more details. See also K. Hintlian, *History of the Armenians in the Holy Land* (Jerusalem: St. James Press, 1976).

186 H. Hagopian, 'The Armenians of Jerusalem and the Armenian Quarter', in *Christians in the Holy Land*, eds. M. Prior and W. Taylor (London: The World of Islam festival Trust, 1994), 125.
187 Ben-Arieh, *The Old City*, p. 193.
188 O'Mahony, 'The Christian Communities of Jerusalem and the Holy Land', 17.
189 Idinopulos, *Weathered by Miracles*, 86-87.
190 Ben-Arieh, *The Old City*, 193.
191 Ibid.
192 Ben-Arieh, *The Old City*, 135; According to a figure provided by the French consul in 1847, there were nearly 1,000 Turkish officials in Jerusalem (Nicault, 'Retour à la Jérusalem Ottoman', 45). We may presume a similar number was stationed at the beginning of the twentieth century as exigencies did not change radically.
193 The foreign presence in Jerusalem is discussed in Chapter 3.

Chapter 2

This Chapter is a revised and expanded version of the article R. Mazza, 'Churches at War: The Impact of the First World War on the Christian Institutions of Jerusalem, 1914-1920', *Middle Eastern Studies*, Vol. 45, No. 2 (2009): 207-227.

1 T. Ware, *The Orthodox Church* (London: Penguin Books, 1963), 18-19; S.P. Colbi, *Christianity* (Tel Aviv: Am Hassefer, 1969), 16.
2 O.L. Yarbrough, 'Early Christian Jerusalem. The City of the Cross', in *Jerusalem. Idea and Reality*, eds. T. Mayer and S. Ali Mourad, 69 (London: Routledge, 2008).
3 S. Roussos, 'The Greek Orthodox Patriarchate and Community of Jerusalem: Church, State and Identity', in *The Christian Communities of Jerusalem and the Holy Land*, ed. A. O'Mahony (Cardiff: University of Wales Press, 2003), 38.
4 Colbi, *Christianity*, 39; J. P. Valognes, *Vie et Mort des Chrétiens d'Orient* (Paris: Fayard, 1994), 503.
5 Ware, *The Orthodox Church*, 59.
6 See D. Chevallier, 'Non-Muslim Communities in Arab Cities', in *Christian and Jews in the Ottoman Empire*, eds. B. Braude and B. Lewis, Vol. 2, 159 (London: Holmes & Meier, 1982). See also 'Dhimma' *Encyclopaedia of Islam, Second Edition*,

http://www.encislam.brill.nl/subscriber/entry?entry=islam_SIM-1823, accessed 14/10/2008.
7   N. Moschopouls, *La Terre Sainte: Essai sur l'Histoire Politique et Diplomatique des Lieux Saints de la Chrétienté* (Athens: 1956), 142-143.
8   A. Pacini, ed, *Christian Communities in the Arab Middle East* (Oxford: Clarendon Press, 1998), 3.
9   C. Wardi, 'The Latin Patriarchate of Jerusalem', *Journal of the Middle East Society* 1, no. 3-4 (Autumn 1947): 6.
10 For a debate on the definition of *millet* see R.H. Davison, 'The Millets as Agents of Change in the Nineteenth Century Ottoman Empire', in B. Braude and B. Lewis (eds.), *Christian and Jews in Ottoman Empire*, Vol. 2, 319-337.
11 Pacini, *Christian Communities*, 5.
12 A. O'Mahony, 'Church, State and the Christian Communities and the Holy Places of Palestine', in *Christians in the Holy Land*, eds. M. Prior and W. Taylor (London: World of Islam Festival, 1994), 15.
13 McCarthy, *The Ottoman Turks*, 345.
14 I. Mancini, 'Cenni Storici sulla Custodia di Terra Santa,' in *La Custodia di Terra Santa e l'Europa*, ed. M. Piccirillo (Rome: Il Veltro Editrice, 1983), 16-17.
15 Colbi, *Christianity*, 62.
16 Ben-Arieh, *The Old City*, 193.
17 Colbi, *Christianity*, 105-106; O.F.A. Meinardus, *The Copts in Jerusalem* (Cairo: Costa Tsoumas & Co., 1960), 70-72.
18 Colbi, *Christianity*, 39.
19 Colbi, *Christianity*, 68.
20 Roussos, 'The Greek Orthodox Patriarchate', 39.
21 For a discussion of the events that affected the Orthodox and Catholic communities see Colbi, *Christianity*, 65-77.
22 W. Zander, 'On the Settlement of Disputes About the Christian Holy Places', *Israel Law Review* 8 (1973): 332.
23 Roussous, 'The Greek Orthodox Patriarchate', 41; Colbi, *Christianity*, 73.
24 T. Hummel, 'Between Eastern and Western Christendom: the Anglican Presence in Jerusalem', in *The Christian Communities of Jerusalem and the Holy Land*, ed. O'Mahony, 147.
25 Colbi, *Christianity*, 78; S. Khoury and N. Khoury, *A Survey of the History of the Orthodox Church of Jerusalem* (Amman: Feras Printing Press, 2002), 121; Roussos, 'The Greek Orthodox Patriarchate', 41.

26 D. Tsimhoni, 'The Greek Orthodox Patriarchate of Jerusalem', *Asian and African Studies* 112, no. 1 (March 1978): 78-84; A. Bertram and J.W.A. Young, eds., *The Orthodox Patriarchate of Jerusalem* (London: Oxford University Press, 1926), 25-33.
27 Capitulations, as privileges granted to foreign traders, existed earlier between the Ottoman Empire and Italian City States. See M. Piccirillo, ed., *La Custodia di Terra Santa e l'Europa* (Rome: Il Veltro Editrice, 1983).
28 B. Collin, 'La Francia e la Custodia di Terra Santa', in *La Custodia di Terra Santa*, ed. Piccirillo, 74.
29 Moschopoulos, *La Terre Sainte*, 10; A. Giovannelli, *La Santa Sede e la Palestine* (Rome: Edizioni Studium, 2000), 6.
30 O'Mahony, 'The Christian Communities of Jerusalem', 7.
31 Possetto, *Il Patriarcato Latino* (Milan: Crociata, 1938), 562-568; Franciscans, *Custodia di Terra Santa* (Jerusalem: Franciscan Printing Press, 1951).
32 See Dominique Trimbur, 'Une Présence Française en Palestine: Notre Dame de France', *Bulletin du CRFJ*, no. 3 (Autumn 1998): 32-58.
33 For details on French pilgrimages see C. Nicault, 'Foi et Politique: Les Pèlerinages Française en Terre Sainte (1850-1914)', in *De Bonaparte á Balfour*, eds. D. Trimbur and R. Aaronsohn (Paris: CNRS Editions, 2001), 311-342. For Italian pilgrimages see L. Rostagno, 'Pellegrinaggi Italiani in età Ottomana: Percorsi, Esperienze, Momenti d'Incontro', *Oriente Moderno*, Vol. XVII, No. 1 (1998): 63-157.
34 Giovannelli, *La Santa Sede*, 6-7.
35 Sanjian, 'The Armenian Church', 63.
36 Sanjian, 'The Armenian Church', 67; Ben-Arieh, *The Old City*, 193.
37 See Sanjian, 'The Armenian Church'; Zürcher, *Turkey. A Modern Turkey*, 119-121; for a survey of the Armenian question see D. Gwynne Dyer, 'Turkish "Falsifiers" and Armenian "Deceivers"', *Middle Eastern Studies* 12 (January 1976): 99-107.
38 See Pacini, *Christian Communities*, 342; Colbi, *Christianity*, 67; A.H. De Groot, 'The Historical Development of the Capitulary Regime in the Ottoman Middle East from the 15th to the 19th Centuries', *Oriente Moderno* 3 (2003): 596.
39 De Groot, 'The Historical Development', 577.
40 J. Thobie, *Intérêts et Impérialism Française dans l'Empire Ottoman (1895-1914)* (Paris: Publications de la Sorbonne, 1977), 14-17; J.B. Angell, 'The Turkish Capitulations', *The American Historical Review* 6, no. 2 (January 1901): 256.

41 M.H. Van den Boogert, *The Capitulations and the Ottoman Legal System* (Leiden: Brill, 2005), 7.
42 D. Goffman, *The Ottoman Empire and Early Modern Europe* (Cambridge: Cambridge University Press, 2002), 187-188.
43 Goffman, *The Ottoman Empire*, 228-229.
44 See Ben-Arieh, *The Old City*.
45 NARA, Consular Post, Vol. 69, Governor of Jerusalem to Glazebrook, 22 September 1914, Jerusalem: 'With the abolition of the capitulations in the Ottoman Empire, the foreign post offices will have to close on the morning of 1 October 1914.'
46 ASMAE, Serie Politica P, Busta 498, Conte Senni to Italian Embassy in Istanbul, 20 September 1914, Jerusalem.
47 Christian Churches relied on income from pilgrims and remittances from foreign countries; however, Churches also established local enterprises. For the economic conditions of Jerusalem in Ottoman times see Gerber, *Ottoman Rule in Jerusalem 1800-1914*.
48 Conde de Ballobar, *Diario de Jerusalen* (Madrid: Nerea, 1996), 63.
49 W. Zander, *Israel and the Holy Places of Christendom* (London: Weidenfeld & Nicolson, 1971), 45.
50 For the whole history of the early documents and Ottoman firmans see P. Baldi, *The Question of the Holy Places*, vol. 1 (Rome: Typographia Pontificia, 1919); see also Zander, *Israel and the Holy Places of Christendom*.
51 The full text of the Firman dated 8 February 1852 is available in: B. Collin, *Pour une Solution des Liuex Saints* (Paris: G.P. Maisonneuve et Larose, 1974), 30-32.
52 R. Heacock, 'La Palestine dans les Relations Internationales 1798-1917', in *De Bonaparte á Balfour*, eds. D. Trimbur and R. Aaronsohn (Paris: CNRS Editions, 2001), 37-39.
53 R. Lapidoth, 'Gerusalemme: Aspetti Politici e Giuridici', in *La Questione di Gerusalemme*, ed. P. Pieraccini (Bologna: Il Mulino, 2005), 39.
54 TNA: PRO FO 371/3061, Allenby's Report, Jerusalem, 11 December 1917.
55 TNA: PRO CAB 27/1, British Desiderata in Turkey in Asia, London, 8 April 1915.
56 TNA: PRO FO 371/3061, Sykes, London, 13 November 1917.
57 ACTS, *Diario della Guerra*, 1917. A discussion about German and Austrian intervention in favour of the local population is to be found in I. Friedman, *Germany, Turkey and Zionism, 1897-1918* (Oxford:

Oxford University Press, 1977); ISA, RG 67, 419/86, German Consul report, Jaffa 11 December 1914.
58 LP, Davidson 398, Renwick to Lord Bryce, Jerusalem, 25 September 1914.
59 Giovannelli, *La Santa Sede*, 19.
60 LP, Davidson 396, Archbishop, 28 September 1914.
61 Hummel, 'Between Eastern and Western Christendom', 160.
62 Hummel, 'Between Eastern and Western Christendom', 160-161.
63 I.M. Okkenhaug, *The Quality of Heroic Living* (Leiden: Brill, 2002), 44.
64 Giovannelli, *La Santa Sede*, 19.
65 TNA: PRO FO 371/3388, Clayton to Sykes, 16 January 1918 see also Khoury and Khoury, *A Survey*, 196-198.
66 Tsimhoni, 'The Greek Orthodox Patriarchate of Jerusalem', 84.
67 Roussos, 'The Greek Orthodox Patriarchate', 44.
68 LP, Davidson 398, Renwick to Lord Bryce, Jerusalem, 25 September 1914.
69 Tsimhoni, 'The Greek Orthodox Patriarchate of Jerusalem', 84-85; Bertram and Anton, *The Orthodox Patriarchate of Jerusalem*, 95-112; Roussos, 'The Greek Orthodox Patriarchate of Jerusalem', 44-46.
70 TNA: PRO FO 371/4000, Pro Memoria, London, 7 August 1918: 'The Greek Brotherhood of the Holy Sepulchre in Jerusalem had found itself in severe financial straits, which were temporarily relieved by means of loans at usurious rates. It is now established that a syndicate of rich Jews have been buying up the bonds of these loans with the object of foreclosing on the termination of the present moratorium, and of thus becoming masters of the property held by the Greek Church for centuries past.'
71 Roussos, 'The Greek Orthodox Patriarchate', 44-45.
72 Conde de Ballobar, *Diario*, 97 and 176. For a description of the Holy Fire ceremony see V. Clark, *Holy Fire. The Battle for Christ's Tomb* (London: Macmillan, 2005).
73 Conde de Ballobar, *Diario*, 176.
74 NARA, Consular Post, Vol. 75, Glazebrook to American Embassy in Istanbul, Jerusalem, 23 June 1916: 'Sometime ago I wired [the] State Department in interest of Greek Patriarchate asking that needs of his community be made as public as possible in America. This appeal brought no result and Patriarch is again urging me to call attention of members of Greek Orthodox Church America to dire financial distress of this Patriarchate […]'
75 Tsimhoni, 'The Greek Orthodox Patriarchate of Jerusalem', 85.

76 Possetto, *Il Patriarcato Latino*, 431-432.
77 For a survey on the American Colony see: M. Shamir, '"Our Jerusalem": Americans in the Holy Land and Protestant Narratives of National Entitlement', *American Quarterly* 55, no.1 (March 2003): 29-60; H. Dudman and R. Kark, eds., *The American Colony* (Jerusalem: Carta, 1998).
78 NARA, Consular Post, Vol. 70, Secretary of State to Glazebrook, Washington DC, 22 December 1915. B. Vester Spafford, 'Jerusalem, My Home', *National Geographic* 126 (December 1964): 838.
79 Vester Spafford, *Our Jerusalem*, 246.
80 Vester Spafford, *Our Jerusalem*, 243-244.
81 Colbi, *Christianity*, 107.
82 TNA: PRO FO 141/666, British Legation Addis Ababa to Sir Reginald Wingate, Addis Ababa, 31 December 1917.
83 TNA: PRO FO 141/666, Arab Bureau to British Legation Addis Ababa, Cairo, 15 January 1918.
84 LP, Davidson 397, MacInnes to Archbishop, Jerusalem, 7 May 1918.
85 Sanjian, 'The Armenian Church', 68.
86 J.H. Melkon Rose, *Armenians of Jerusalem: Memories of Life in Palestine* (London: The Radcliffe Press, 1993), 79; Sanjian, 'The Armenian Church', 69; LP, Davidson 397, MacInnes to Archbishop, Jerusalem, 7 May 1918.
87 Mancini, 'Cenni Storici sulla Custodia di Terra Santa', 16.
88 Giovannelli, *La Santa Sede*, 3.
89 ASMAE, Archivio di Gabinetto, Pacco 185, Diotallevi to Cimino, Jerusalem, 6 March 1918.
90 As explained earlier, Ottoman law permitted only individuals, and not institutions, to be the owners of religious estates. A change took place in 1912, allowing for property to be in the name of an institution rather than an individual; however, ownership still belonged to the individual, and not the institution.
91 Fr Eutimio Castellani was in charge of the daily business of the Custody due to the absence of the *Custos*, who after travelling to Istanbul was recalled to Italy.
92 ACTS, Diario della Guerra, 1914.
93 ACTS, Diario della Guerra, November 1914: '3 November. [...] 24 Franciscan nuns, 19 Carmelitan nuns, 20 Benedictine nuns, 17 Franciscan of the tertiary order nuns, 60 orphans and other 12 nuns came to Casa Nova.' '7 November 15 White Fathers came to St Saviour.'

94 ACTS, Diario di Guerra, 1915.
95 ASV, *Segreteria di Stato-Guerra-111*, Card Gasparri to Card Dolci, Vatican City, 3 September 1915.
96 ASV, *Sacra Congregazione degli Affari Ecclesiastici Straordinari Africa-Asia-Oceania*, Pos. 13. Fasc. 5, Card Dolci to Card Gasparri, Istanbul, 5 April 1915.
97 NARA, Consular Post, Vol. 69, Governor of Jerusalem to Glazebrook, Jerusalem, 22 December 1914.
98 NARA, Consular Post, Vol. 69, Government of Jerusalem, 20 December 1914.
99 ACTS, Diario della Guerra, 1915.
100 NARA, Consular Post, Vol. 73, Custody of the Holy Land, 8 November 1915.
101 ACTS, Diario della Guerra, April-June 1916.
102 Giovannelli, *La Santa Sede*, 4.
103 TNA: PRO CAB 27/23 Balfour to De Salis reported to Wingate, 23 January 1918.
104 ASMAE, Archivio di Gabinetto, Pacco 185, Diotallevi to Cimino, Jerusalem, 6 March 1918.
105 TNA: PRO CAB 27/23, From G.O.C. to C.I.G.S., Cairo, 25 January 1918.
106 MAE, Jérusalem Série B, Carton 157 2-6, Card Gasparri to Denys Cochin, Vatican City, 26 June 1917.
107 B. Collin, *Les Lieux Saints* (Paris: Les Editions International, 1948), 149.
108 Giovannelli, *La Santa Sede*, 27. On 10 April 1924 Cardinal Gasparri sent a telegram to the Latin Patriarch ordering him to suspend the liturgical honours granted to the French. S. Minerbi, *The Vatican and Zionism* (Oxford: Oxford University Press, 1990), 56.
109 Giovannelli, *La Santa Sede*, 36; Collin, *Les Lieux Saints*, 149-150.
110 D. Fabrizio, ed., *Diario di Terra Santa* (Milan: Edizioni Biblioteca Francescana, 2002).
111 Fabrizio, *Diario di Terra Santa*, 12-13.
112 See tables in Chapter 1.
113 O'Mahony, 'The Christian Communities of Jerusalem', 17-20.
114 Pappe, *A History of Modern Palestine*, 56-62.
115 Khalidi, *Palestinian Identity*, 20.
116 According to Ilan Pappe the Christian-Muslim association represented the first ever political party in Palestine; *A History of Modern Palestine*, 80.

117 A. O'Mahony, 'Palestinian Christians: Religion, Politics and Society, c. 1800-1948', in *Palestinian Christians*, ed. O'Mahony (London: Melisende, 1999), 45-53.
118 J. Gray, *A History of Jerusalem* (London: Robert Hale, 1969), 297.
119 ASV, *Segr. Stato, Affari Eccl. Straordinari, Africa-Asia-Oceania*, Pos. 53, Fasc. 39, Committee 'Hijos de Palestina' to Latin Patriarchate, Mexico, 5 January 1919.
120 ASV, *Segr. Stato, Affari Eccl. Straordinari, Africa-Asia-Oceania*, Pos. 53, Fasc. 39, Apostolic See Bolivia to Secretary of State Card Gasparri, La Paz, 30 November 1918.
121 Jacobson, 'From Empire to Empire', 251.
122 ISA, RG 2, 4/140, Ronald Storrs, Jerusalem, 4 November 1918. It is not clear how the delegation addressed Storrs and how Storrs reacted.
123 O'Mahony, 'The Christian Communities of Jerusalem', 19.
124 TNA: PRO FO 608/96, J.M. Camp. (Asst. Political Officer), to Chief Administrator OETA and Military Governor, Jerusalem, 12 August 1919.
125 P. Pieraccini, 'Le Patriarcat Latin de Jérusalem et la France', in *De Balfour à Ben Gourion*, eds. D. Trimbur and R. Aaronsohn (Paris: CRFJ, 2008), 319.
126 MAE, Nantes, Jérusalem, Série B, Carton 114, Report by Durieux, Jerusalem, 30 January 1919.
127 Pieraccini, 'Le Patriarcat Latin de Jérusalem et la France', 321.
128 NARA, Consular Post, Vol. 87, Supreme Commission of the Palestine Assemblies to the Government of the United States of America, Haifa, 27 November 1919.
129 NARA, Consular Post, Vol. 87.
130 NARA, Consular Post, Vol. 87, Literary Club to American Representative in Jerusalem, Jerusalem, 20 August, 1919.
131 ASV, *Segr. Stato, Affari Eccl. Straordinari Asia-Africa-Oceania*, Pos. 53, Fasc. 40, Christian Muslim Association to Vatican, 21 October 1919.
132 ASV, *Segr. Stato, Affari Eccl. Straordinari Asia-Africa-Oceania*, Pos. 53, Fasc. 40, Arab Committee, Jerusalem, 17 May 1920.
133 ASV, *Segr. Stato, Affari Eccl. Straordinari Asia-Africa-Oceania*, Pos. 53, Fasc. 42, Literary Club to Vatican, Jerusalem, 21 September 1919.
134 NARA, Consular Post Vol. 91, Islamic-Christian Conference to American Representative, Nablus, 16 January 1920.
135 PC, The Paper of Sir Ronald Storrs, Reel 7, Box III, Report 4613/G, Storrs, November 1921.

136 MAE, Nantes, Jérusalem Série B, Carton 114, Report by Durieux (Delegate of the French High Commissioner), Jerusalem, 30 January 1919.
137 O'Mahony, 'The Christian Communities of Jerusalem', 20.
138 TNA: PRO FO 608/99, Report by General Money, Jerusalem, 31 March 1919.

Chapter 3

1 M. Grindea, *The Image of Jerusalem* (New York: University of Rochester, 1968), 134-136.
2 R. Saunders, *The Concept of the Foreign* (Oxford: Lexington Books, 2003), 3.
3 Pappe, *A History of Modern Palestine*, 33.
4 Pappe, *A History of Modern Palestine*, 32-33.
5 Pappe, *A History of Modern Palestine*, 6.
6 See some definitions in E. Badone and S.R. Roseman, 'Approaches to the Anthropology of Pilgrimage and Tourism', in *Intersecting Journeys*, eds. E. Badone and S.R. Roseman (Chicago: University of Illinois, 2004), 10.
7 S. Coleman and J. Elsner, eds. *Pilgrimage* (Cambridge MA: Harvard University Press, 1995), 6.
8 See J. Krammer, 'Austrian Pilgrimage to the Holy Land', in *Austrian Presence in the Holy Land in the 19th and early 20th Century*, ed. M. Wrba (Tel Aviv: Austrian Embassy, 1996), 66-80.
9 The Nebi Musa Festival expressed Muslim reverence for the Prophet Moses; it coincided with the Christian Easter festivities, and consisted of many pilgrimages and marches to and from the burial site of Moses on the road to Jericho from Jerusalem. See T.A. Idinopulos, *Jerusalem Blessed, Jerusalem Cursed* (Chicago: Ivan R. Dee, 1991), 271-272.
10 D. Hopwood, 'The Resurrection of Our Eastern Brethren: Russia and Orthodox Arab Nationalism in Jerusalem', in *Studies on Palestine During the Ottoman Period*, ed. M. Ma'oz (Jerusalem: Magnes Press, 1975), 395-396.
11 ISA, RG 123.1, 790/12, H.E. Satow, Report on Consular District Year 1911. See also Y. Ben-Arieh, *Jerusalem in the 19th Century. The New City* (New York: St Martin's Press, 1984), 304-305.
12 Tsimhoni, 'The Greek Orthodox Patriarchate of Jerusalem,' 84; Roussos, 'The Greek Orthodox Patriarchate', 44.

13 Nicault, 'Retour à la Jérusalem Ottomane', 65-67.
14 In relation to this event see all material available in MAE, Nantes, Série B, Carton 33.
15 Idinopulos, *Weathered by Miracles*, 17.
16 Trimbur, 'Une Présence Française en Palestine', 35-38.
17 See the publication 'L'Italia e la Palestina' in MAE, Archivio di Gabinetto, Pacco 163, S. Benigno, 1917.
18 See D. Hopwood, *The Russian Presence in Syria and Palestine 1843-1914* (Oxford: Clarendon Press, 1969).
19 Y. Ben-Arieh, 'The Growth of Jerusalem in the Nineteenth Century', *Annals of the Association of American Geographers* 65, no. 2 (June 1975): 263.
20 Ben-Arieh, *The New City*, 300.
21 G.G. Gilbar, 'The Growing Economic Involvement of Palestine with the West, 1865-1914', in *Palestine in the Late Ottoman Period*, ed. D. Kushner (Leiden: E.J. Brill, 1986), 202. More information can be found in the 'Bulletin de la Chambre de Commerce d'Industrie e d'Agriculture de Palestine' from 1909.
22 For an overview of the tourist guides of Jerusalem see: E. Bosworth, 'The Land of Palestine in the Late Ottoman Period as mirrored in Western Guide Books', *British Society for Middle Eastern Studies (Bulletin)* 13, no. 1 (1986):36-44.
23 Ben-Arieh, *The Old City*, 56; Idinopulos, *Weathered by Miracles*, 109-110.
24 C.M. Watson, *The Story of Jerusalem* (London: J.M. Dent & Sons, 1912), 286.
25 Ben-Arieh, *The New City*, 388-389.
26 ISA, RG 123.1, 790/12, H.E. Satow, Report on Consular District Year 1911.
27 Ibid.
28 Quoted in Ben-Arieh, *The New City*, 389.
29 Ben-Arieh, *The New City*, 385-390; Khalidi, *Palestinian Identity*, 47.
30 Locals were employed in hotels, restaurants, hospitals, shops and transport: L. Harry Charles, *A Guide to Jerusalem and Judea* (London: Thomas Cook & Son, 1924); E. Reynolds-Ball, *Jerusalem* (London: A. & C. Black Ltd, 1924). For a discussion of the local economy before 1914 see Gilbar, 'The Growing Economic Involvement', 188-210.
31 Ben-Arieh, *The New City*, 389.
32 Matson, *Guidebook to Jerusalem*, 17-18.

33 TNA: PRO, FO 195/2084, Dickson to de Bunsen, Jerusalem, 13 November 1900; TNA: PRO, FO 195/2084, Wheeler and Masterman to Dickson, Jerusalem 13 November 1900.
34 Ben-Arieh, *The New City*, 388.
35 J. Thobie, *Intérêts et Impérialism Français dans l'Empire Ottoman*, 158-161.
36 NARA, Consular Post, Vol. 69A, Report on Commerce and Industries of the Jerusalem Consular District, Jerusalem, 15 March 1915.
37 R. Kark, *American Consuls in the Holy Land* (Jerusalem: The Magnes Press, 1994) 29.
38 S.M. Paul and W.G. Dever, eds., *Biblical Archaeology* (Jerusalem: Keter, 1973), ix.
39 Y. Ben-Arieh, *The Rediscovery of the Holy Land in the Nineteenth Century* (Jerusalem: The Magnes Press, 1979), 133-139.
40 Krammer, 'Austrian Pilgrimage', 67.
41 See Idinopulos, *Weathered by Miracles*, 86-106.
42 A.L. Tibawi, *British Interest in Palestine 1800-1901* (Oxford: Oxford University Press, 1961), 185; Ben-Arieh, *The Rediscovery of the Holy Land*, 195. The Founding meeting of the Exploration Fund proclaimed that the aims of the Palestine Exploration Fund were the investigation of the archaeology, geography, geology, and natural history of Palestine.
43 For a history of the Palestine Exploration Fund see: J.J. Moscrop, *Measuring Jerusalem* (London: Leicester University Press, 2000).
44 Moscrop, *Measuring Jerusalem*, 123.
45 Kark, and Oren-Nordheim, *Jerusalem and Its Environs*, 294-297.
46 Y. Ben-Arieh, 'Jerusalem Travel Literature as Historical Source and Cultural Phenomenon', in *Jerusalem in the Mind of the Western World*, eds. Y. Ben-Arieh and M. Davis (London: Praeger, 1997), 29.
47 M. Eliav, 'The German and Austrian Consular Archives in Jerusalem as a Source for the History of Palestine and its Population in the Late Ottoman Empire', in *Palestine in the Late Ottoman Empire*, ed. D. Kushner (Leiden: E.J. Brill, 1986), 372-373.
48 MAE, Nantes, Série B, Carton 35, various reports on foreign consulates in Jerusalem.
49 M. Eliav, *Britain in the Holy Land* (Jerusalem: The Magnes Press, 1997), 15-16.
50 The six consulates were France and Russia (1893), Persia (1901), Greece and Italy (1902), Germany (1914). Nicault, 'Retour à la Jérusalem Ottomane', 89-90.
51 Tibawi, *British Interests in Palestine*, 29-57.

52 M. Eliav, 'German Interests and the Jewish Community', in *Palestine in the Late Ottoman Empire*, ed. D. Kushner (Leiden: E.J. Brill, 1986), 426-427.
53 D. Kushner, 'The Foreign Relations of the Governors of Jerusalem Toward the End of the Ottoman Period', in Kushner, *Palestine in the Late Ottoman Empire*, 301-311.
54 Kark, *American Consuls in the Holy Land*, 236.
55 S. Minerbi, 'Italian Economic Penetration in Palestine 1908-1919', in *Studies on Palestine During the Ottoman Period*, ed. M. Ma'oz (Jerusalem: Magnes Press, 1975), 466-482.
56 See Chapter 1.
57 Kushner, 'The Foreign Relations of the Governors of Jerusalem', 312.
58 Kushner, 'The Foreign Relations of the Governors of Jerusalem', 312-313.
59 See MAE, Nantes, Ambassade Costantinople, Série D, Carton 15.
60 Tibawi, *British Interests in Palestine*, 31.
61 B. Wasserstein, *Divided Jerusalem* (London: Profile Books, 2001), 52-53.
62 Tibawi, *British Interests in Palestine*, 33-34.
63 TNA: PRO, FO 195/2452 William Hough to McGregor, Jaffa, 27 October 1913.
64 There are many examples available regarding the attempt of the Ottoman authorities to stop Jewish immigration in A. Hyamson, *The British Consulate in Jerusalem*, Vol. 2 (London: E. Goldstone, 1941) and in Eliav, *Britain in the Holy Land*.
65 Kark, *American Consuls in the Holy Land*, 143; Kushner, 'The Foreign Relations of the Governors of Jerusalem', 313. MAE, Ambasciata d'Italia in Turchia, Busta 239, Italian Consul in Jerusalem to the Italian Ambassador in Istanbul, Jerusalem, 26 November 1896.
66 TNA: PRO, FO 95/2199, J. Dickson to O'Conor, Jerusalem, 31 July 1905.
67 TNA: PRO, FO 368/1139, McGregor to Foreign Office, 29 January 1914; McGregor to Foreign Office, 29 January 1914.
68 TNA: PRO, FO 368/1139/6143, McGregor to Foreign Office, Jerusalem, 29 January 1914. V. Lemire, 'L'Eau, le Consul et l'Ingénieur', 136-137.
69 TNA: PRO, FO 368/1139/6144, McGregor to Foreign Office, Jerusalem, 29 January 1914.
70 ISA, RG 83/28, Ekrem Bey to Istanbul, 15 November 1906.
71 NARA, Consular Post, Vol. 69, Governor of Jerusalem to Glazebrook, Jerusalem 22 September 1914: 'with the abolition of the capitulations

in the Ottoman Empire, the foreign post offices will have to close on the morning of 1 October 1914.' Vester Spafford, *Our Jerusalem*, 231.
72 NARA, Consular Post, Vol. 69/A, Deputy Consul to Trade Office, Jerusalem, 4 September 1914.
73 OA, DH.EUM.MEM. 41/19, Mutasarrıf of Jerusalem to Ministry of Interior, November 1913; DH.EUM.MEM. 91/39, Mutasarrıf of Jerusalem to Ministry of Interior, 1917.
74 Conde de Ballobar, *Diario*, 63.
75 NARA, Consular Post, Vol. 68, Glazebrook to American Embassy Istanbul, Jerusalem 14 September 1914; TNA: PRO, FO 369/332, J. Morgan to Foreign Secretary, Jerusalem, 14 December 1910.
76 ACTS, Diario della Guerra, October-November 1914. Vester Spafford, *Our Jerusalem*, 231.
77 NARA, RG 59, Department of State 711.673/69, Embassy in Istanbul to Secretary of State, 9 March 1916.
78 NARA, RG 59, Department of State 711.673/107, Oscar S. Heizer to High Commissioner in Istanbul, Jerusalem, 22 September 1920.
79 NARA, RG 59, Department of State 711.673/120, Memorandum, Division of Near Eastern Affairs, March 1919: 'Capitulations may be remodelled (however) Turkey must be made to apply them in their entirety as they stood prior to their attempt to abrogate them.'
80 For instance the American consul Glazebrook sent to Cemal Paşa a list of American citizens and of other nationalities under his protection (120 Americans, 25 Italians, 35 English, 30 Russians, and 3 Serbs). NARA, Consular Post, Vol. 70, Glazebrook to Cemal Paşa, Jerusalem, 22 July 1915.
81 Vester Spafford, *Our Jerusalem*, 232.
82 W. Hough, 'History of the British Consulate in Jerusalem', *Journal of the Middle East Society*, no. 1 (October-December 1946): 13-14.
83 Conde de Ballobar, *Diario*, 64-65.
84 Eliav, *Britain in the Holy Land*, 91. See also TNA: PRO, FO 369/776, Hough to Sir Grey, Cairo 21 November 1914. In this report the British consul reports the details of circumstances of his departure from Jerusalem. NARA, Consular Post, Vol. 69, Glazebrook to Morgenthau, 23 November 1914: 'The archives of the British consulate had already been moved to this consulate and their premises completely evacuated. Likewise the few articles belonging to the Belgian consulate had been placed under my charge. The Serbians have no consulate here.' NARA, Consular Post, Vol. 69, Glazebrook to American Embassy Istanbul, Jerusalem, 2 November 1914: 'French

consul now requests the consulate to take charge of French interest stop.'
85 NARA, Consular Post Vol. 70, Glazebrook to Embassy in Istanbul, Jerusalem 3 February 1915: 'The Jewish subjects of those [Great Britain, France and Russia] countries were either expelled or had to become Ottoman subjects.' TNA: PRO FO 369/776, W. Hough to E. Gray, Jerusalem, 21 November 1914: 'Practically all convents, religious institutions, schools, hospitals etc., under the protection of the Entente Powers were seized by the Military authorities.' ASV, *Segr. Stato Guerra (1914-1918)*, 306, Card. Gasparri to Mons. Marchetti, Vatican City, 26 May 1917.
86 TNA: PRO, FO 369/776, Hough to Sir Grey, Cairo, 21 November 1914.
87 Conde de Ballobar, *Diario*, 65.
88 The German consul at the beginning of the conflict was Edmund Schmidt, who was replaced by Johann Wilhelm H. Brode after his death in 1916. Schmidt was buried in the Protestant cemetery of Jerusalem on Mt Zion, in the gravesite a245; the Austrian consul was Friedrich Kraus.
89 G. Hintlian, 'The First World War in Palestine and Msgr. Franz Fellinger', in *Austrian Presence in the Holy Land in the 19th and early 20th Century*, ed. M. Wrba (Tel Aviv: Austrian Embassy, 1996), 180; Friedman, *Germany, Turkey, and Zionism*, 211-214.
90 NARA, Consular Post, Vol. 72, Governor of Jerusalem to Glazebrook, Jerusalem 5 August 1915.
91 V.D. Lipman, *Americans and the Holy Land through British Eyes* (London: V.D. Lipman Self-Publishing, 1989).
92 NARA, Consular Post, Vol. 72, Glazebrook to Morgenthau, Jerusalem, 29 May 1915.
93 M. Eliav, 'The Austrian Consulate in Jerusalem. Activities and Achievements', *Austrian Presence in the Holy Land in the 19th and early 20th Century*, ed. M. Wrba (Tel Aviv: Austrian Embassy, 1996), 48.
94 ACTS, Diario della Guerra, Jerusalem, 11 October 1915.
95 For the episode of the expulsion of the Jews from Jaffa see Friedman, *Germany, Turkey and Zionism*, 347-373; Eliav, 'The Austrian Consulate in Jerusalem', 48. See also Conde de Ballobar, *Diario*, 197.
96 M. Levene, 'The Balfour Declaration: a Case of Mistaken Identity', *The English Historical Review* 107, no. 422 (January 1992): 76; see also J. Renton, *The Zionist Masquerade: the Birth of the Anglo-Zionist Alliance 1914-18* (Basingstoke: Palgrave Macmillan, 2007).

97 NARA, Consular Post, Vol. 69, Governor of Jerusalem to Glazebrook, Jerusalem, 29 December 1914.
98 NARA, Consular Post, Vol. 69, Glazebrook to Cemal Paşa, Jerusalem, 30 December 1914.
99 For the Nili episode see A. Engle, *The Nili Spies* (London: Hogarth Press, 1959); P. Goldstone, *Aaronsohn's Map: the Untold Story of the Man Who Might Have Created Peace in the Middle East* (Orlando: Harcourt, 2007); H. Halkin, *A Strange Death* (London: Weidenfeld & Nicolson, 2006).
100 Conde de Ballobar, *Diario*, 196; Friedman, *Germany, Turkey and Zionism*, 350-351.
101 See, NARA, Consular Post, Vol. 72, Governor of Jerusalem to Glazebrook, Jerusalem, 5 August. 1915; NARA, Consular Post, Vol. 75, Governor of Jerusalem to Glazebrook, Jerusalem, 23 January 1916.
102 NARA, Consular Post, Vol. 72, Governor of Jerusalem to Glazebrook, Jerusalem, 5 August 1915.
103 See Lipman, *Americans and the Holy Land*, 253.
104 NARA, Consular Post, Vol. 75, Governor of Jerusalem to Glazebrook, Jerusalem, 23 January 1916.
105 NARA, Consular Post, Vol. 72, American Embassy to Department of State, Istanbul, 22 January 1915.
106 NARA, State Department Record, 867.40 – 867.4016/125, Roll No. 43, Morgenthau to Secretary of State, Istanbul, 10 April 1915: 'Letter from Yellin dated Jerusalem March 25 states that present situation of Jews very satisfactory.'
107 NARA, Consular Post, Vol. 75, Central Committee for the Relief of Jews to Glazebrook, New York, 10 February 1916. TNA: PRO, FO 371/2480, Foreign Office to French Ambassador, London, 16 December 1914.
108 NARA, Consular Post, Vol. 75, Central Committee for the Relief of Jews to Glazebrook, New York, 10 February 1916.
109 I.C. Clarke, *American Women and the World War* (New York: D. Appleton and Company, 1918), Ch. XXXI.
110 D. Heddesheimer, 'The First Holocaust' (Chicago: Theses and Dissertations Press, 2003), 33; see also M. Engelman, *Fifteen Years of Effort on Behalf of World Jewry* (New York: Ference Press, 1929).
111 Most of the biographical references are from Kark, *American Consuls in the Holy Land*, 333-334.
112 Kark, *American Consuls in the Holy Land*, 333-334.
113 Vester Spafford, *Our Jerusalem*, 239.

114 Vester Spafford, *Our Jerusalem*, 242-243.
115 NARA. Consular Post, Vol. 81, Glazebrook to American Film Company, Jerusalem, 9 December 1916.
116 See Renton, *The Zionist Masquerade: the Birth of the Anglo-Zionist Alliance*; he argues that the British Government and Zionists sought to create and spread the idea that the Jewish nation was about to be reborn in order to capture Jewish support around the world for the British cause in the war: however the commitment of the British was vague and eventually 'hijacked' by Zionists.
117 See NARA, Consular Post, Vol. 70, Consular Agent in Jaffa to Glazebrook, Jaffa, 2 July 1915.
118 Conde de Ballobar, *Diario*, 233-235; Friedman, *Germany, Turkey, and Zionism*, 373.
119 NARA, Consular Post, Vol. 83, Consul Conde Ballobar, Jerusalem, 9 May, 1917.
120 NARA, Consular Post, Vol. 73, Glazebrook to Morgenthau, Jerusalem 6 August 1915.
121 Conde de Ballobar, *Diario*, 179.
122 Conde de Ballobar, *Diario*, 25-26.
123 AMAE, Madrid, P481/33813, Personnell files Antonio de la Cierva y Lewita.
124 The reasons for the argument between the Spanish consular mission and the Custody are discussed in P.G. Barrioso, *España en la Historia de Tierra Santa*, Vol. II (Madrid: Ministerio de Asuntos Exteriores, 1992-94), 625-630.
125 AMAE, P481/33813, Personnel files Antonio de la Cierva y Lewita.
126 AMAE, P481/33813, Minutes of Secretary of State, 22 October 1921, Madrid.
127 AMAE, P481/33813, Spanish Embassy to the Holy See, 21 May 1939, Vatican City.
128 A complete picture of the positions offered is to be found in the personnel files. MAE, P481, Personnel files Antonio de la Cierva y Lewita.
129 Officially, the Spanish government did not recognise the State of Israel; however, Franco wanted to open a consulate in Jerusalem in order to open a dialogue with the Israeli authorities. It was only in 1986 that full diplomatic relations were established between Spain and Israel.

[130] For a brief summary of anthropological studies of food see Sidney Mintz and Christine M. Du Bois, 'The Anthropology of Food and Eating', *Ann. Rev. Anthropol.* 31 (2002): 99-119.
[131] Segev, *One Palestine, Complete*, 17.
[132] See James E. Young, 'Interpreting Literary Testimony: A Preface to Rereading Holocaust Diaries and Memoirs', *New Literary History* 18 (1987): 403-423.
[133] Conde de Ballobar, *Diario*, 65. Ballobar moved his residence on 16 November 1916 and he went to live in the house of Guerassimo, director of the Credit Lyonnais in Jerusalem. Ballobar noted that this was the most comfortable and chic house in the city.
[134] Edward Said, *Orientalism* (London: Pantheon Books, 1978), 205-209.
[135] Conde de Ballobar, *Diario*, 91.
[136] Conde de Ballobar, *Diario*, 111.
[137] Conde de Ballobar, *Diario*, 95.
[138] Conde de Ballobar, *Diario*, 179.
[139] AMAE, H3025/020, Spanish Embassy in Berlin, copy of the German report on the evacuation of Jaffa, 9 June 1917, Berlin. This episode is thoroughly debated by Friedman, *Germany, Turkey, and Zionism*, 347-373.
[140] Conde de Ballobar, *Diario*, 199-200; *The New York Times*, 3 June 1917.
[141] ASMAE, Archivio di Gabinetto, Italian Consular Mission in Egypt, 30 may 1917, Cairo; *New York Times*, 22 May 1917.
[142] Friedman, *Germany, Turkey, and Zionism*, 356.
[143] ASV, *Segr. Stato, Guerra (1914-1918)* – 130, Card Dolci to Card Gasparri, 3 June 1917, Istanbul.
[144] David Fromkin, *A Peace to End All Peace* (New York: Owl Books, 2001), 296.
[145] AMAE, H3025/020, Spanish Ambassador to Ministry of State, 10 August 1917, Istanbul.
[146] Conde de Ballobar, *Diario*, 200.
[147] AMAE, H3078/005, Ministry of State to Diplomatic Mission in Palestine, 13 April 1918, Madrid.
[148] AMAE, H3078/005, Ministry of State to German Embassy, 8 August 1918, San Sebastian.
[149] Conde de Ballobar, *Diario*, 200.
[150] AMAE, H3069/008, Ballobar to Ministry of State, list of payments, 10 October 1917, Jerusalem.
[151] Conde de Ballobar, *Diario*, 209.
[152] Conde de Ballobar, *Diario*, 245.

153 For details on Wasif Jawhariyyeh see, Salim Tamari, 'Jerusalem's Ottoman Modernity: The Times and Lives of Wasif Jawhariyyeh', *Jerusalem Quarterly File*, No. 9 (2000): 5-27.
154 See for instance Alan Beardsworth and Teresa Keil (eds.), *Sociology on the Menu* (New York: Routledge, 1997). Beardsworth and Keil have attempted to study in sociological terms the experience of food-related issues – in particular food production and consumption. Also see David Bell and Gill Valentine (eds.), *Consuming Geographies* (New York: Routledge, 1997). Bell and Valentine argues that food and eating is packed with social, cultural and symbolic meanings; they also suggest that every meal can tell us something about the persons involved, in both the action of eating and their place in society.
155 Geoffrey Hunt, 'The Middle Class Revisited: Eating and Drinking in an English Village', *Western Folklore* 50 (1991): 401-402; R. Barthes, 'Toward a Psychosociology of Contemporary Food Consumption', in *Food and Culture: a Reader*, eds. C. Counihan and P. Van Esterik (London: Routledge, 1997), 21.
156 P. Farb and G. Armelagos (eds.), *Consuming Passions: The Anthropology of Eating* (Boston: Houghton Mifflin, 1980), 103.
157 A. Warde, *Consumption, Food & Taste* (London: SAGE, 1997), 10-11.
158 Barthes, 'Toward a Psychosociology of Contemporary Food Consumption', 25.
159 A. Jacobson, 'Negotiating Ottomanism in Times of War: Jerusalem During World War I Through the Eyes of a Local Muslim Resident', *Int. J. Middle East Studies* 40 (2008): 75.
160 Tamari, 'Jerusalem's Ottoman Modernity', 5-27; Jacobson, 'From Empire to Empire', 94.
161 Conde de Ballobar, *Diario*, 68-69.
162 NARA, Washington DC, Consular Post Vol. 69/A, Governor of Jerusalem, 3 August 1914.
163 Conde de Ballobar, *Diario*, 91.
164 Conde de Ballobar, *Diario*, 105-106.
165 Mintz and Du Bois, 'The Anthropology of Food and Eating', 105.
166 Conde de Ballobar, *Diario*, 147.
167 Conde de Ballobar, *Diario*, 145-148.
168 Conde de Ballobar, *Diario*, 154-155.
169 Conde de Ballobar, *Diario*, 148: 'According to the *Berliner Tageblatt* the invasion of Palestine by 300,000 British troops is imminent. I am not really sure about this.'
170 Conde de Ballobar, *Diario*, 205.

171 Conde de Ballobar, *Diario*, 233.
172 AMAE, H1927, Ballobar to Secretary of State, 20 November 1917, Jerusalem.
173 Conde de Ballobar, *Diario*, 235. Ballobar was asked to take care of some Jews in May 1917, after the Spanish Ministry of State petitioned the Austrian government to give protection to 5,000 Jews. AMAE, H3025-020, Ministry of State to Spanish Consul in Vienna, 18 May 1917, Madrid.
174 Conde de Ballobar, *Diario*, 253-254.
175 Storrs, *The Memoirs*, 303-304.
176 TNA: PRO, FO 371/3061, Mark Sykes, 13 November 1917.
177 TNA: PRO, FO 141/746/3, Lieutenant Deedes's report, Jerusalem, 16 December 1917.
178 The history of Jerusalem under British military rule is discussed in detail in Chapter 5.
179 MAE, Archivio di Gabinetto, Pacco 185, *Custos* of Holy Land to Foreign Minister, Cairo, 20 February 1918. TNA: PRO, CAB 27/23, Headquarters Egypt to Foreign Office, Cairo, 25 January 1918. Ballobar was often defined as the universal consul in Jerusalem; the British did not want to interfere with his activities of protection of foreign interests, but as they did not allow any official consul in the city when they took over, they informed Ballobar that if he was to leave Jerusalem he may not be allowed to return to the city.
180 A. Gabellini, *L'Italia e l'Assetto della Palestina 1916-1924* (Florence: SeSaMO, 2000), 39.
181 S. Minerbi, *L'Italie et la Palestine* (Paris: Presses Universitaire de France, 1970), 157.
182 Nicault, *Une Histoire de Jérusalem*, 172.
183 The full question cannot be discussed here; however it has been discussed quite thoroughly by Nicault, *Une Histoire de Jérusalem 1850-1967*; Gabellini, *L'Italia e l'Assetto della Palestina*.
184 Minerbi, *L'Italie et la Palestine*, 248-249.
185 Nicault, *Une Histoire de Jérusalem*, 171.
186 MAE, Nantes, Série B, Jérusalem, Carton 291. In this folder it is possible to see how the new French High Commissioner Le Caix tried to promote some anti-British and anti-Zionist propaganda in Palestine through the French consul at the end of 1919.
187 MAE, Nantes, Série B, Jérusalem, Carton 113, Note on the administration of the territories occupied by British troops in Palestine, Paris, 23 November 1917.

188 Nicault, *Une Histoire de Jérusalem*, 172.
189 NARA, Consular Post, Vol. 85, Glazebrook to Secretary of State, Jerusalem, 28 March 1919.
190 Gabellini, *L'Italia e l'Assetto della Palestina*, 41.

Chapter 4

1 T. Tasso, *Gerusalemme Liberata*, ed. A.M. Esolen (Baltimore: JHU Press, 2000), 22.
2 E. Bar-Yosef, 'The Last Crusade? British Propaganda and the Palestine Campaign 1917-18', *Journal of Contemporary History* 36, no. 1 (2001): 87-88.
3 J.M. Winter, 'Propaganda and the Mobilization of Consent', in *First World War*, ed. H. Strachan (Oxford: Oxford University Press, 1998), 216.
4 F. Ahmad, 'War and Society Under the Young Turks', in *The Modern Middle East*, eds. Hourani, Khoury and Wilson, 126; Hanioğlu, *A Brief History of the Late Ottoman Empire*, 177.
5 Hanioğlu, *A Brief History of the Late Ottoman Empire*, 133.
6 Hanioğlu, *A Brief History of the Late Ottoman Empire*, 190.
7 Ottoman intelligence has been discussed by T. Lüdke, *Jihad Made in Germany: Ottoman and German Propaganda and Intelligence Operations in the First World War* (Münster: Lit, 2005),
8 E. Köroğlu, *Ottoman Propaganda and Turkish Identity* (London: I.B.Tauris, 2007), 6-11.
9 R. Ovendale, *The Origins of the Arab-Israeli Wars* (London: Longman, 1992), 17. See also L. Von Sanders, *Cinq Ans de Turquie* (Paris: Payot, 1923); Lüdke, *Jihad Made in Germany*, 48-54.
10 Ahmad, 'War and Society Under the Young Turks', 134.
11 TNA: PRO FO 882/14, Intelligence News, Cairo, 20 September 1914. Though this report is of great interest, it is should be read with caution as it was written very early in the conflict and any suggestion of occupation was quite premature; on the other hand, it does show how the British exploited this report to underline the positive attitudes of the locals towards the British. It is not clear whether Anis el-Gamal was working for the British.
12 B. Wasserstein, *The British in Palestine* (Oxford: Basil Blackwell, 1991), 5.
13 Wasserstein, *The British in Palestine*, 6.

14 OA, DH.EUM. 4 ŞB 23/5, Macid Şevket to Minister of the Interior, Jerusalem, 15 August 1914.
15 NARA, Consular Post Vol. 69/A, Glazebrook to American Consular Agent, Jerusalem, 4 May 1914.
16 NARA, Consular Post Vol. 69/A, Consular Agent to Glazebrook, Jaffa, 6 May 1914.
17 NARA, Consular Post Vol. 69/A, Consular Agent to Glazebrook, Jaffa, 6 May 1914.
18 NARA, Consular Post Vol. 69/A, Governor of Jerusalem, 3 August 1914; ASMAE, Serie Politica P, 498, Conte Senni to Italian Embassy in Istanbul, 7 August 1914.
19 NARA, Consular Post Vol. 69, Glazebrook to Morgenthau, Jerusalem, 12 August 1914.
20 LP, DAVIDSON 398, p. 38, Mr. Renwick to Lord Bryce, 25 September 1914.
21 ASMAE, Serie Politica P, 498, Senni to Italian Embassy in Istanbul, Jerusalem, 7 August 1914.
22 Jacobson, 'From Empire to Empire', 47.
23 NARA, Consular Post Vol. 69/A, Glazebrook to American Agent in Beirut, 18 August 1914.
24 Jacobson, 'Negotiating Ottomanism in Times of War', 73.
25 Ibid.
26 See Renton, *The Zionist Masquerade*.
27 See S. Tamari, 'The Short Life of Private Ihsan: Jerusalem 1915', *Jerusalem Quarterly File* 30 (2007): 26-58. MAE, Nantes, Le Caire Ambassade, Carton 513, Report on Syria, 24 April 1915.
28 F.A.K., Yasamee, 'Ottoman Empire', in *Decisions for War 1914*, ed. K. Wilson (London: UCL Press, 1995), 250.
29 A. Forder, *In Brigand's Hands & Turkish Prison 1914-1918* (London: Marshall Brothers, 1919), 18.
30 LP, Davidson 398, Memorandum Archbishop, 7 October 1914.
31 NARA, Consular Post Vol. 69, File 824, Governor of Jerusalem to Glazebrook, Jerusalem, 8 August 1914.
32 ASMAE, Serie Politica P, 498, Senni to Italian Embassy in Istanbul, Jerusalem, 29 August 1914.
33 ASMAE, Serie Politica P, 498, Senni Italian Embassy in Istanbul, Jerusalem, 7 August 1914.
34 NARA, Consular Post Vol. 69/A, Glazebrook to Morgenthau, Jerusalem, 17 November 1914.

35 ASMAE, Serie Politica P, 498, Senni to Italian Embassy in Istanbul, Jerusalem, 29 August 1914.
36 ASV, *Segr. Stato. Affari Eccl.*, Africa Asia Oceania, Pos. 13 Fasc. 5, Senni to Italian Foreign Minister, 11 December 1914.
37 ASMAE, Serie Politica P, 498, Senni to Italian Embassy in Istanbul, 5 September 1914. According to the Italian consul 40 cannons were delivered to Jerusalem, with others expected to follow.
38 H. Kayalı, 'Wartime Regional and Imperial Integration of Greater Syria during World War I', in *The Syrian Land: Process of Integration and Fragmentation*, eds. T. Philipp and B. Schaebler (Stuttgart: Franz Steiner Verlag, 1998), 301.
39 Kayalı, 'Wartime Regional and Imperial Integration of Greater Syria', 303-304.
40 Jacobson, 'From Empire to Empire', 38.
41 NARA, Consular Post, Vol. 69, Macid Şevket to Glazebrook, 22 September 1914. Also M.J. Lagrange, 'A Jerusalem Pendant la Guerre', *Le Correspondent*, February 1915, 646.
42 OA, DH.KMS. 27/37, File 31, Macid Şevket to Minister of the Interior, Jerusalem, 22 September 1914.
43 NARA, Consular Post, Vol. 69A, File 811.1, Governor of Jerusalem to Glazebrook, 16 November 1914.
44 Cemal, for instance, allowed the cutting of 40% of all kinds of trees, damaging some of the local industries. Kayalı, 'Wartime Regional', 300.
45 TNA: PRO WO 106/178, Memorandum by General W.R. Robertson, London, 19 July 1917.
46 Robert Nivelle was nominated Commander in Chief of the French Army in December 1916. As officer of Artillery, he planned to use new artillery tactics in order to break through the German lines; nevertheless his plans proved to be a failure and eventually Nivelle was replaced in April 1917. See J. Keegan, *The First World War* (Toronto: Vintage Canada, 2000), 322-329.
47 Ibid; K. Robbins, *The First World War* (Oxford: Oxford University Press, 1993).
48 Fromkin, *A Peace to End All Peace*, 234.
49 M. Hughes, *Allenby and British Strategy in the Middle East 1917-1919* (London: Frank Cass, 1999), 33.
50 General Allenby was appointed commander of the Egyptian Expeditionary Force early in 1917.
51 Hughes, *Allenby and British Strategy*, 30.

52 BL, Resume of Operation in Palestine and Arabia since 20th March 1917, in Priestland, *Records of Jerusalem*, vol. 1, 89.
53 Bullock, *Allenby's War*, 66.
54 Bar-Yosef, 'The Last Crusade? British Propaganda', 87-109.
55 TNA: PRO FO 141/473 MacInnes to High Commissioner of Egypt, Cairo, 2 May 1917.
56 Fromkin, *A Peace to End All Peace*, 100-101.
57 TNA: PRO FO 395/152, Notice D. 607, 15 December 1917.
58 Bar-Yosef, 'The Last Crusade? British Propaganda', 89.
59 For a long-term assessment of the British occupation of Palestine, see: Segev, *One Palestine, Complete*.
60 I would like to thank Abigail Jacobson for this image of the 'changing hands'.
61 R.D. Adelson, 'The Formation of British Policy Towards the Middle East 1914-1918' (PhD thesis, Washington University, 1972), 353; A.P. Wavell, *Allenby Soldier and Statesman* (London: George G. Harrap, 1946), 14.
62 D.L. Bullock, *Allenby's War* (London: Blandford Press, 1988), 63.
63 Hughes, *Allenby and British Strategy*, 13.
64 For the biography of Allenby see: B. Gardner, *Allenby* (London: Cassell, 1965); Wavell, *Allenby Soldier*; Hughes, *Allenby and British Strategy*.
65 Hughes, *Allenby and British Strategy*, 31.
66 Hughes, *Allenby and British Strategy*, 45; A. Bruce, *The Last Crusade* (London: John Murray, 2002), 115.
67 Bruce, *The Last Crusade*, 112.
68 Bruce, *The Last Crusade*, 115; Hughes, *Allenby and British Strategy*, 56.
69 Hughes, *Allenby and British Strategy*, 48-50.
70 Hughes, *Allenby and British Strategy*, 56-59.
71 Hughes, *Allenby and British Strategy*, 57.
72 Bruce, *The Last Crusade*, 154.
73 TNA: PRO FO 141/773, Archbishop to Bishop MacInnes, London, 18 July 1917.
74 TNA: PRO FO 371/3061, Prisoner of War Department to Lord Robert Cecil, London, 8 November 1917.
75 TNA: PRO FO 371/3061, Mark Sykes Report, London, 13 November 1917.
76 TNA: PRO FO 371/3061, Mark Sykes Report, London, 13 November 1917.

77 TNA: PRO FO 371/3061 Report of Mark Sykes on 13 November 1917.
78 TNA: PRO FO 371/3061, Foreign Office to Wingate, London, 17 November 1917.
79 TNA: PRO FO 371/3061, Wingate to Foreign Office, Cairo, 19 November 1917.
80 Laurens, *La Question de Palestine*, Vol. 1, 372-373.
81 TNA: PRO FO 371/3061, War Office to Headquarters Cairo, London, 21 November 1917.
82 TNA: PRO FO 371/3061, War Office to Headquarters in Cairo, 21 November 1917. Only the points which vary from the first drafts are reported. 'Prime Minister wishes to make first announcement of occupation of Jerusalem in House of Commons in following terms. (1) Manner in which you were received by the population. (2) That you entered Holy city on foot. (5) That Mosque of Omar and area around it has been placed under Moslem control. (7) That Tomb at Hebron has been placed under exclusive Moslem control and guards established at Bethlehem and on Rachel's tomb. [..] Please wire me in above terms as far as you may be able to comply with them.'
83 TNA: PRO FO 371/3383, Foreign Office to Wingate, London, 2 January 1918.
84 See T.S. Asbridge, *The First Crusade: a New History* (London: Free, 2004); M. Foss, *People of the First Crusade* (London: M. O'Mara Books, 1997); A. Maalouf, *The Crusade Through Arab Eyes* (London: Al Saqi, 1984).
85 IWM, Film and Video Archive, IWM 145.
86 See for instance IWM, Film and Video Archive 45, 'With the Crusaders in the Holy Land. Allenby: the Conqueror', 1919; see also *The Times* (London), December 11, 1917.
87 For Godfrey see T.S. Asbridge, *The First Crusade*, 316-319.
88 C. Falls, *Military Operations Egypt and Palestine*, vol. 1 (London: HMSO, 1930); The Marquess of Anglesey, *A History of the British Cavalry*, vol. 5 (London: Leo Cooper, 1994).
89 Bruce, *The Last Crusade*.
90 Field Marshal Lord Carver, *The National Army Museum Book of the Turkish Front 1914-18* (London: Pan Books, 2003), 212-222.
91 Bruce, *The Last Crusade*, 155. A direct order to the XXI Corps stated: 'No operations are to be undertaken within a six miles radius of Jerusalem.' Quoted in The Marquess of Anglesey, *A History of British Cavalry*, 205.

92 Bruce, *The Last Crusade*, 156.
93 Bruce, *The Last Crusade*, 157.
94 Bruce, *The Last Crusade*, 159; Bullock, *Allenby's War*, 91; Falls, *Military Operations*, 235-236.
95 Falls, *Military Operations*, 234-235.
96 Bruce, *The Last Crusade*, 160; Bullock, *Allenby's War*, 92-93.
97 TNA: PRO 395/237, 'The Last Days of Jerusalem under the Turk', V. Jabotinsky, 4 February 1918; *The Palestine News* (Jerusalem), March 7, 1918.
98 Falls, *Military Operations*, 252.
99 T. Canaan, 'Two Documents on the Surrender of Jerusalem', *The Journal of the Palestine Oriental Society* 10, no. 1 (1930): 27-32.
100 T. Canaan, 'Two Documents', 28.
101 Vester Spafford, *Our Jerusalem*, 255.
102 A. Amireh, 'My Last Days as an Ottoman Subject', *Jerusalem Quarterly File*, Issue 9 (Summer 2000): 31-32.
103 Conde de Ballobar, *Diario*, 236.
104 V. Gilbert, *The Romance of the Last Crusade* (London: Appleton & C., 1928), 166. Gilbert reported the name 'Murch' rather than 'Church'; however it seems plausible the correct spelling is 'Church', considering that all other sources used this last name.
105 Falls, *Military Operations*, 252.
106 Ibid.
107 Ibid; Bertha Vester Spafford also reported Major Cooke as being present at the meeting; however from the sources available it appears Major Cooke arrived later and was ordered to take over the post office.
108 IWM, Bayley Papers.
109 A zealous soldier saved some of these pictures for no apparent reason. The pictures mentioned are conserved in the photographic collection of the Imperial War Museum, London. Segev, *One Palestine, Complete*, 54; argues that when Shea learned that pictures had been taken of Watson he immediately ordered that the negatives be destroyed.
110 Bruce, *The Last Crusade*, 162-163; Falls, *Military Operations*, 254.
111 TNA: PRO FO 141/473, Press Communiqué No. 137, Cairo, 12 December 1917.
112 *Daily Mail* (London), December, 1917. Press cuttings from Allenby's Paper, 4/3.
113 TNA: PRO FO 371/3061, General Allenby Reports, Jerusalem, 11 December 1917.

[114] TNA: PRO FO 882/14, 'The Politics of Jerusalem', 29 December 1916; ACTS, 'Cronaca di Terra Santa', Fr E. Castellani.
[115] Conde Ballobar, *Diario*, 237.
[116] Ibid.
[117] Gilbert, *The Romance*, 174.
[118] Amireh, 'My Last Days', 32.
[119] There is an interesting debate about the memories of the Crusades in the Muslim imaginary; originally Muslims looked at the Crusaders as *ifrang*, Westerners, therefore not in religious terms; it was only later with the arrival of the Zionists and the imperial policies of the British that the Muslims evoked the ancient memory of the Crusades. See P.M. Holt, *The Age of the Crusades* (London: Longman, 1986); J.P. Berkey, *The Formation of Islam* (Cambridge: Cambridge University Press, 2003); see also D.R. Woodward, *Hell in the Holy Land* (Lexington: The University Press of Kentucky, 2006), 138-141.
[120] Bar-Yosef, 'The Last Crusade? British Propaganda', 98-99; B. Brian, *The First World War and British Military History* (Oxford: Clarendon Press, 1991), 192.
[121] *The Times* (London), December 11, 1917.
[122] A. Bluett, *With Our Army in Palestine* (London: Andrew Melrose, 1919), 222; Gilbert, *The Romance*, 178.
[123] ACTS, Diario della Guerra, 8 December 1917.
[124] Amireh, 'My Last Days', 31; also Tamari, 'Jerusalem's Ottoman Modernity'.
[125] Amireh, 'My Last Days'; Tamari, 'Jerusalem's Ottoman Modernity', 7-9.
[126] W.T. Massey, *How Jerusalem Was Won* (London: Constable and Company, 1919), 201.
[127] LP, H5672 J4 4, Document 12.
[128] *Daily Telegraph* (London), December 12, 1917. Press cuttings from Allenby's Papers 4/3, Liddle Hart Centre from Military Archives, King's College, London.
[129] TNA: PRO FO 371/3388, Sir Mark Sykes to Clayton, London, 14 January 1918.
[130] Massey, *How Jerusalem Was Won*, 190.
[131] *The Jewish Chronicle* (London), December 14, 1917.
[132] Vladimir Jabotinsky was born in 1880 in Odessa (Russia). He studied in many European countries and, in 1903, joined the Zionist Movement. Until 1914 he worked as journalist in Russia, and then became a war correspondent in Egypt. Between 1915 and 1917,

Jabotinsky conducted a campaign for the creation of a Jewish legion under British command. In 1920 he was involved in the Nebi Musa riots, creating a self-defence armed unit (*Haganah*). Tried and convicted by British authorities, he travelled across Europe and then moved to the United States. He became the promoter of the revisionist movement within Zionism, and died in 1940 while campaigning for the creation of a Jewish army to fight the Nazis. For biographical details see Y. Benari, *Zeev Vladimir Jabotinsky* (Tel Aviv: Jabotinsky Institute, 1977); J.B. Schechtman, *The Life and Times of Vladimir Jabotinsky*, vol. 1 (Silver Spring MD: Eshel Books, 1986).

[133] TNA: PRO FO 395/237, Jabotinsky, 'The Last Days of Jerusalem Under the Turks', February 1918.

[134] TNA: PRO FO 395/237, Jabotinsky, 'No Idlers', July 1918.

[135] TNA: PRO FO 395/237, Jabotinsky, 'No Idlers', July 1918.

[136] LP, Davidson 400, Greek Church in London to Archbishop, 11 December 1917.

[137] LHCMA, Allenby's Paper, *The Universe*, 21 December 1917.

[138] MAE, Archivio Politico e Gabinetto, Pacco 185, Italian Ambassador to Italian Foreign Office, Paris, 24 December 1917.

[139] ASV, *Segr. Stato, Affari Eccl., Straordinari, Africa Asia Oceania*, Pos. 53(2), Fasc. 34, On. Orlandi, 12 December 1917.

[140] L. Rostagno, *Terrasanta o Palestina? La Diplomazia Italiana e il Nazionalismo Palestinese (1861-1939)* (Rome: Bardi Editore, 1996), 49-50.

[141] E. Julien (Bishop of Arras), *La Délivrance de Jérusalem. Allocution Prononcée à l'Occasion du 'Te Deum' Chanté dans la Basilique Notre Dame de Boulogne le Dimanche 16 Décembre 1917* (Boulogne sur Mer: Imprimeries Réunies, 1917); also quoted in Nicault, *Un Histoire de Jérusalem*, 138.

[142] Laurens, *La Question de Palestine 1799-1922*, Vol. 1, 374-375.

[143] L. Buzzetti and S. Sorani eds., *Il Distaccamento Italiano di Palestina 1917-1921* (Milan: Silvano Sorani Editore, 1976), 15-21. A copy of the Italian poster is reproduced.

[144] Giovannelli, *La Santa Sede*, 22.

[145] MAE, Nantes, Jérusalem, Série B, Carton 113, French Embassy in Rome to Pichon, Rome, 11 December 1917.

[146] ASV, *Segr. Stato Guerra*, Propaganda Fide to Cardinal Gasparri, Rome, 14 December 1917.

[147] TNA: PRO FO 141/666. British Legation to High Commissioner Egypt, Addis Ababa, 31 December 1917.

[148] CW Papers, Vol. VIII, Letter 25, to Herbert Samuel, London, 12 December 1917.

149 See figures reported in Chapter 1.
150 Quoted in ASV, *Segr. Stato, Affari Eccl. Straordinari Africa Asia Oceania*, Pos. 53 (2), Fasc. 34, *Osservatore Romano*, 14 December 1917.TNA: PRO FO 371/3061, W. Towley to Foreign Office, The Hague, 12 December 1917.
151 Quoted in ASV, *Segr. Stato, Affari Eccl. Straordinari Africa Asia Oceania*, Pos. 53 (2), Fasc. 34, *Osservatore Romano*, 14 December 1917.
152 TNA: PRO FO 371/3061, W. Towley to Foreign Office, The Hague, 12 December 1917.
153 E. Siberry, *The New Crusaders* (Aldershot: Ashgate, 2000), 87-88.
154 E. Siberry, *The New Crusaders*, 90.
155 Bar-Yosef, 'The Last Crusade? British Propaganda', 87.
156 J. Bowes, *The Aussie Crusaders* (London: Oxford University Press, 1920); F.H. Cooper, *Khaki Crusaders* (Cape Town: Central News Agency, 1919); F.L. Stevenson, *The Great Crusade* (London: Hodder and Stoughton, 1918); M.C. Adams, *The Modern Crusaders* (London: Routledge & Sons, 1920).
157 Adams, *The Modern Crusaders*, 84.
158 A. Marrin, *The Last Crusade* (Durham NC: Duke University Press, 1974), 124.
159 Marrin, *The Last Crusade*, 124.
160 Bar-Yosef, 'The Last Crusade? British Propaganda', 89.
161 E. Bar-Yosef, *The Holy Land in English Culture* (Oxford: Clarendon Press, 2005), 250.
162 E. McFayden, 'The Last Crusade – 1915', *Songs of the Last Crusade* (North Sydney: Winn & Co., 1917).
163 Marrin, *The Last Crusade*, 136.
164 C. Sommers, *Temporary Crusaders* (London: John Lane, 1919), v.
165 C. Sommers, *Temporary Crusaders*, vi.
166 C. Sommers, *Temporary Crusaders*, 77.
167 Bar-Yosef, 'The Last Crusade? British Propaganda', 95.
168 Siberry, *The New Crusaders*, 101.
169 L. Davidson, *America's Palestine. Popular and Official Perceptions from Balfour to Israeli Statehood* (Gainsville: University Press of Florida, 2005), 21-26.
170 Bowes, *The Aussie Crusaders*; Cooper, *Khaki Crusaders*.
171 J. Newell, 'Allenby and the Palestine Campaign', in *The First World War and British Military History*, ed. B. Bond (Oxford: Clarendon Press, 1991), 191.
172 Siberry, *The New Crusaders*, 96.

Chapter 5

1. See for instance Wasserstein, *The British in Palestine*; Segev, *One Palestine, Complete*; N. Shepherd, *Ploughing Sand* (New Brunswick: Rutgers University Press, 2000).
2. Segev, *One Palestine, Complete*, 87.
3. N. Bentwich, *England in Palestine* (London: Kegan Paul, 1932), 20.
4. J.J. McTague, 'The British Military Administration in Palestine 1917-1920', *Journal of Palestine Studies* 7, no. 3 (Spring 1978): 57.
5. S. Huneidi, *A Broken Trust* (London: I.B.Tauris, 2001), 27.
6. Huneidi, *A Broken Trust*, 27.
7. Wasserstein, *The British in Palestine*, 20; McTague, 'The British Military', 56.
8. TNA: PRO FO 371/3384, Allenby to War Office, 23 October 1918: 'Turkish system of government will be continued and the existing machinery utilised [...]'.
9. H.C. Luke and E. Keith-Roach (eds), *The Handbook of Palestine and Trans-Jordan* (London: MacMillan and Co., 1930), 312-315; *Palestine Royal Commission*, London, 1937, 112; Bentwich, *England in Palestine*, 28; TNA: PRO FO 371/3384, Allenby to War Office, 23 October 1918, 'Turkish system of government will be continued and the existing machinery utilised [...] Chief Administrators are reminded that the administration is a military and provisional one.'
10. Wasserstein, *The British in Palestine*, 18.
11. Laurens, *La Question de Palestine*, Vol. 1, 389.
12. *Palestine Royal Commission* (1937), 112.
13. According to Ronald Storrs, General Clayton was quite optimistic and to him 'no problem seemed insoluble'. Furthermore, Storrs wrote that Clayton was too busy to think about the real administration of Palestine as he (Clayton) 'was never in the way and never out of the way'. Storrs, *The Memoirs*, 306.
14. Wasserstein, *The British in Palestine*, 18.
15. M.F. Abcarius, *Palestine Through the Fog of Propaganda* (London: Hutchinson & Co., 1946), 59-60.
16. TNA: PRO, FO 141/746, Military Administrator's Report, Jerusalem 15 December 1917; TNA: FO 141/688, Clayton to Headquarters, Jerusalem, 22 December 1917.

17 *Palestine Royal Commission Report*, Secretary of State for the Colonies, London, 1937, 113.
18 *Annual Report of the Department of Health*, Government of Palestine, 1921, 1-7.
19 Bentwich, *England in Palestine*, 29.
20 *Annual Report of the Department of Health* (1921), 1.
21 *Palestine Royal Commission Report* (1937), 113.
22 *Palestine Royal Commission Report* (1937), 113.
23 *Report on Palestine Administration*, Government of Palestine, London, 1922, 84-85.
24 Luke and Keith-Roach, *The Handbook of Palestine*, 213; Shepherd, *Ploughing Sand*, 31.
25 Luke and Keith-Roach, *The Handbook of Palestine*, 213-219.
26 TNA: PRO, 141/688, Samuel to Curzon, Jerusalem, 20 November 1920.
27 A.L. Tibawi, *Arab Education in Mandatory Palestine* (London: Luzac & C., 1956), 23-25.
28 D. Fabrizio, *La Battaglia delle Scuole in Palestina* (Milan: FrancoAngeli, 2003), 18.
29 J.S. Bentwich, *Education in Israel* (London: Routledge, 1945), 17-18; N. Nardi, *Education in Palestine* (Washington DC: Zionist Organization of America, 1945), 22-23.
30 Luke and Keith-Roach, *The Handbook of Palestine*, 240-242.
31 C.R. Ashbee, *A Palestine Notebook 1918-1923* (London: William Heinemann, 1923), 79.
32 Storrs, *The Memoirs*, 308.
33 Luke and Keith-Roach, *The Handbook of Palestine*, 222-223.
34 Luke and Keith-Roach, *The Handbook of Palestine*, 222-223 and 227. See also *Report on Palestine Administration* (1922), 3; S.J. Shaw, 'The Nineteenth-Century Ottoman Tax Reforms and Revenue System', *International Journal of Middle East Studies*, no. 6 (1975): 13: '[…] local roads were constructed by the fief holders and tax farmers, mainly by forced labor which they were able to impose on the cultivators living nearby through law and tradition'.
35 TNA: PRO, T1/12286, General Routine Order, 18 January 1918.
36 TNA: PRO, T1/12286, Foreign Office to Clayton, London, 7 November 1918.
37 Conde de Ballobar, *Diario*, 252; 'The streets are honestly clean and the commerce, almost inexistent during Turkish rule, was livelier and the farmers coming to the city in order to sell their products are helped.'

38 Storrs, *The Memoirs*, 333. For the Chamber of Commerce see MAE, Nantes, Jérusalem, Série B, Carton 8, Bulletin de la Chambre de Commerce d'Industrie et d'Agriculture No.1, Jerusalem, 1909.
39 CZA, L3/10/1, O.E.T.A. to Zionist Commission, Jerusalem 5 September 1919.
40 NARA, Consular Post, Vol. 87, Glazebrook to The Diamond Chain & Mfg. Co., Jerusalem, 10 May 1919.
41 NARA, Consular Post, Vol. 87, Glazebrook to Van Siclen & C., Jerusalem, 8 November 1919.
42 *Palestine Royal Commission Report* (1937), 114.
43 E. Horne, *A Job Well Done* (Essex: The Anchor Press, 1982), 16; G.W. Swanson, 'The Ottoman Police', *Journal of Contemporary History* 7, no.1/2 (January-April 1972): 253.
44 Horne, *A Job Well Done*, 15.
45 Horne, *A Job Well Done*, 35.
46 Storrs, *The Memoirs*, 348.
47 Horne, *A Job Well Done*, 15.
48 CZA, L3/52, Zionist Commission to Military Governorate, Jerusalem 23 February 1920.
49 CZA, L3/52, O.E.T.A. to Zionist Commission, Jerusalem 18 June 1919; Zionist Commission report, Jerusalem, 20 August, 1919.
50 Wasserstein, *The British in Palestine*, 18; Segev, *One Palestine, Complete*, 87.
51 Storrs, *The Memoirs*, 297; Laurens, *La Question de Palestine*, Vol. 1, 389.
52 PC, The Papers of Sir Ronald Storrs, Reel 10, Box III, Liverpool Post, 10 January 1918: 'The Appointment of Mr. Ronald Storrs as Governor of Jerusalem in succession to Borton Pasha is regarded in official circles here as a happy one. Though only thirty six years of age, Mr. Storrs has had considerable experience of administrative affairs in Egypt, and he has shown himself to be possessed of exceptional ability and of great tact in the handling of native people.'
53 Wasserstein, *The British in Palestine*, 21.
54 McTague, 'The British Military', 56; Huneidi, *A Broken Trust*, 30; Nicault, *Une Histoire de Jérusalem*, 180.
55 TNA: PRO FO 371/3394 Foreign Office to War Office, London, 25 January 1918.
56 TNA: PRO FO 371/3394 Foreign Office to War Office, London, 25 January 1918. An interesting discussion of the Commission in Jerusalem is to be found in Laurens, *La Question de Palestine*, 400-406.

57 TNA: PRO FO 371/3384 Allenby to War Office, 23 October 1918; TNA: PRO FO 141/688, Clayton to G.H.Q., Jerusalem 22 December 1917.
58 Pappe, *A History of Modern Palestine*, 79; Wasserstein, *The British in Palestine*, 15; Laurens, *La Question de Palestine*, Vol. 1, 392.
59 See Ch 4 for a more thorough discussion of the distribution of relief after the war.
60 Storrs, *The Memoirs*, 308.
61 See Y. Porath, *The Emergence of the Palestinian-Arab National Movement* (London: Frank Cass, 1974).
62 Pappe, *A History of Modern Palestine*, 79-81; see also Ch 2 for a more detailed discussion on the Christian-Muslim Associations.
63 Pappe, *A History of Modern Palestine*, 80; Khalidi, *Palestinian Identity*, 147-153.
64 Wasserstein, *The British in Palestine*, 25; Huneidi, *A Broken Trust*, 30.
65 TNA: PRO FO 371/3386, Money to GHQ, 20 November 1920.
66 Wasserstein, *The British in Palestine*, 23
67 TNA: PRO FO 371/85, Bols to Allenby, 12 April 1920.
68 Shepherd, *Ploughing Sand*, 39.
69 McTague, 'The British Military', 65-66.
70 Segev, *One Palestine, Complete*, 94.
71 TNA: PRO FO 371/3392, Foreign Office to Wingate, London, 13 February 1918; TNA: PRO FO 371/3394, Foreign Office to War Office, London 25 January 1918.
72 Segev, *One Palestine, Complete*, 94; Shepherd, *Ploughing Sand*, 40; see also J. Ershow, 'Conspiracies and Commitments: the British in Palestine', in *Yale Israel Journal*, no. 5 (Winter 2005): 21.
73 TNA: PRO, FO 141/665, Foreign Office to Clayton, London, 24 January 1918.
74 See several reports on the Orthodox Church, mainly by the French agent Fr Jaussen, MAE, Nantes, Jérusalem, Série B, Carton 140.
75 Storrs, *The Memoirs*, 313-315.
76 Storrs, *The Memoirs*, 327.
77 LP, LC 105, Bishop MacInnes to the Lambeth Conference, Jerusalem, 7 July 1920.
78 LP, Davidson 395, MacInnes to Archbishop, Jerusalem, 19 January 1918.
79 PC, The Paper of Sir Ronald Storrs, Reel 10, Box III, Evening News, 21 December 1920.

80 The biographical information regarding Storrs has been gathered through: Storrs, *The Memoirs*; Segev, *One Palestine, Complete*; Shepherd, *Ploughing Sand*; A.J. Sherman, *Mandate Days* (Slovenia: Thames and Hudson, 1997); G.S. Georghallides, *Cyprus and the Governorship of Sir Ronald Storrs* (Nicosia: Cyprus Research Centre, 1985).
81 Georghallides, *Cyprus*, 1-2.
82 For the question of buildings and damages of war see Chapter 3.
83 Storrs, *The Memoirs*, 343,458.
84 MAE, Nantes, Londres, Série K, Carton 387, Note of the French Foreign Office, Paris, 25 January 1918.
85 MAE, Nantes, Londres, Série K, Carton 387, Defrance to Ministry of Foreign Affaires, Cairo, 23 February 1918.
86 Georghallides, *Cyprus*.
87 See D. Birn, ed., *Middle East Politics and Diplomacy* (Marlborough: Adam Matthew, 1999).
88 Ashbee, *Jerusalem 1918-1920*, vii.
89 Ashbee, *Jerusalem 1918-1920*, vii.
90 B. Hyman, 'British Planners in Palestine 1918-1936' (PhD thesis, LSE, London, 1994), 352.
91 B. Hyman, 'British Planners in Palestine 1918-1936', 360.
92 Shepherd, *Ploughing Sand*, 49.
93 Hyman, British Planners," 362.
94 Segev, *One Palestine, Complete*, 61. For the naming of the streets see also Storrs, *The Memoirs*, 331-332.
95 Segev, *One Palestine, Complete*, 61-62.
96 In relation to street naming, I am indebted to Yair Wallach, 'Reading in Conflict: Public Text in Modern Jerusalem' (PhD thesis, Birkbeck College, London, 2008).
97 Storrs, *The Memoirs*, 331-332.
98 Wallach, 'Reading in Conflict', 138-139.
99 Shepherd, *Ploughing Sand*, 51.
100 See for instance K. Armstrong, *Jerusalem: One City, Three Faiths* (London: Harper Collins, 1996); Gilbert, *Jerusalem in the Twentieth Century*; M. Benvenisti, *City of Stone* (Los Angeles: University California Press, 1996).
101 Wallach, 'Reading in Conflict', 148.
102 Storrs, *The Memoirs*, 326. Public Notice 34, April 1918.
103 Ashbee, *Jerusalem 1918-1920*, 37.
104 Ashbee, *Jerusalem 1918-1920*, 37.

105 PC, The Papers of Sir Ronald Storrs, Reel 6, Box III, The Globe, New York, 1919; PRO, CO 742/1, Official Gazette, Jerusalem, 16 March 1920.
106 See M. Shilo, 'Women as Victims of War: the British Conquest (1917) and the Blight of Prostitution in the Holy City', *Nashim: A Journal Of Jewish Women's Studies & Gender Issues* 6 (Fall 2003): 72-83.
107 *The Palestine News* (Jerusalem), Gazette no. 5, August 1, 1918; MAE, Nantes, Jérusalem, Série B, Carton 113, Avis No. 43, 'Maison Publiques.'
108 Storrs, *The Memoirs*, 416.
109 ASV, *Sacra Congregazione degli Affari Ecclesiastici Straordinari*, Pos. 102 Fasc. 69, Latin Patriarch to Gasparri, Jerusalem 4 February 1921; See also Pos. 102, Fasc. 70, Latin Patriarch to Gasparri, Appendix 2, Jerusalem, April 1921.
110 See comments of Weizmann in relation to the British Administration in Letters and Papers of Chaim Weizmann, Weizmann to Zionist Executive, 25 March 1920, in I. Friedman, *Riots in Jerusalem, San Remo Conference, April 1920* (London: Garland, 1987), 2; CTS, Diario della Guerra, see comments written in relation to the British Occupation of Jerusalem.
111 Wallach, 'Reading in Conflict', 132-133.
112 Hyman, 'British Planners', 85 and 362.
113 *The New York Times* (New York), July 21, 1921.
114 Kark and Oren-Nordheim, *Jerusalem and Its Environs*, 142.
115 Benvenisti, *City of Stone*, 136.
116 Hyman, 'British Planners', 39-40; E. Efrat and A. Noble, 'Planning Jerusalem', *Geographical Review* 78, no. 4 (October 1988): 392.
117 S. Shapiro, 'Planning Jerusalem: the First Generation, 1917-1968', in *Urban Geography of Jerusalem*, eds. D. Amiran, A. Shachar and I. Khimi (Jerusalem: Masada Press, 1973), 141.
118 Hyman, 'British Planners', 53.
119 Baruch Guini was the city engineer of the municipality under Ottoman rule and it seems he carried out this role under the new British administration as well. See Kark and Oren-Nordheim, *Jerusalem and its Environs*, 35.
120 Kark and Oren-Nordheim, *Jerusalem and its Environs*, 70, 91 and 95.
121 For information in relation to Patrick Geddes see P. Boardman, *The Worlds of Patrick Geddes* (London: Routledge, 1978).
122 *The Jewish Chronicle* (London), August 29, 1919; *The New York Times* (New York), September 20, 1919.

[123] Hyman, 'British Planners', 113.
[124] Hyman, 'British Planners', 297.
[125] J. McTague, *British Policy in Palestine 1917-1922* (Lanham MD: University Press of America, 1983): 54.
[126] Wasserstein, *The British in Palestine*, 71.
[127] Wasserstein, *The British in Palestine*, 58-72.
[128] Khalidi, *Palestinian Identity*; Porath, *The Emergence*; L. Fishman, 'The 1911 Haram al-Sharif Incident: Palestinian Notables Versus the Ottoman Administration', *Journal of Palestine Studies* 3, Vol. XXXIV (Spring 2005): 6-22.
[129] Segev, *One Palestine, Complete*, 127-144.
[130] Segev, *One Palestine, Complete*, 141.
[131] B. Morris, *Righteous Victims* (New York: Vintage Books, 2001), 96.
[132] Pappe, *A History of Modern Palestine*.
[133] Y. Benari, *El Pogrom de Jerusalem en el Año 1920* (Buenos Aires: Congreso Judio Latinoamericano, 1975).
[134] Y. Benari, *El Pogrom de Jerusalem*, 3-20.
[135] Idinopulos, *Weathered by Miracles*, 166; Segev, *One Palestine, Complete*, 127; Wallach, 'Reading in Conflict', 105.
[136] Porath, *The Emergence*, 6; Esco Foundation for Palestine, *Palestine: a Study of Jewish, Arab and British Policies* (New Haven: Yale University Press, 1947), 132.
[137] Shepherd, *Ploughing Sand*, 41-42; Wasserstein, *The British in Palestine*, 64.
[138] Segev, *One Palestine, Complete*, 129-130.
[139] S.J. Tambiah, *Leveling Crowds* (London: University of California Press, 1996), 213-220; D.L. Horowitz, *The Deadly Ethnic Riot* (New Delhi: Oxford University Press, 2001), 9-28; P. Van der Veer, 'Riots and Rituals: The Construction of Violence and Public Space in Hindu Nationalism', in *Riots and Pogroms*, ed. P.R. Brass (New York: New York University Press, 1996), 154-159; D. Veer Mehta, *Sociology of Communal Violence* (New Delhi: Amnol Publications, 1998), 1-12.
[140] Horowitz, *The Deadly Ethnic Riot*, 6-7 and 227-229.
[141] Horowitz, *The Deadly Ethnic Riot*, 89-94. Horowitz calls 'the Lull' a particular atmosphere before the riot; Brass, *Riots and Pogroms*, 8-9.
[142] Pappe, *A History of Modern Palestine*, 82.
[143] Wasserstein, *The British in Palestine*, 60.
[144] Wasserstein, *The British in Palestine*, 63; Shepherd, *Ploughing Sand*, 195.
[145] Segev, *One Palestine, Complete*, 85-101; Wasserstein, *The British in Palestine*, 34-57.

146 Letters and Papers of Chaim Weizmann, Weizmann to Zionist Executive, 25 March 1920, in *Riots in Jerusalem, San Remo Conference*, ed. I. Friedman, 2 (London: Garland, 1987).
147 Shepherd, *Ploughing Sand*, 38-40; TNA: PRO WO 32/9614, Report of the Court of Enquiry into the Riots in Jerusalem During Last April, Jerusalem, April 1920; Wasserstein, *The British in Palestine*, 47; Khalidi, *Palestinian Identity*; TNA: PRO FO 371/5034, Director of the Arab Club (Mohammed Derweesh) to Allenby, Jerusalem April 1920.
148 TNA: PRO FO 371/5034, Director of the Arab Club (Mohammed Derweesh) to Allenby, Jerusalem April 1920: 'We declare that we cannot accept the Jews in our Country. [...] We declare that we do not accept the Jews neither as guests nor as neighbours in Palestine.'
149 Khalidi, *Palestinian Identity*, 126; Q. Shomali, 'La Presse Arabe en Palestine dans la Période Ottomane', in *de Bonaparte à Balfour*, 452-454.
150 Khalidi, *Palestinian Identity*, 126.
151 Letters and Papers of Chaim Weizmann, Weizmann to Zionist Executive, 25 March 1920, in *Riots in Jerusalem, San Remo Conference*, ed. I. Friedman, 2.
152 Wasserstein, *The British in Palestine*, 62-63.
153 CZA, Z4/16078/66, Storrs to Jewish Self-Defence League, 31 March 1920.
154 TNA: PRO FO 371/5034, Meinertzhagen to Curzon, Cairo, 31March 1920.
155 Quoted in Segev, *One Palestine, Complete*, 131.
156 TNA: PRO FO 371/5034, Mohammed Derweesh (Director of the Arab Club) to Allenby, Jerusalem, April 1920.
157 PC, The Paper of Sir Ronald Storrs, Reel 7, Box III, Storrs to Samuel, Jerusalem 18 August 1920.
158 See a list of proximate causes of communal rioting in D. Veer Mehta, *Sociology of Communal Violence*, 2-4.
159 AMAE, H2687, Pedro Marrades to Diplomatic Agency Cairo, Jerusalem, 10 April 1920.
160 N. Caplan, *Palestine Jewry and the Arab Question 1917-1925* (London: Frank Cass, 1978), 58.
161 TNA: PRO WO 32/9614, Report of the Court of Enquiry into the Riots in Jerusalem During Last April, Jerusalem April 1920.
162 Morris, *Righteous Victims*, 95.
163 Segev, *One Palestine, Complete*, 128; TNA: PRO WO 32/9614, Report of the Court of Enquiry into the Riots in Jerusalem During Last April, Jerusalem, April 1920.

164 TNA: PRO WO 32/9614, Report of the Court of Enquiry into the Riots in Jerusalem During Last April, Jerusalem, April 1920.
165 Abcarius, *Palestine Through the Fog of Propaganda*, 67; TNA: PRO WO 32/9614, Report of the Court of Enquiry into the Riots in Jerusalem During Last April, Jerusalem, April 1920.
166 TNA: PRO WO 32/9614, Report of the Court of Enquiry into the Riots in Jerusalem During Last April, Jerusalem, April 1920.
167 MAE, Nantes, Jérusalem, Série B, Carton 94, French Consul to General Gouraud, Jerusalem, 8 April 1920.
168 TNA: PRO WO 32/9614, Report of the Court of Enquiry into the Riots in Jerusalem During Last April, Jerusalem, April 1920.
169 TNA: PRO WO 32/9614, Report of the Court of Enquiry into the Riots in Jerusalem During Last April, Jerusalem, April 1920. The Indian Muslim police was deployed, from the British occupation of the city, in the old city in order to protect Muslim sacred shrines.
170 TNA: PRO WO 32/9614, Report of the Court of Enquiry into the Riots in Jerusalem During Last April, Jerusalem, April 1920.
171 TNA: PRO WO 32/9614, Report of the Court of Enquiry into the Riots in Jerusalem During Last April, Jerusalem, April 1920.
172 TNA: PRO WO 32/9614, Report of the Court of Enquiry into the Riots in Jerusalem During Last April, Jerusalem, April 1920. Letters and Papers of Chaim Weizmann, Weizmann to Lloyd George, Beirut 10 April 1920, in *Riots in Jerusalem, San Remo Conference*, ed. I. Friedman, 22; CZA Z4/16084, Zionist Commission Memorandum, Jerusalem, 11 April 1920.
173 Brass, *Riots and Pogroms*, 21-26; Horowitz, *The Deadly Ethnic Riot*, 124-128.
174 Brass, *Riots and Pogroms*, 21.
175 Horowitz, *The Deadly Ethnic Riots*, 7.
176 Brass, *Riots and Pogroms*, 25.
177 Brass, *Riots and Pogroms*, 23.
178 Segev, *One Palestine, Complete*, 137-138, 143-144.
179 CZA, Z4/16084, Zionist Commission Memorandum, Jerusalem 11 April 1920. A later statement of the Zionist Organisation in London, however, changed the tone and 'victims' became 'casualties'; see TNA: PRO FO 371/5117, Secretary of the Zionist Organisation (Samuel Landman) to Under Secretary of Foreign Affairs, London 16 April 1920.
180 TNA: PRO FO 371/5114, Muslim-Christian Society to Storrs, Jerusalem April 1920.

NOTES 231

[181] For population figures see Ch 1.
[182] TNA: PRO WO 32/9614, Report of the Court of Enquiry into the Riots in Jerusalem During Last April, Jerusalem, April 1920.
[183] Brass, *Riots and Pogroms*, 12-13.
[184] Horowitz, *The Deadly Ethnic Riot*, 74-75.
[185] Horowitz, *The Deadly Ethnic Riot*, 231-252; Brass, *Riots and Pogroms*, 26-32.
[186] TNA: PRO WO 32/9614, Report of the Court of Enquiry into the Riots in Jerusalem During Last April, Jerusalem, April 1920.
[187] TNA: PRO WO 32/9614, Report of the Court of Enquiry into the Riots in Jerusalem During Last April, Jerusalem, April 1920: '[…] Colonel Storrs inclines to consider the actual danger at the Nebi Musa Festival itself was greater in the preceding year. The majority of witnesses are not of his opinion.'
[188] TNA: PRO FO 371/5117, Landman (Secretary of the Zionist Organisation) to the Under Secretary of State for the Foreign Affairs, London, 16 April 1920.
[189] TNA: PRO WO 32/9614, Report of the Court of Enquiry into the Riots in Jerusalem During Last April, Jerusalem, April 1920.
[190] TNA: PRO WO 32/9614, Report of the Court of Enquiry into the Riots in Jerusalem During Last April, Jerusalem, April 1920.
[191] TNA: PRO FO 371/5119, P. Kerr to Foreign Office, London, 19 May 1920.
[192] R. Meinertzhagen, *Middle East Diary* (London: Cresset Press, 1959), 79-84.
[193] Meinertzhagen, *Middle East Diary*, 79-84.
[194] See for instance TNA: PRO FO 371/5119, Philip Kerr to Campbell (FO), 29 May 1920: '[…]The existing administration is taking no effective steps to prevent such an outbreak ….'
[195] Brass, *Riots and Pogroms*, 33.
[196] Brass, *Riots and Pogroms*, 33.
[197] Horowitz, *The Deadly Ethnic Riot*, 20.
[198] Meinertzhagen, *Middle East Diary*, 79-84.
[199] *The Jewish Chronicle* (London), April 16, 1920.

Epilogue

[1] Jacobson, 'From Empire to Empire', 293.

BIBLIOGRAPHY

Archival Material:

Archives des Affaires Étrangères, Nantes
Archivo General des Asuntos Exteriores, Madrid
Archivio Segreto Vaticano, Vatican City
Archivio Storico Ministero degli Affari Esteri, Rome
Central Zionist Archives, Jerusalem
Custodia di Terra Santa, Jerusalem
Imperial War Museum, London
Israel State Archives, Jerusalem
Lambeth Palace Library, London
National Archives and Record Administration, College Park MD
Osmanlı Arşivi Daire Başkanlığı (Ottoman Archives), Istanbul
The National Archives: Public Record Office, Kew

Private Papers:

The Papers of Sir Ronald Storrs, Pembroke College, Cambridge.
Allenby's Papers, Liddell Hart Centre for Military Archives, King's College, London.

Official Publications:

Ashbee, C.R., ed. *Jerusalem 1918-1920, Being the Records of the Pro-Jerusalem Council during the period of the British Military Administration.* London: John Murray, 1921.
Falls, Cyril, ed. *Military Operations Egypt & Palestine.* 2 Vols., London: HMSO, 1930.

Farhat, Edmond, ed. *Gerusalemme nei Documenti Pontifici*. Citta' del Vaticano: Libreria Editrice Vaticana, 1987.
Friedman, I., ed. *Riots in Jerusalem, San Remo Conference, April 1920*. London: Garland, 1987.
Government of Palestine. *Annual Report of the Department of Health*. 1921.
Government of Palestine. *Report on Palestine Administration*. London, 1922.
Luke, Harry Charles and Edward Keith-Roach, eds. *The Handbook of Palestine and Trans-Jordan*. London: MacMillan and Co., 1930.
Palestine Royal Commission. London: HMSO, 1937.
Priestland, Jane, ed. *Records of Jerusalem*. Oxford: Archive Editions, 2002.
Secretary of State for the Colonies. Palestine Royal Commission Report. London, 1937.
Report of the Commission Appointed by His Majesty's Government of Palestine to Inquire into the Affairs of the Orthodox Patriarchate of Jerusalem. London, 1921.
Report of the Joint Palestine Survey Commission. London, 1928.
Royal Institute of International Affairs. Great Britain and Palestine. London, 1946.

Newspapers:

L'Osservatore Romano, Vatican City, 1914-1920
The Jewish Chronicle, London, 1914-1920
The New York Times, New York, 1914-1920
The Manchester Guardian, Manchester, 1914-1920
The Palestine News, Jerusalem, 1918-1920
The Times, London, 1914-1920
The Truth, Jerusalem, 1912-1915
The War Illustrated, London, 1917-1918

Memoirs, Diaries and Tourist Guides:

Adams, M.C. *The Modern Crusaders*. London: Routledge & Sons, 1920.
Ashbee, C.R. *A Palestine Notebook 1918-1923*, London: William Heinemann, 1923.
Bein, Alex, ed. *Arthur Ruppin: Memoirs, Diaries, Letters*, London: Weidenfeld and Nicolson, 1971.
Bentwich, N. & H. *Mandate Memoirs 1918-1948*, London: The Hogarth Press, 1965.
Bluett, Antony. *With Our Army in Palestine*, London: Andrew Melrose, 1919.
Blyth, Estelle. *When We Lived in Jerusalem*, London: John Murray, 1927.
Bowes, J. *The Aussie Crusaders*, London: Oxford University Press, 1920.
Conde de Ballobar. Edited by Eduardo Manzano Moreno. *Diario de Jerusalén 1914-1919*, Madrid: Nerea, 1996.
Cook, Thomas Ltd. *A Guide to Jerusalem and Judea*. London: Thomas Cook & Son, 1924.
Cooper, F.H. *Khaki Crusaders*. Cape Town: Central News Agency, 1919.
Dane, Edmund. *British Campaigns in the Nearer East*. London: Hodder and Stoughton, 1918.
Fabrizio, Daniela, ed. *Diario di Terrasanta*. Milan: Edizioni Biblioteca Francescana, 2002.
Gilbert, Vivian. *The Romance of the Last Crusade*. London: Appleton & Co, 1928.
Goodsall, Robert H. *Palestine Memories 1917-1918-1925*. Canterbury: Cross and Jackman, 1925.
Lloyd George, David. *War memoirs of David Lloyd George*. 2 vols., London: Odhams Press, 1938.
Lock, H.O. *With the British Army in the Holy Land*. London: Robert Scott, 1919.
Luke, Harry Charles. *A Guide to Jerusalem and Judea*. London: S. M. H. K. & Co., 1924.

Luncz. *Eretz Israel Almanac 19.* 1912-13.
Matson, Olaf. *Guidebook to Jerusalem and Environs.* Jerusalem: Fr. Vester & Co. The American Colony, 1920.
Massey, W.T. *How Jerusalem Was Won.* London: Constable & Co, 1919.
Meinertzhagen, Richard. *Army Diary 1899-1926.* London: Oliver and Boyd, 1960.
Reynolds-Ball, E. *Jerusalem.* London: A. & C. Black Ltd, 1924.
Sommers, Cecil. *Temporary Crusaders.* London: John Lane, 1919.
Stevenson, F.L. *The Great Crusade.* London: Hodder and Stoughton, 1918.
Storrs, Ronald. *The Memoirs of Sir Ronald Storrs.* New York: G.P. Putnam's Sons, 1937.
— *Orientations.* London: Nicholson & Watson, 1943.
Vester Spafford, Bertha. *Our Jerusalem.* New York: Arno Press, 1977.
Von Sanders, Liman. *Cinq Ans de Turquie.* Paris: Payot, 1923.
Weisgal, W. Meyer, ed. *The Letters and Papers of Chaim Weizmann.* Jerusalem: Transaction Books, 1977.
Yellin, David. *Jerusalem of Yesterday* (Hebrew), Jerusalem: Rubin-Mass, 1972.

Unpublished Material:

Adelson, Roger D. 'The Formation of British Policy Towards the Middle East 1914-1918', PhD thesis, Washington University, Washington, 1972.
Harouvi, Eldad. 'The Criminal Investigation Department of the Palestine Police Force 1920-1948', PhD thesis, University of Haifa, 2002.
Heddesheimer, D. 'The First Holocaust', Thesis and Dissertations Press, Chicago, 2003.
Hyman, Benjamin. 'British Planners in Palestine 1918-1936', PhD thesis, London School of Economics, 1994.
Jacobson, Abigail. 'From Empire to Empire: Jerusalem in the Transition Between Ottoman and British Rule 1912-1920', PhD thesis, Chicago University, 2006.

Mayer, Henry D. 'Records of the United States Consulate and Consulate General at Jerusalem, Palestine, 1857-1935', Washington DC: unpublished, 1976.

Schoenberg, Philip E. 'Palestine in the Year 1914', PhD thesis, New York University, 1978.

Wallach, Yair, 'The 1920s Street-Naming Campaign and the British Reshaping of Jerusalem', Amman: WOCMES, June 2006.

— 'Reading in Conflict: Public Text in Modern Jerusalem', PhD thesis, Birkbeck College, London, 2008.

Internet sources:

British – Israelism/ Anglo – Israelism.
http://religiousmovements.lib.virginia.edu/nrms/britisrael.html

Virginia Military Institute Archives. 'Otis Glazebrook.'
http://www.vmi.edu/archives/

Encyclopaedia of Islam.
http://www.encislam.brill.nl/

Books:

Abcarius, M.F. *Palestine Through the Fog of Propaganda*. London: Hutchinson & Co., 1946.

Abitbol, Michel. *France and the Middle East*. Jerusalem: Hebrew University Magnes Press, 2004.

Amiran, David, Shachar, Ariel and Kimhi, Israel, eds. *Urban Geography of Jerusalem*. Jerusalem: Masada Press, 1973.

Anderson, B. *Imagined Community*. London: Verso, 2006.

Andrews, F.F. *The Holy Land Under Mandate*, Vol. 2, Boston: Houghton Mifflin Company, 1931.

Armstrong, Karen. *Jerusalem: One City, Three Faiths*. London: Harper Collins, 1996.

Asali, Kamil J., ed. *Jerusalem in History*. Essex: Scorpion Publishing, 1989.

Asbridge, T.S. *The First Crusade: a New History*. London: Free, 2004.

Ateek, N. and Prior, Michael, eds. *Holy Land Hollow Jubilee*. London: Melisende, 1999.
Avcı, Yasemin. *Değişim Sürecinde Bir Osmanlı Kenti: Kudüs 1890-1914*. Ankara: Phoenix, 2004.
Badone, Ellen and Roseman, Sharon R., eds. *Intersecting Journeys*. Chicago, University of Illinois Press, 2004.
Baer, Gabriel and Amnon Cohen, eds. *Egypt and Palestine: A Millennium of Association*. New York: St Martin's Press, 1984.
Baldi, Paschal. *The Question of the Holy Places*. 2 vols., Rome: Typographia Pontificia, 1919.
Barriuso, Garcia. *España en la Historia de Tierra Santa*. Vol. II, Madrid: Ministerio de Asuntos Exteriores, 1992-94.
Bar-Yosef, Eitan. *The Holy Land in English Culture*. Oxford: Clarendon Press, 2005.
Beardsworth, Alan, and Keil, Teresa, eds. *Sociology on the Menu*. New York: Routledge, 1997.
Bell, David and Valentine, Gill, eds. *Consuming Geographies*. New York: Routledge, 1997.
Benari, Y. *El Pogrom de Jerusalem en el Año 1920*. Buenos Aires: Congreso Judio Latinomaericano, 1975.
— *Zeev Vladimir Jabotinsky*. Tel Aviv: Jabotinsky Institute, 1977.
Ben-Arieh, Yehoshua. *Jerusalem in the 19th Century. The Old City*. New York: St Martin's Press, 1984.
— *Jerusalem in the 19th Century. The New City*. New York: St Martin's Press, 1986.
— *The Rediscovery of the Holy Land in the Nineteenth Century*. Jerusalem: The Magnes Press, 1979.
— and Davis, Moshe, ed. *Jerusalem in the Mind of the Western World*. London: Praeger, 1997.
Ben Dor, Gabriel, ed. *The Palestinians and the Conflict*. Haifa: Haifa University, 1982.
Benbassa, E. and A. Rodrigue, eds. *Sephardi Jewry: a History of the Judeo-Spanish Community 15th to 20th Centuries*. Berkeley: University of California Press, 2000.
Bentwich, Norman. *England in Palestine*. London: Kegan Paul, 1932.
— *Palestine of the Jews*. London: Kegan Paul, 1919.
Bentwich, Joseph S. *Education in Israel*. London: Routledge & Kegan Paul, 1965.

Benvenisti, Meron. *City of Stone*. Los Angeles: University California Press, 1996.
Berkey, J.P. *The Formation of Islam*. Cambridge: Cambridge University Press, 2003.
Bertram, Anton and Young, J.W.A. *The Orthodox Patriarchate of Jerusalem*. London: Oxford University Press, 1926.
Biger, G. *An Empire in the Holy Land*. New York: St Martin's Press, 1994.
Binns, John. *The Christian Orthodox Churches*. Cambridge: Cambridge University Press, 2002.
Birn, D., ed. *Middle East Politics and Diplomacy*. Marlborough: Adam Matthew, 1999.
Boardman, Philip. *The Worlds of Patrick Geddes*. London: Routledge, 1978.
Bond, Brian, ed., *The First World War and British Military History*. Oxford: Clarendon Press, 1991.
Brass, P.R. *Riots and Pogroms*. New York: New York University Press, 1996.
Braude, Benjamin and Bernard Lewis, eds. *Christians and Jews in the Ottoman Empire*. Vol. 1-2, London: Holmes & Meier, 1982.
Breger, Marshall and Ahimeir, Ora, eds. *Jerusalem a City and Its Future*. Syracuse: Syracuse University Press, 2002.
Bruce, Anthony. *The Last Crusade*. London: John Murray, 2002.
Brunelli, Roberto. *Storia di Gerusalemme*. Milan: Oscar Mondadori, 1990.
Bullock, David L. *Allenby's War*. London: Blandford Press, 1988.
Buzzetti, L. and Sorani, S., eds. *Il Distaccamento Italiano di Palestina 1917-1921*. Milan: Silvano Sorani Editore, 1976.
Caplan, Neil. *Palestine Jewry and the Arab Question 1917-1925*. London: Frank Cass, 1978.
Carr, E.H. *What is History?* London: Penguin, 1990.
Cassini de Perinaldo, Francesco. *La Orden Franciscana en Tierra Santa*. Barcelona: Tipografia Catolica, 1907.
Cattan, Henry. *Jerusalem*. London: Saqi Books, 2000.
Clark, Victoria. *Holy Fire. The Battle for Christ's Tomb*. London: Macmillan, 2005.
Clarke, I.C. *American Women and the World War*. New York: D. Appleton and Company, 1918.

Cohen, Amnon. *Palestine in the 18th Century*. Jerusalem: The Magnes Press, 1973.
Colbi, Saul P. *Christianity in the Holy Land*. Tel Aviv: Am Hassefer, 1969.
Coleman, Simon and Elsner, John, eds. *Pilgrimage*. Cambridge MA: Harvard University Press, 1995.
Collin, Bernardin. *Pour une Solution au Probleme des Lieux Saints*. Paris: G.P. Maisonneuve et Larose, 1974.
— *Les Lieux Saints*. Paris: Les Editions International, 1948.
Counihan, C. and Van Esterik, P., eds. *Food and Culture: a Reader*. London: Routledge, 1997.
Davidson, Lawrence. *America's Palestine. Popular and Official Perceptions from Balfour to Israeli Statehood*. Gainsville: University Press of Florida, 2005.
Davison, Roderic H. *Nineteenth Century Ottoman Reforms and Diplomacy*. Istanbul: Isis Press, 1999.
Deringil, Selim. *The Well-Protected Domains*. London: I.B.Tauris, 1999.
Divine, Donna Robinson. *Politics and Society in Ottoman Palestine*. Boulder: Lynne Rienner, 1994.
Doumani, Beshara. *Rediscovering Palestine*. London: University of California Press, 1995.
Dudman, H. and Kark, Ruth. *The American Colony*. Jerusalem: Carta, 1998.
Dumper, Michael. *The Politics of Jerusalem Since 1967*. New York: Columbia University Press, 1997.
Eliav, Mordechai. *Britain and the Holy Land*. Jerusalem: The Magnes Press, 1997.
Engelman, M. *Fifteen Years of Effort on Behalf of World Jewry*. New York: Ference Press, 1929.
Engle, Anita. *The Nili Spies*. London: Hogarth Press, 1959.
Epstein, Elias M. *Jerusalem Correspondent 1919-1958*. Jerusalem: The Jerusalem Post Press, 1964.
Epstein, Lawrence J. *Zion's Call*. Boston: University Press of America, 1984.
Erickson, Edward J. *Ordered to Die*. Westport: Greenwood Press, 2001.

Esco Foundation, ed. *Palestine a Study of Jewish, Arab and British Policies.* Vol. 1, New Haven: Yale University Press, 1947.
Fabrizio, Daniela. *La Battaglia delle Scuole in Palestina.* Milan: FrancoAngeli, 2003.
Farb, P. and Armelagos, G., eds. *Consuming Passions: The Anthropology of Eating.* Boston: Houghton Mifflin, 1980.
Field Marshal Lord Carver. *The National Army Museum Book of the Turkish Front 1914-18.* London: Pan Books, 2003.
Findley, C.V. *Bureaucratic Reform in the Ottoman Empire.* Princeton: Princeton University Press, 1980.
Forder, Alfred. *In Brigand's Hands & Turkish Prison 1914-1918.* London: Marshall Brothers, 1919.
Foss, M. *People of the First Crusade.* London: M. O'Mara Books, 1997.
Franciscans. *Custodia di Terra Santa.* Jerusalem: Franciscan Printing Press, 1951.
Friedlander, Dov and Goldscheider, Calvin, eds. *The Population of Israel.* New York: Columbia University Press, 1979.
Friedman, Isaiah. *Germany, Turkey and Zionism, 1897-1918.* Oxford: Oxford University Press, 1977.
Fromkin, David. *A Peace to End All Peace.* New York: Henry Holt, 1989.
Gabellini, Andrea. *L'Italia e l'Assetto della Palestine (1916-1924).* Florence: SeSaMO, 2000.
Gardner, Brian. *Allenby.* London: Cassell, 1965.
Georghallides, G.S. *Cyprus and the Governorship of Sir Ronald Storrs.* Nicosia: Cyprus Research Centre, 1985.
Gerber, Haim. *Ottoman Rule in Jerusalem 1800-1914.* Berlin: Klaus Schwarz Verlag, 1985.
Gilbar, Gad G. *Ottoman Palestine 1800-1914.* Leiden: E.J. Brill, 1990.
Gilbert, Martin. *Jerusalem in the Twentieth Century.* London: Chatto & Windus, 1996.
— *Jerusalem Rebirth of a City.* London: Chatto & Windus, 1985.
Giovannelli, Andrea. *La Santa Sede e la Palestina.* Rome: Edizioni Studium, 2000.
Glass, Jospeh and Kark, Ruth. *Sephardi Entrepreneurs in Jerusalem: The Valero Family 1800-1948.* Jerusalem: Gefen Publishing House, 2007.

Goffman, D. *The Ottoman Empire and Early Modern Europe*. Cambridge: Cambridge University Press, 2002.
Goldstone, Patricia. *Aaronsohn's Map: the Untold Story of the Man Who Might Have Created Peace in the Middle East*. Orlando: Harcourt, 2007.
Gray, John. *A History of Jerusalem*. London: Robert Hale, 1969.
Grindea, Miron, ed. *The Image of Jerusalem*. New York: University of Rochester, 1968.
Halkin, Hillel. *A Strange Death*. London: Weidenfeld & Nicolson, 2006.
Hanioğlu, Şükrü. *A Brief History of the Late Ottoman Empire*. Princeton: Princeton University Press, 2008.
Hintlian, Kevork. *History of the Armenians in the Holy Land*. Jerusalem: St. James Press, 1976.
Holt, P.M. *The Age of the Crusades*. London: Longman, 1986.
Hopwood, D. *The Russian Presence in Syria and Palestine 1843-1914*. Oxford: Clarendon Press, 1969.
Horne, Edward. *A Job Well Done*. Essex: The Anchor Press, 1982.
Horowitz, D.L. *The Deadly Ethnic Riot*. New Delhi: Oxford University Press, 2001.
Hourani, Albert. *A History of the Arab Peoples*. London: Faber and Faber, 1991.
— P. Khoury and M.C. Wilson, eds. *The Modern Middle East*. London: I.B.Tauris, 1993.
Hughes, Matthew. *Allenby and British Strategy in the Middle East 1917-1919*. London: Frank Cass, 1999.
Huneidi, S. *A Broken Trust*. London: I.B.Tauris, 2001.
Hurewitz, J.C. *Diplomacy in the Near and Middle East*. Vol. 2, New Haven: Yale University Press, 1975.
Hyamson, Albert. *The British Consulate in Jerusalem*. Vol. 2, London: E. Goldstone, 1941.
— *Palestine: a Policy*. London: Methuen & Co., 1942.
Idinopulos, Thomas A. *Weathered by Miracles*. Chicago: Ivan R. Dee, 1998.
— *Jerusalem Blessed, Jerusalem Cursed*. Chicago: Ivan R. Dee, 1991.
Jacobs, Louis. *The Jewish Religion*. Oxford: Oxford University Press, 1995.

Kark, Ruth. *American Consuls in the Holy Land 1832-1914*. Jerusalem: The Magnes Press, 1994.
Kark, R. and Oren-Nordheim, M. *Jerusalem and Its Environs*. Jerusalem: The Hebrew University Magnes Press, 2001.
Keegan, J. *The First World War*. Toronto: Vintage Canada, 2000.
Kent, Marian, ed. *The Great Powers and the end of the Ottoman Empire*. London: George Allen & Unwin, 1984.
Khalidi, Rashid. *Palestinian Identity*. New York: Columbia University Press, 1997.
— *British Policy Towards Syria and Palestine 1906-1914*. London: Ithaca Press, 1980.
Khoury, Philip S. *Urban Notables and Arab Nationalism*. Cambridge: Cambridge University Press, 1983.
Khoury, Shahadeh and Khoury, Nicola. *A Survey of the History of the Orthodox Church of Jerusalem*. Amman: Feras Printing Press, 2002.
Kimmerling, B. and Migdal, J.S. *Palestinians*. New York: The Free Press, 1993.
Köroğlu, Erol. *Ottoman Propaganda and Turkish Identity*. London: I.B.Tauris, 2007.
Kushner, David, ed. *Palestine in the Late Ottoman Period*. Leiden: E.J. Brill, 1986.
— *To Be Governor of Jerusalem*. Istanbul: Isis Press, 2005.
Lafi, Nora, ed. *Municipalités Méditerranéennes*. Berlin: Klaus Schwarz Verlag, 2005.
Laurens, Henry. *La Question de Palestine 1799-1922*. Paris: Fayard, 1999.
Leppäkari, Maria. *Apocalyptic Representations of Jerusalem*. Leiden: E.J. Brill, 2006.
Lewis, Bernard. *The Middle East*. London: Phoenix, 2003.
— *The Emergence of Modern Turkey*. 3rd edn. Oxford: Oxford University Press, 2002.
Lipman, V.D. *Americans and the Holy Land Through British Eyes*. London: Self Publishing Associations, 1989.
Lüdke, Tilman. *Jihad Made in Germany: Ottoman and German Propaganda and Intelligence Operations in the First World War*. Münster: Lit, 2005.
Maalouf, A. *The Crusade Through Arab Eyes*. London: Al Saqi, 1984.

Ma'oz, Moshe, ed. *Studies on Palestine During the Ottoman Period.* Jerusalem: Magnes Press, 1975.
— *Palestine During the Ottoman Period.* Jerusalem: The Hebrew University of Jerusalem, 1970.
Marcus, Amy Dockser. *Jerusalem 1913. The Origins of the Arab-Israeli Conflict.* New York: Viking Penguin, 2007.
Marrin, Albert. *The Last Crusade.* Durham NC: Duke University Press, 1974.
Mayer, Tamar and Ali Mourad, Suleyman, eds. *Jerusalem. Idea and Reality.* London: Routledge, 2008.
McCarthy, Justin. *The Ottoman Turks.* London: Longman, 1997.
McFayden, E. 'The Last Crusade – 1915', *Songs of the Last Crusade.* North Sydney: Winn & Co., 1917.
McTague, John J. *British Policy in Palestine 1917-1922.*Lanham MD: University Press of America, 1983.
Meinardus, O.F.A. *The Copts in Jerusalem.* Cairo: Costa Tsoumas & Co., 1960.
Meistermann, Bernabé. *La Ciudad de David: Estudio Topografico.* Jerusalem: Tipografia de Los PP. Franciscanos, 1907.
Melkon Rose, John H. *Armenians of Jerusalem.* London: The Radcliffe Press, 1993.
Minerbi, I. Sergio. *L'Italie et la Palestine 1914-1920.* Paris: Presses Universitaires de France, 1970.
— *The Vatican and Zionism: Conflict in the Holy Land 1895-1925.* New York: Oxford University Press, 1990.
Mombelli, A. *La Custodia di Terra Santa.* Jerusalem: Franciscan Printing Press, 1934.
Momigliano, Felice. *La Conquista di Gerusalemme e l'Avvenire della Palestina.* Rome: Nuova Antologia, 1918.
Moschopoulos, Nicephore. *La Terre Sainte.* Athens, 1956.
Moscrop, John J. *Measuring Jerusalem.* London: Leicester University Press, 2000.
Morris, B. *Righteous Victims.* New York: Vintage Books, 2001.
Nardi, Noah. *Education in Palestine 1920-1945.* Washington: Zionist Organisation of America, 1945.
Nashashibi, Nasser Eddin. *Jerusalem's Other Voice.* Exeter: Ithaca Press, 1990.

Nevakivi, Jukka. *Britain, France and the Arab Middle East*. London: The Athlone Press, 1969.
Nicault, Catherine, ed. *Jérusalem 1850-1948*. Paris: Éditions Autrement, 1999.
— *Une Histoire de Jérusalem 1850-1967*. Paris: CNRS Éditions, 2008.
Nicolle, David. *The Ottoman Army 1914-18*. London: Osprey, 1994.
Noja, Sergio. *Storia dei Popoli dell'Islam. L'Islam Moderno*. Vol. 4, Milan: Oscar Mondadori, 1990.
Okkenhaug, Inger Marie. *The Quality of Heroic Living*. Leiden: E.J. Brill, 2002.
O'Mahony, Anthony, ed. *The Christian Communities of Jerusalem and the Holy Land*. Cardiff: University of Wales Press, 2003.
— *Palestinian Christians*. London: Melisende, 1999.
Ovendale, Ritchie. *The Origins of the Arab-Israeli Wars*. London: Longman, 1992.
Pacini, Andrea, ed. *Christian Communities in the Arab Middle East*. Oxford: Clarendon Press, 1998.
Pappe, Ilan. *A History of Modern Palestine*. Cambridge: Cambridge University Press, 2004.
Paul, Shalom M. and Dever, William G., eds. *Biblical Archaeology*. Jerusalem: Keter, 1973.
Perry, Yaron. *British Mission to the Jews in 19th Century Palestine*. London: Frank Cass, 2003.
Philipp, Thomas, ed. *The Syrian Land in the 18th and 19th Century*. Stuttgart: Steiner, 1992.
— and Schaebler, B., eds. *The Syrian Land: Process of Integration and Fragmentation*. Stuttgart: Franz Steiner Verlag, 1998.
Piccirillo, Michele, ed. *La Custodia di Terra Santa e l'Europa*. Rome: Il Veltro Editrice, 1983.
Pieraccini, Paolo, ed. *La Questione di Gerusalemme*. Bologna: Il Mulino, 2005.
Porath, Y. *The Emergence of the Palestinian-Arab National Movement 1918-1929*. London: Frank Cass, 1974.
Possetto, Alessandro. *Il Patriarcato Latino di Gerusalemme*. Milan: Crociata, 1938.
Prior, Michael and Taylor, William, eds. *Christians in the Holy Land*. London: World of Islam Festival Trust, 1994.

Renton, James. *The Zionist Masquerade: the Birth of the Anglo-Zionist Alliance 1914-18*. Basingstoke: Palgrave Macmillan, 2007.
Robbins, K. *The First World War*. Oxford: Oxford University Press, 1993.
Rostagno, Lucia. *Terrasanta o Palestina? La Diplomazia Italiana e il Nazionalismo Palestinese (1861-1939)*. Rome: Bardi Editore, 1996.
Roubiçek, Marcel. *Modern Ottoman Troops 1790-1915*. Jerusalem: Franciscan Printing Press, 1978.
Ruppin, Arthur. *Syria: an Economic Survey*. New York: Provisional Zionist Committee, 1918.
Said, Edward. *Orientalism*. London: Penguin Books, 2003.
Saunders, Rebecca, ed. *The Concept of the Foreign*. Oxford: Lexington Books, 2003.
Schechtman, J.B. *The Life and Times of Vladimir Jabotinsky*. Vol. 1, Silver Spring MD: Eshel Books, 1986.
Schölch, Alex. *Palestine in Transformation 1865-1882*. Washington DC: Institute for Palestine Studies, 2006.
Segev, Tom. *One Palestine, Complete*. New York: Henry Holt, 2001.
Shaw, Stanford and Ezel Kural Shaw, eds. *History of the Ottoman Empire and Modern Turkey*. Vol. 2, Cambridge: Cambridge University Press, 1977.
Shepherd, Naomi. *Ploughing Sand*. New Brunswick: Rutgers University Press, 2000.
Sherman, A.J. *Mandate Days*. Slovenia: Thames and Hudson, 1997.
Siberry, Elizabeth. *The New Crusaders*. Aldershot: Ashgate, 2000.
Sidebotham, Herbert. *Great Britain and Palestine*. London: MacMillan & Co., 1937.
Singer, Amy. *Palestinian Peasants and Ottoman Officials*. Cambridge: Cambridge University Press, 1994.
Stone, Michael E., Roberta R. Ervine and Nira Stone, eds. *The Armenians in Jerusalem and the Holy Land*. Leuven: Peeters, 2002.
Strachan, Hew, ed. *First World War*. Oxford: Oxford University Press, 1998.
Sykes, Christopher. *Cross Roads to Israel*. London: Collins, 1965.
Tamari, Salim, ed. *Jerusalem 1948*. Jerusalem: The Institute of Jerusalem Studies, 1999.
Tambiah, S.J. *Leveling Crowds*. London: University of California Press, 1996.

The Marquess of Anglesey. *A History of the British Cavalry*. Vol. 5, London: Leo Cooper, 1994.
Thobie, Jacques. *Intérêts et Impérialism Française dans l'Empire Ottoman (1895-1914)*. Paris: Publications de la Sorbonne, 1977.
Tibawi, A.L. *Anglo-Arab Relations*. London: Luzac & Co., 1947.
— *Arab Education in Mandatory Palestine*. London: Luzac & Co., 1956.
— *British Interests in Palestine 1801-1901*. Oxford: Oxford University Press, 1961.
Trimbur, Dominique and Aaronsohn, Ran, eds. *De Bonaparte á Balfour: la France, L'Euorope Occidentale et la Palestine 1799-1917*. Paris: CNRS Editions, 2001.
— *De Balfour à Ben Gourion*. Paris: CRFJ, 2008.
Trumpener, Ulrich. *Germany and the Ottoman Empire*. New York: Caravan Books, 1989.
Tsimhoni, Daphne. *Christian Communities in Jerusalem and the West Bank Since 1948*. Westport CT: Praeger, 1993.
Tuchman, Barbara. *Bible and Sword*. London: Alvin Redman Ltd., 1957.
Tütüncü, Mehmet. *Turkish Jerusalem 1516-1917*. Harlem: SOTA, 2006.
Valognes, J.P. *Vie et Mort des Chrétiens d'Orient*. Paris: Fayard, 1994.
Van den Boogert, Maurits H. *The Capitulations and the Ottoman Legal System*. Leiden: E.J. Brill, 2005.
Veer Mehta, D. *Sociology of Communal Violence*. New Delhi: Amnol Publications, 1998.
Warde, Alan. *Consumption, Food & Taste*. London: SAGE, 1997.
Ware, Thimoty. *The Orthodox Church*. London: Penguin Books, 1963.
Wasserstein, Bernard. *The British in Palestine*. Oxford: Basil Blackwell, 1991.
— *Herbert Samuel: a Political Life*. Oxford: Clarendon Press, 1992.
— *Divided Jerusalem*. London: Profile Books, 2001.
Watson, C.M. *The Story of Jerusalem*. London: J.M. Dent & Sons, 1912.
Wavell, A.P. *Allenby Soldier and Statesman*. London: George G. Harrap, 1946.

Willner, Dorothy. *Nation-Building and Community in Israel.* Princeton: Princeton University Press, 1969.
Wilson, Keith, ed. *Decisions for War 1914.* London: UCL Press, 1995.
Woodward, David R. *Hell in the Holy Land.* Lexington: The University Press of Kentucky, 2006.
Wrba, Marian, ed. *Austrian Presence in the Holy Land in the 19th and early 20th Century.* Tel Aviv: Austrian Embassy, 1996.
Young, George. *Corps de Droit Ottoman.* Vol. 1, Paris, 1905.
Zander, Walter. *Israel and the Holy Places of Christendom.* London: Weidenfeld & Nicolson, 1971.
Zürcher, Erik. J. Turkey. *A Modern History.* London: I.B.Tauris, 1993.

Articles and Chapters:

Abir, Mordechai. 'Local Leadership and Early Reforms in Palestine 1800-1834', In *Studies on Palestine During the Ottoman Period.*
Abu Manneh, Butrus. 'Jerusalem in the Tanzimat Period: The New Ottoman Administration and the Notables', *Die Welt des Islams* 30, no. 1/4 (1990): 1-44.
— 'The Rise of the Sanjak of Jerusalem in the Late Nineteenth Century', In *The Palestinians and the Conflict.*
Aghazarian, A. 'The Significance of Jerusalem to Christians', In *Christians in the Holy Land.*
Ahmad, Feroz. 'The Late Ottoman Empire', In *The Great Powers and the End of the Ottoman Empire.*
— 'War and Society Under the Young Turks, 1908-1918', In *The Modern Middle East.*
Amireh, A. 'My Last Days as an Ottoman Subject', *Jerusalem Quarterly File*, no. 9 (Summer 2000).
Angell, James B. 'The Turkish Capitulations', *The American Historical Review* 6, no. 2 (January 1901): 254-259.
Atran, Scott. 'The Surrogate of Colonization of Palestine 1917-1939', *American Anthropologist* 16, no. 4 (November 1989): 719-744.
Avcı, Y. and Lemire, V. 'De la Modernité Administrative à la Modernisation Urbain: une Réévaluation de la Municipalité

Ottomane de Jérusalem 1867-1917', In *Municipalités Méditerranéennes*.
Badone, E. and Roseman, S.R. 'Approaches to the Anthropology of Pilgrimage and Tourism', In *Intersecting Journeys*.
Baer, Gabriel. 'Jerusalem's Families of Notables and the Wakf in the early 19th Century', In *Palestine in the Late Ottoman Period*.
Barthes, R. 'Toward a Psychosociology of Contemporary Food Consumption', In *Food and Culture: a Reader*.
Bar-Yosef, Eitan. 'The Last Crusade? British Propaganda and the Palestine Campaign, 1917-1918', *Journal of Contemporary History* 36, no. 1 (2001): 87-109.
Ben-Arieh, Yehoshua. 'The Growth of Jerusalem in the Nineteenth Century', *Annals of the Association of American Geographers* 65, no. 2 (June 1975): 252-269.
— 'Jerusalem Travel Literature as Historical Source and Cultural Phenomenon', In *Jerusalem in the Mind of the Western World*.
Bosworth, Edmund. 'The Land of Palestine in the Late Ottoman Period as Mirrored in Western Guide Books', *Bulletin British Society for Middle Eastern Studies* 13, no. 1 (1986): 36-44.
Buheiry, Marwan R. 'The Agricultural Exports of Southern Palestine 1885-1914', *Journal of Palestine Studies* 10, no. 4 (Summer 1981): 61-81.
Canaan, T. 'Two Documents on the Surrender of Jerusalem', *The Journal of the Palestine Oriental Society* 10 (1930): 27-31.
Charteris, M.M.C. 'A Year as an Intelligence Officer in Palestine', *Journal of the Middle East Society*, no. 1 (October-December 1946): 15-23.
Chevallier, A. 'Non-Muslim Communities in Arab Cities', In *Christians and Jews in the Ottoman Empire*, Vol. 2.
Clark, Edward C. 'The Ottoman Industrial Revolution', *International Journal of Middle Eastern Studies*, no. 5 (1974): 65-76.
Collin, B. 'La Francia e la Custodia di Terra Santa', In *La Custodia di Terra Santa e l'Europa*.
— 'Questione e Problema dei Luoghi Santi', in *Custodia di Terra Santa*.
Davison, Roderic H. 'The Millets as Agents of Change in the Nineteenth Century Ottoman Empire', In *Christian and Jews in the Ottoman Empire*, Vol. 2.

De Groot, Alexander H. 'The Historical Development of the Capitulary Regime in the Ottoman Middle East from the 15th to the 19th Centuries', *Oriente Moderno* 22 (2003): 575-604.

Doumani, Beshara B. 'Rediscovering Ottoman Palestine: Writing Palestinians into History', *Journal of Palestine Studies* 21, no. 2 (Winter 1992): 5-28.

Dunn, J. 'Egypt's Nineteenth Century Armament Industry', *The Journal of Military History* 61, no. 2 (April 1997): 231-254.

Efrat, Elisha and Noble, Allen G.. 'Planning Jerusalem', *Geographical Review* 78, no. 4 (October 1988): 387-404.

El-Aref, Aref. 'The Closing Phase of Ottoman Rule in Jerusalem', In *Studies on Palestine During the Ottoman Period*.

Eliav, M. 'The German and Austrian Consular Archives in Jerusalem as a Source for the History of Palestine and its Population in the Late Ottoman Empire', In *Palestine in the Late Ottoman Period*.

— 'German Interests and the Jewish Community', In *Palestine in the Late Ottoman Period*.

— 'The Austrian Consulate in Jerusalem. Activities and Achievements', In *Austrian Presence in the Holy Land in the 19th and early 20th Century*.

Ershow, Jeremy. 'Conspiracies and Commitments: the British in Palestine', in *Yale Israel Journal*, no. 5 (Winter 2005): 20-30.

Farhi, D. 'Documents on the Attitude of the Ottoman Government Towards the Jewish Settlement in Palestine After the Revolution of the Young Turks', In *Studies on Palestine During the Ottoman Period*.

Findley, Carter V. 'The Evolution of Provincial Administration', In *Palestine in the Late Ottoman Period*.

Fishman, Louis. 'The 1911 Haram al-Sharif Incident: Palestinian Notables Versus the Ottoman Administration', *Journal of Palestine Studies* 34, no. 3 (Spring 2005): 6-22.

Gilbar, G.G. 'The Growing Economic Involvement of Palestine with the West, 1865-1914', In *Palestine in the Late Ottoman Period*.

Gerber, Haim. 'The Ottoman Administration of Sanjaq of Jerusalem 1890-1908', *Asian and African Studies* 12, no. 1 (March 1978): 32-76.

— 'A New Look at the Tanzimat: The Case of the Province of Jerusalem', In *Palestine in the Late Ottoman Period*.
Gwynne, Dyer. 'Turkish "Falsifiers" and Armenian "Deceivers"', *Middle Eastern Studies* 12 (January 1976): 99-107.
Hagopian, H. 'The Armenians of Jerusalem and the Armenian Quarter', In *Christians in the Holy Land*.
Heacock, R. 'Palestine dans les Relations Internationales 1798-1917', In De *Bonaparte á Balfour*.
Hintlian, G. 'The First World War in Palestine and Msgr. Franz Fellinger', In *Austrian Presence in the Holy Land in the 19th and early 20th Century*.
Hofman, Yitzhak. 'The Administration of Syria and Palestine under Egyptian Rule (1831-1840)', In *Studies on Palestine During the Ottoman Period*.
Hopwood, D. 'The Resurrection of Our Eastern Brethren: Russia and Orthodox Arab Nationalism in Jerusalem', In *Studies on Palestine During the Ottoman Period*.
Hough, William. 'History of the British Consulate in Jerusalem', *Journal of the Middle East Society*, no. 1 (October-December 1946): 3-14.
Hourani, Albert. 'Ottoman Reforms and the Politics of Notables', In *The Modern Middle East*.
Hudson, M.C. 'The Transformation of Jerusalem 1917-1984 AD', In *Jerusalem in History*.
Hummel, T. 'Between Eastern and Western Christendom: The Anglican Presence in Jerusalem', In *The Christian Communities of Jerusalem and the Holy Land*.
Hunt, G. 'The Middle Class Revisited: Eating and Drinking in an English Village', *Western Folklore* 50 (1991): 401-402.
Incelli, G. 'Le Scuole di Terra Santa', In *Custodia di Terra Santa*.
Jacobson, A. 'Negotiating Ottomanism in Times of War: Jerusalem During World War I Through the Eyes of a Local Muslim Resident', *Int. J. Middle East Studies* 40 (2008): 69-88.
Jung, Peter. 'Austria's Desert War. The Austro-Hungarian Army in the Middle East 1914-1918', In *Austrian Presence in the Holy Land in the 19th and early 20th Century*.
Kark, Ruth. 'The Jerusalem Municipality at the End of the Ottoman Rule', *Asian and Africa Studies*, no. 14 (1980): 117-141.

— 'The Contribution of the Ottoman Regime to the Development of Jerusalem and Jaffa 1840-1914', In *Palestine in the Late Ottoman Period*.

— 'Land Registry Maps in Palestine during the Ottoman Period', *The Cartographical Journal* 21 (June 1984): 30-32.

Katz, Itamar and Ruth Kark. 'The Greek Orthodox Patriarchate of Jerusalem and its Congregation: Dissent Over Real Estate', *International Journal of Middle Eastern Studies*, no. 37 (2005): 509-534.

Kayalı, H. 'Wartime Regional and Imperial Integration of Greater Syria during World War I', In *The Syrian Land: Process of Integration and Fragmentation*.

Klieman, Aaron S. 'Britain's War Aims in the Middle East in 1915', *Journal of Contemporary History* 3, no. 3 (July 1968): 237-251.

Kolatt, Israel. 'The Organisation of the Jewish Population of Palestine and the Development of its Political Consciousness Before World War I', In *Studies on Palestine During the Ottoman Period*.

Krammer, J. 'Austrian Pilgrimage to the Holy Land', In *Austrian Presence in the Holy Land in the 19th and early 20th Century*.

Kushner, David. 'Intercommunal Strife in Palestine During the Late Ottoman Period', *Asian and African Studies*, no. 18 (1984): 187-204.

— 'The Ottoman Governors of Palestine 1864-1914', *Middle Eastern Studies 23* (July 1987): 274-290.

— 'The Foreign Relations of the Governors of Jerusalem Toward the End of the Ottoman Period', In *Palestine in the Late Ottoman Period*.

Lagrange, M.J. 'A Jerusalem Pendant la Guerre', *Le Correspondent* (February 1915): 641-658.

Lapidoth, R. 'Gerusalemme: Aspetti Politici e Giuridici', In *La Questione di Gerusalemme*.

Lemire, V. 'L'Eau, le Consul et l'Ingénieur: Hydropolitique et Concurrences Diplomatique à Jérusalem, 1908-1914', In *France and the Middle East*.

Levene, Mark. 'The Balfour Declaration. A Case of Mistaken Identity', *The English Historical Review* 107, no. 422 (January 1992): 54-77.

Libertun de Duren. 'Jerusalem at the Beginning of the Twentieth Century', *City Vision*, MIT (2004).

Lipman, Vivian D. 'Britain in the Holy Land: 1830-1914', In *With Eyes Toward Zion III*.

Mancini, I. 'Cenni Storici sulla Custodia di Terra Santa', In *La Custodia di Terra Santa e l'Europa*.

Manna, Adel. 'Continuity and Change in the Socio-Political Elite in Palestine During the Late Ottoman Period', In *The Syrian Land in the 18th and 19th Century*.

Manuel, Frank E. 'The Palestine Question in Italian Diplomacy, 1917-1920', *The Journal of Modern History* 27, no.3 (Sept. 1995): 263-280.

Mazza, Roberto. 'Churches at War: The Impact of the First World War on the Christian Institutions of Jerusalem, 1914-20', *Middle Eastern Studies* 45, no. 2, (March 2009): 207-227.

McTague, John J. Jr. 'The British Military Administration in Palestine 1917-1920', *Journal of Palestine Studies* 7, no. 3 (Spring 1978): 55-76.

Minerbi, I. Sergio. 'L'Italie et le Protectorat Religiuex Français en Palestine 1914-1920', *Asian and African Studies* 4 (1968): 23-55.

— 'Italian Economic Penetration in Palestine 1908-1919', In *Studies on Palestine During the Ottoman Period*.

Mintz, S. and Du Bois, C.M. 'The Anthropology of Food and Eating', *Ann. Rev. Anthropol.* 31 (2002): 99-119.

Nassar, I. 'Jerusalem in the Late Ottoman Period', In *Jerusalem Idea and Reality*.

Nicault, Catherine. 'Retour à la Jérusalem Ottoman', In *Jérusalem 1850-1948*.

— 'Foi et Politique: Les Pèlerinages Française en Terre Sainte (1850-1914)', In *De Bonaparte á Balfour*.

Newell, Jonathan. 'Allenby and the Palestine Campaign', In *The First World War and British Military History*.

O'Mahony, Anthony. 'The Christian Communities of Jerusalem and the Holy Land: A Historical and Political Survey', In *The Christian Communities of Jerusalem and the Holy Land*.

— 'Church, State and the Christian Communities and the Holy Places of Palestine', In *Christians in the Holy Land*.

— 'Palestinian Christians: Religion, Politics and Society, c. 1800-1948', In *Palestinian Christians*.
Pappe, Ilan. 'The Husayni Family Faces New Challenges', *Jerusalem Quarterly File*, Issue 11-12 (2001).
— 'The Rise and Fall of the Husaynis, 1840-1922', *Jerusalem Quarterly File*, Issue 10 (2000).
Pieraccini, Paolo. 'Le Patriarcat Latin de Jérusalem et la France', In *De Balfour à Ben Gourion*.
Reimer, M.J. 'Becoming Urban: Town Administration in Jordan', *Int. J. Middle East Studies*, no. 37 (2005): 189-211.
Reinharz, Jehuda. 'The Balfour Declaration and Its Makers: a Reassessment', *The Journal of Modern History* 64, no. 3 (September 1992): 455-499.
Rostagno, Lucia. 'Pellegrinaggi Italiani in età Ottomana: Percorsi, Esperienze, Momenti d'Incontro', *Oriente Moderno*, Vol. XVII, No. 1 (1998): 63-157.
Roussos, S. 'The Greek Orthodox Patriarchate and Community of Jerusalem: Church, State and Identity', In *The Christian Communities of Jerusalem and the Holy Land*.
Sanjian, A. 'The Armenian Church', In The Christian Communities of Jerusalem and the Holy Land.
Schmelz, U.O. 'Population Characteristics of Jerusalem and Hebron Regions According to Ottoman Census of 1905', In *Ottoman Palestine 1800-1914*.
Schölch, Alexander. 'Britain in Palestine, 1838-1882: The Roots of the Balfour Declaration', *Journal of Palestine Studies 22*, no. 1 (Autumn 1992): 39-56.
— 'Jerusalem in 19th Century 1831-1917 AD', In *Jerusalem in History*.
Schwake, Norbert. 'Le Développement du Réseau Hospitalier en Palestine', In *De Bonaparte à Balfour*.
Shamir, Milette. 'Our Jerusalem: Americans in the Holy Land and Protestant Narratives of National Entitlement', *American Quarterly 55*, no. 1 (March 2003): 29-60.
Shamir, S. 'Egyptian Rule (1832-1840) and the Beginning of the Modern Period in the History of Palestine', In *Egypt and Palestine: A Millennium of Association*.

Shapiro, A. 'Planning Jerusalem: the First Generation, 1917-1968', In *Urban Geography of Jerusalem*.

Shaw, Stanford J. 'The Nineteenth-Century Ottoman Tax Reforms and Revenue System', *Int. J. of Middle East Studies*, no. 6 (1975): 421-459.

Shilo, M. 'Women as Victims of War: the British Conquest (1917) and the Blight of Prostitution in the Holy City', *Nashim: A Journal Of Jewish Women's Studies & Gender Issues 6* (Fall 2003): 72-83.

Shomali, Q. 'La Presse Arabe en Palestine dans la Période Ottomane', In *De Bonaparte à Balfour*.

Stevens, Richard P. 'The Vatican, the Catholic Church and Jerusalem', *Journal of Palestine Studies 10*, no. 3 (Spring 1981): 100-110.

Swanson, Glen. 'The Ottoman Police', *Journal of Contemporary History 7*, no 1/2 (January-April 1972): 243-260.

Tamari, S. 'Jerusalem's Ottoman Modernity: The Times and Lives of Wasif Jawhariyyeh', *Jerusalem Quarterly File*, Issue 9 (Summer 2000).

— 'The Short Life of Private Ihsan: Jerusalem 1915', *Jerusalem Quarterly File 30* (2007): 26-58.

Trimbur, Dominique. 'Une Présence Française en Palestine: Notre Dame de France', *Bulletin du CRFJ*, no. 3 (Autumn 1998): 32-58.

Trumpener, Ulrich. 'Germany and the End of the Ottoman Empire', In *The Great Powers and the end of the Ottoman Empire*.

Tsimhoni, Daphne. 'The Greek Orthodox Patriarchate of Jerusalem', *Asian and African Studies 12*, no 4 (March 1978): 77-121.

Van der Veer, P. 'Riots and Rituals: The Construction of Violence and Public Space in Hindu Nationalism', In *Riots and Pogroms*.

Vereté, M. 'The Balfour Declaration and Its Makers', In *From Palmerston to Balfour: collected Essays of Mayir Vereté*.

Vester Spafford, Bertha. 'Jerusalem, My Home', *National Geographic* (December 1964): 826-847.

Wardi, C. 'The Latin Patriarchate of Jerusalem', *Journal of the Middle East Society 1*, no. 3-4 (Autumn 1947): 5-12.

Winter, J.M. 'Propaganda and the Mobilization of Consent', In *First World War*.

Yarbrough, O.L. 'Early Christian Jerusalem. The City of the Cross', In *Jerusalem. Idea and Reality*.

Yasamee, F.A.K. 'Ottoman Empire', In *Decisions for War 1914*.

Young, J.E. 'Interpreting Literary Testimony: A Preface to Rereading Holocaust Diaries and Memoirs', *New Literary History 18* (1987): 403-423.

Zander, Walter. 'On the Settlement of Disputes About the Christian Holy Places', *Israel Law Review 8* (1973): 331-366.

INDEX

A

Abdülhamid II 21, 33, 114
Abyssinians 142
Administrative Council 24, 26-27, 33, 180
aliyah 41
Allenby, General Edmund 57, 107-108, 113, 122, 124-131, 135-137, 139, 146, 148-149, 154, 156, 164, 171, 175-176, 215-216
Alliance Israélite Universelle 25, 151
American 39, 44-45, 55, 61, 71, 80-85, 89-91, 93, 95-96, 104, 107, 109, 117, 153, 206; consul 6, 26, 39, 60, 65, 82, 88-90, 93-96, 115, 153, 206; consulate 37, 39, 85, 94, 100; government; institutions 83, 93-94, 150
American Colony 61, 95, 107, 132-133, 150, 181, 199
Anglican Church 163
Anglicans 44, 58-59, 83
Antebi, Albert 104
Arab Bureau 34, 37, 39
Arab Club 70, 171-172

Arab Nationalism 174
Arab Revolt 158
Aref, Aref-el 172
Armenian Quarter 43, 54
Armenians 42-43, 51, 54, 62, 105, 157
Ashbee, C.R. 151, 160-161, 164-165
Ashkenazim 41-42, 193
Austria (Austrian) 16, 44, 52, 54, 58, 63-65, 77-79, 84, 88-93, 97, 104, 107, 120-121, 127-128, 132-133, 143, 197, 207, 212

B

Balfour, Arthur James 166
Balfour, Declaration 58, 68, 72, 92, 95, 122, 129, 138, 147, 150, 165, 169, 179-180
Balkan Wars 50, 81, 113
Ballobar, Conde de 6, 60, 90, 92, 95-108, 134, 137, 158, 210, 212
Barluzzi, Antonio 80
Bentwich, Norman 37-39
Beersheba 19, 125-126, 185
Bilad al-Sham 12-13, 17

British 4, 15, 17, 20, 35, 40, 45, 58, 61, 63, 65, 67, 70-72, 76, 82, 84, 86, 89-90, 93, 98, 102, 104-106, 108-109, 112, 114, 120-124, 126, 129, 132, 134, 136-137, 140, 142-143, 147-149, 151-153, 155-156, 160-162, 165-166, 177-182, 191, 209, 212, 213, 219; administration (authorities, census, officials) 2, 5-6, 35, 37-38, 40, 57-58, 69, 77, 107, 110, 123-124, 127-128, 136, 147-148, 150, 152, 155-157, 161, 163-165, 167, 169, 175-176, 180-181, 192, 220, 227; army (troops) 17, 61, 65-55, 67, 111-112, 115, 121, 125, 130-140, 143, 145-147, 154, 157, 170, 172-173, 175, 180, 211-212, 220; consul 37, 45, 78, 81, 87, 90, 191, 206; consulate 16, 84, 90, 206; empire 124, 140, 145, 160, 166, 182; Foreign Office 58, 67, 123, 127-130, 137, 139-140, 142, 148-150, 152, 154-157, 166, 176-178, 180; government 45, 55, 58, 77, 83, 86, 92, 95, 123, 135, 138, 141-143, 150, 158, 178, 180, 209; intelligence 59, 123; Mandate 2, 56, 67, 140, 151; policies 57, 123, 126, 136, 148, 171, 180; rule 33, 38, 107, 111, 120, 140, 147, 152, 161, 180-181, 212; War Office 37, 83, 123, 126, 128-129, 139, 148, 150, 154
Brode, Johann 58, 91-92, 105, 207
Bols, General 148, 156, 176

C

Cairo 13, 34, 59, 61, 125, 127, 139, 154, 158-159
Caliphate 133
Camassei, Filippo 60-61, 90, 142
Capitulations 50, 52, 54-56, 58, 67, 76, 79, 85-86, 89, 108-109, 114, 196-197, 205-206
Catholic Church (Institutions) 43-44, 48, 51, 53, 57, 63, 67, 70, 85, 120, 141-142
Catholics 43-44, 50-53, 58, 61-63, 66-67, 70, 73, 79, 85, 108, 138, 141-142, 195
Cemal Paşa 60-62, 90-92, 96, 99, 101, 104-106, 117, 120, 206, 215
Church of the Holy Sepulchre 49-51, 62, 83, 108, 128, 133, 198
Christians 14, 16, 27, 33, 35, 39-40, 43, 49-50, 56, 58-59, 68-69, 72-73, 78, 80, 85, 89, 91, 93, 116-117, 119, 126, 130, 137-139, 157, 163, 168, 173-174, 179-180, 187-188
Clayton, Gilbert 149, 156, 222

INDEX 259

Committee of Union and Progress (CUP) 18-19, 33-34, 104, 112-114, 116, 136, 157
Consulates 55, 79, 82, 84-87, 89-90, 110, 116, 118, 204
Consuls 14, 21, 23-25, 30, 35, 44, 56, 63, 65, 76, 85-92, 95-96, 102, 104, 109, 118, 132, 153, 181
Cook's Travel Agency 80, 82, 136, 146
Coptic Church 50
Copts 44, 50
Corruption 14-15, 162
Courts 32, 85, 151
Crimean War 16, 85
Crusaders 6, 48-49, 130, 138, 140, 144, 146, 217
Custody of the Holy Land 5, 39, 50, 53, 58, 62-68, 83-84, 97, 119, 199, 209
Custos 50, 58, 62-64, 66-68, 199
Curzon, Lord 171

D

Damascus 12, 14, 21, 31, 42, 90, 97, 117, 125, 142, 167
Damascus Gate 105, 162
Damianos, Patriarch 60
De Bunsen Committee 57
Diotallevi, Ferdinando 66-68
Dolci, Cardinal 64, 142
Druses 192

E

Eastern Front 112, 121-123, 125
Egypt 12-13, 16-17, 45, 58, 61, 63, 72, 80, 114-116, 120, 123, 125, 128, 130, 137, 150, 164, 175, 219, 224
Egyptian Expeditionary Force (EEF) 122, 125, 135, 138, 142, 149, 215
Ekrem Bey 1, 21, 24, 87, 186
Ethiopians 44
Europe 41-42, 55, 77-78, 84, 88, 95, 101, 105, 113, 115, 117, 121-123, 220
Europeans 3, 13-14, 16, 20, 23, 55-56, 80, 82, 96

F

Faysal, Prince 169, 172
Firman 51, 56-57, 197
First World War 2, 17-18, 28, 51, 53, 69, 85, 98, 113, 121, 125
France 16, 41, 44, 52-53, 55, 66-67, 78, 84-85, 108, 112, 120, 127, 140-141, 146, 204, 207
Franciscans 50, 52-53, 64-66, 79, 96, 119, 138, 157
French 4, 13, 16, 24, 44-45, 54, 58, 63, 65, 67, 72, 79, 82, 85, 87, 90, 107-109, 128, 141, 146, 149, 154, 159, 163, 196, 200-201, 212, 225; army (troops) 13, 108, 121, 136, 142, 158, 215; consul 84, 90, 172, 191, 194, 206,

212; consulate 57;
government 52, 57, 85, 109,
127, 141, 159; institutions
16, 53, 67, 79

G
Gasparri, Cardinal 66-67,
101, 142, 200
Gaza 19, 27, 100, 124-127,
130-131
Geddes, Patrick 164-165, 227
Gendarmerie 117, 153
German 44-45, 63, 65, 77,
81-84, 91, 95, 101-102, 106-
107, 114-115, 127-128, 193;
army (troops) 60-61, 76,
100, 114, 121, 126, 131-135,
215; consul 58, 89, 91, 93,
104-105, 132, 207
Germany 16, 41, 61, 85, 88-
90, 92-93, 105, 112, 120,
122, 133, 143, 193, 204
Glazebrook, Otis 6, 60-61,
89-90, 93-96, 100, 102, 153,
158, 206
Great Britain 66, 120, 207
Greece 60, 104, 204
Greeks 60, 105
Greek Orthodox Church 43,
48, 51-52, 59, 140, 157, 198

H
Haganah 140, 169, 174, 220
Haifa 71
Hebrew University 164
Hebron 12, 19, 27, 129, 131,
172, 217

Holy Fire ceremony
(procession of) 60, 198
Holy Land 13-14, 44, 50, 53,
55-56, 59, 64, 66, 76-77, 79-
80, 82-83, 85, 107-108, 119,
130, 144
Holy Places 3, 13, 16, 48, 50,
52-54, 56-58, 63, 67-68, 76,
127-129, 133, 136, 142, 153,
157
Holy See: see Vatican
Husayni Family 15, 32-34,
41, 69-70, 91, 155
Husayni, Salim 15, 133-135,
149, 155

I
Ibrahim Paşa 13-15
Islam 12, 18, 49, 69, 105,
123-124, 144, 146, 186
Israel 12, 165, 209
Istanbul 19-22, 24-25, 33, 43,
51-52, 54, 56, 58, 64-65, 85-
87, 89, 91, 93-94, 101, 113-
115, 120, 188, 199
Italy 29, 64-66, 78, 85, 90,
104, 108, 113, 127, 141-142,
199, 204
Italian 4, 29, 44-45, 54, 63,
65, 72, 79, 84-85, 107-109,
121, 128, 141, 149, 154,
163, 196, 206; army (troops)
121, 136, 142; consul 29, 87,
90, 104, 109, 118, 215;
government 28-29, 57, 64,
108, 127, 141; institutions
28-29, 79, 109
Italian Hospital 28-29

Izzet Bey 132-133

J
Jaffa 19, 27, 45, 65, 70, 81-82, 85, 91-92, 100-101, 115, 130, 150, 181, 188, 207
Jaffa Gate 61, 82, 136, 164, 171-172, 175
Jaffa-Jerusalem Railway 81
Jaffa Road 79-80, 82, 131, 134, 162, 171
Jabotinsky, Vladimir 140. 169, 171, 174, 219
Jawhariyyeh, Wasif 5, 102-103, 134, 137-138, 190, 211
Jerusalem, as Capital 148, 165, 181; Chamber of Commerce of 152, 224; conquest (capture) of 40, 43, 66, 69, 98, 111-112, 122-131, 137, 139-140, 142-143, 147, 158; demography of 34; governor of 1, 6, 21, 25, 40-41, 56-57, 59, 86-88, 105, 116, 118, 128, 132-133, 148-149, 154, 158, 180, 186, 224; as Holy City 112 124, 126, 132, 140, 152, 162, 181, 217; as imaginary city 11, 180; schools (colleges) of 53, 56, 59, 63-64, 77, 89, 105, 119-120, 151, 181, 207
Jewish Chronicle 140, 164, 177
Jews 25, 28, 33, 35, 39-42, 49, 61, 68-69, 71, 73, 78, 80, 83, 85-86, 89, 91-95, 101, 106-107, 116-117, 119, 124, 138-140, 155-156, 166-168, 170-174, 176-177, 179-181, 188, 192-193, 198, 207-208, 212, 229
Judaism 144

K
Kaiser Wilhelm II 81, 136
Khalidi Family 32-33, 69, 91
Kressenstein, Kress von 107, 131

L
Land Registry 28
Latins 43, 49-52, 70
Latin Patriarch 60, 63, 66, 70, 90, 142, 163, 200
Latin Patriarchate 49-50, 52, 67-70
Lawrence, T.E. 158
Lloyd George, David 121-122, 124, 143, 166
London 41, 80, 125-127, 129-130, 138, 140, 143, 149, 154, 158-159, 166, 170, 177, 218, 230
London Society for Promoting Christianity Amongst the Jews 58, 86

M
MacInnes, Rennie Bishop in Jerusalem 59, 61, 123, 127, 150, 157
Madrid 98
Massey, W.T. 138, 140
Husayn-McMahon Correspondence 122
McLean, William 164-165

Meclis-i Idare 26-29
Meclis-i Umumi 26, 28
Mesopotamia 122
Millet 12, 34, 49-50, 183, 195
Muhammad 'Ali 13, 16-17, 45, 55
Morgenthau, Henry 89, 91, 93, 95
Mount of Olives 11, 164
Mount Zion 104
Mufti 15, 27, 33
Muslims 16, 26-27, 32-33, 39-41, 48-49, 61, 68-69, 72-73, 78, 91, 120, 123, 126, 129, 137, 141, 153, 163, 173-174, 179-180, 187-188, 219
Muslim-Christian Associations 69-70, 72-73, 155, 169
Mutasarrıf 20-21, 25, 28-29, 86, 115, 118
Mutasarrıflık 20

N
Napoleon 13, 45
Nashashibi Family 32, 41, 69-70, 91
Nebi Musa festival 78, 168, 170-171, 176, 231
Nebi Musa riots 6, 71, 147-148, 153, 155-156, 159, 165-168, 175, 177-178, 182, 220
New York Times 101, 146, 164
Notables 12, 14-15, 21, 27-28, 30-34, 40, 68-70, 73, 90-91, 93, 102, 110, 133, 135, 155-156, 171, 174, 180

Notre Dame de France 53, 120

O
Occupied Enemy Territory Administration (OETA) 73, 148-150, 178
Old City 43, 53, 120, 137, 163-164, 176, 230
Ottoman administration 4-5, 11, 30-32, 44-45, 51, 79, 82, 87, 180-181; army (troops) 24, 31, 54, 58, 60, 62, 64, 90-91, 100, 106, 115, 117, 120, 126, 131, 133-134; Empire 14, 16-22, 28, 30, 43, 54-55, 57, 77-78, 85, 88-90, 102, 104-106, 112-114, 123, 143, 149, 196-197, 204, 206; government 34, 39, 53, 55, 64, 86, 89, 91, 103, 113, 133, 157
Ottomanism 18, 33

P
Palestine 2, 12-14, 16-17, 23-24, 27, 33-34, 38, 41-45, 49, 52-54, 56, 61-64, 66-73, 75, 77-80, 82-86, 90, 92-93, 95-97, 101, 105, 107-110, 112, 115, 117, 121, 123-126, 129-130, 136-139, 141-151, 153-158, 163-166, 169-172, 176, 178, 181, 184, 187, 211-212, 216, 222
Palestine Exploration Fund 83, 204
Palestine Police Force 153

Paris 57, 82, 141
Perier Company 24
Picot, Georges 108-109, 128, 149
Pilgrimage 16, 53, 57, 59, 64, 78-80, 82, 168, 171, 196, 202
Pilgrims 43, 48, 53, 55, 60, 76-81, 85, 108, 119, 172, 181, 197
Police 23-24, 28, 33, 64, 117, 120, 127, 134-135, 153-154, 171-173, 175-176, 187, 230
Post Office 55-56, 88, 120, 152, 197, 206, 218
Pro-Jerusalem Society 157, 160-161, 163
Protestants 44, 61, 83
Provincial Law: see *Vilayet* Law
Prussia 16, 22, 85, 186
Public Debt Administration 44

Q
Quds, al- 183

R
Rome 48, 50, 67, 159
Ruppin, Arthur 37, 105
Russia 16, 28, 41-43, 52, 57, 59-60, 78, 85, 167, 204, 207, 219
Russian Compound 53, 80
Russian Government 16, 59, 85
Russian Orthodox Church 78

S
Salah al-Din 49, 139, 168
Sancak 12, 18-21, 26, 86, 185
St George's College 59
St Stephen's Gate 132, 172
Samuel, Herbert 142, 178
San Remo Conference 71-72, 177
Senni, Carlo Conte (consul) 29, 90, 118
Sephardim 41-42
Spain 16, 41, 63, 66, 85, 90, 97-98, 104, 107, 209
Spanish 44, 63, 65, 97; consul 4, 6, 60, 63, 65, 88, 90, 92, 95-98, 101, 103-105, 108, 134, 171; consulate 97, 106, 209; government 98, 102, 171, 209, 212; institutions 97
Status Quo (Holy Places) 54, 56-58, 63, 66, 128, 157
Status Quo ante Bellum 149-150, 154-155, 160, 163-165, 178-179
Storrs, Ronald 6, 37, 40-41, 70, 107, 148-150, 152-155, 157-165, 170-172, 174-176, 180, 201, 222, 224, 226, 231
Sykes, Mark 57, 123, 126-128, 132, 136, 139, 156
Sykes-Picot Agreement 122, 128, 141
Syria 12-14, 17, 20-21, 49, 60-61, 73, 90, 108-109, 120, 139, 143, 150, 153, 169, 172, 187

T

Tanzimat 14, 16-22, 32, 50, 185
Tapu, 28
Tel Aviv 140
Tourism 16, 80-82, 181
Tuozzi, Alberto 109
Turkey 17, 59-60, 65, 88, 124, 142, 178, 206
Turkish 11, 21, 29, 32, 40, 45, 54, 58-60, 62-66, 91, 114, 132, 153, 159, 194, 205
Twain, Mark 80

U

United States of America 53, 60-61, 71, 78, 85, 90-91, 93-96, 98, 102, 104, 146, 193, 220
Urban Planning 23

V

Valero Family 31
Vali 21
Vatican (Holy See), 64, 66-72, 98, 101, 139, 142
Vester Spafford, Bertha 61, 133-134, 218
Von Falkenhayn, Erich 60, 107, 131
Von Sanders, Liman 114
Vilayet 18, 20-21, 26-27, 188
Vilayet Law (Provincial Law) 18, 22, 26-27

W

Waqf 128, 151

Weizmann, Chaim 142, 156, 167, 169-171, 227
Wilson, Woodrow 71, 94
Wingate, Reginald Colonel 128-129

Y

Young Turks 16, 18, 21, 26, 33-34, 50, 113

Z

Zionism 3-4, 33, 48, 67-70, 73, 91-93, 106, 155-156, 163, 166, 170, 174, 178, 180, 220
Zionist Commission 95, 110, 140, 147, 150-151, 154-157, 164, 166, 169-170, 174, 177-178, 180
Zionist Organisation 45, 150, 154, 165, 192, 230

Illustration 1: Jerusalem. Street scene inside the Jaffa Gate.
(Matson Photograph Collection, Library of Congress, 06546)

Illustration 2: Mayor of Jerusalem and Turkish Official, 1914-1917.
(Matson Photograph Collection, Library of Congress, 07438)

Illustration 3: Enver Paşa visiting the Dome of the Rock, 1916.
(Matson Photograph Collection, Library of Congress, 11599)

Illustration 4: Jews at the Wailing Wall.
(Matson Photograph Collection, Library of Congress, 04803)

Illustration 5: Mosque of Omar, northeast side.
(Matson Photograph Collection, Library of Congress, 06628)

Illustration 6: Ceremony of the Holy Fire at the Holy Sepulchre.
(Matson Photograph Collection, Library of Congress, 00873)

Illustration 7: St George's Cathedral.
(*Matson Photograph Collection, Library of Congress, 06676*)

Illustration 8: Turkish column out to drill in Jerusalem, 1914.
(*Matson Photograph Collection, Library of Congress, 60015*)

Illustration 9: Ceremony of the Washing of the Feet. Holy Sepulchre, 1898-1914.
(Matson Photograph Collection, Library of Congress, 06566)

Illustration 10: Military review by Cemal Paşa, 1917.
(Matson Photograph Collection, Library of Congress, 08132)

Illustration 11: Zaky Bey and his staff, 1914.
(*Matson Photograph Collection, Library of Congress, 14622*)

Illustration 12: Austrian Post Office in Jerusalem.
(*Matson Photograph Collection, Library of Congress, 08716*)

Illustration 13: Turkish troops Jaffa Gate.
(*Matson Photograph Collection, Library of Congress, 11594*)

Illustration 14: Turkish military. Man dancing with a sword.
(*Matson Photograph Collection, Library of Congress, 14238*)

Illustration 15: Turkish prisoner of war, 9 December 1917.
(*Matson Photograph Collection, Library of Congress, 05789*)

Illustration 16: Turkish aeroplane in Jerusalem.
(*Matson Photograph Collection, Library of Congress, 13838*)

Illustration 17: American Consulate.
(*Matson Photograph Collection, Library of Congress, 08303*)

Illustration 18: British troops on parade, Russian Compound, December 1917.
(*Matson Photograph Collection, Library of Congress, 11528*)

Illustration 19: Military review by Allenby, 11 December 1917.
(Matson Photograph Collection, Library of Congress, 50017)

Illustration 20: Entry of Allenby in Jerusalem, Jaffa Gate.
(Matson Photograph Collection, Library of Congress, 02225)

Illustration 21: Franciscan monk reading the proclamation in Italian, 11 December 1917.
(*Matson Photograph Collection, Library of Congress, 00173*)

Illustration 22: Italian guard at the Church of the Holy Sepulchre, 1918.
(Matson Photograph Collection, Library of Congress, 00734)

Illustration 23: OETA Headquarters.
(*Matson Photographic Collection, Library of Congress, 13291*)

Illustration 24: Local gendarmerie, Jerusalem 1918.
(*Matson Photograph Collection, Library of Congress, 13291*)

Illustration 25: Ronald Storrs at the Shrine of Nebi Musa, 1918.
(*Matson Photograph Collection, Library of Congress, 13291*)

Illustration 26: Last Turkish celebration of Nebi Musa, 1917.
(*Matson Photograph Collection, Library of Congress, 00749*)

Illustration 27: A Greek priest is searched, 8 April 1920.
(Matson Collection, Library of Congress, 00753)

Illustration 28: Nebi Musa festival, April 1920.
(Matson Photograph Collection, Library of Congress, 04653)

www.ingramcontent.com/pod-product-compliance
Lightning Source LLC
Chambersburg PA
CBHW050338230426
43663CB00010B/1900